Danksagung

Wir danken Hans Reitz für die Idee zu diesem Buch, Nurjahan Begum, die unsere Bangladesch-Reisen als perfekte Gastgeberin arrangierte, Golam Morshed Mohammed, der uns auf allen Reisen mit höchster sozialer und inhaltlicher Kompetenz begleitete, Annika Kamphausen und Elke Lies für ihre redaktionelle Mitarbeit vor Ort, die es erst ermöglichte, die persönlichen Geschichten der fotografierten Menschen in diesem Buch zu dokumentieren, sowie Shankar Patrick Costa und Md. Abdus Salam für ihre Fotoassistenz.

Außerdem danken wir allen fotografierten Menschen, die uns unabhängig von Geschlecht, sozialem Stand und Religionsangehörigkeit bereitwillig Portrait standen.

Roger Richter und Peter Spiegel

Acknowledgement

Our special thanks go to Hans Reitz, for the idea of creating this book; to Nurjahan Begum, a perfect host, who arranged our trips to Bangladesh; to Golam Morshed Mohammed, a travel guide of the highest social competence, and dedicated to the project; to Annika Kamphausen and Elke Lies for their on-the-spot editorial assistance, which was essential in order to document the individual stories behind the photographs in this book; as well as to the assistant photographers Shankar Patrick Costa and Md. Abdus Salam.

Above all, however, we want to express our deepest gratitude to the people of Bangladesh for their hospitality and willingness to be portrayed by us, irrespective of gender, social standing and religion.

Roger Richter and Peter Spiegel

DIE KRAFT DER WÜRDE
THE POWER OF DIGNITY

THE POWER OF DIGNITY

DIE KRAFT DER WÜRDE

THE GRAMEEN FAMILY

❖ Den Kindern der Grameen-Kreditnehmerinnen steht eine andere Zukunft offen. **SETU AKTER,** 8 Jahre, besucht die 2. Klasse der Grundschule im Dorf Nagar Kosba.

❖ A different future is possible for the children of the Grameen borrowers. **SETU AKTER,** 8 years old, attends the second grade of the elementary school in the village of Nagar Kosba.

VORWORT DES FRIEDENS-NOBELPREISTRÄGERS PROFESSOR MUHAMMAD YUNUS

Menschen, die in Armut leben, sind ganz anders als das Bild, das wir von ihnen haben. Um ihre Situation verändern zu können, müssen wir uns „die Armen" erst einmal genau ansehen. Ich habe immer gesagt, dass die Armut nicht von den Armen selbst geschaffen wird – Armut wird von den Institutionen und Rahmenbedingungen verursacht, die wir ins Leben gerufen haben. Und die Armut besteht weiter, zum Teil deshalb, weil wir viele der Bedingungen als unabänderlich akzeptiert haben, die ursächlich für das Entstehen der Armut sind.

Ich bezeichne die Armen gern als „Bonsai-Menschen", denn sie sind wie Bonsai-Bäume. Da ist nichts falsch mit den Samen der Bonsai-Bäume, sie bringen jegliches Potenzial mit, um zu großen, wunderbaren Bäumen heranzuwachsen. Aber weil wir sie in einen kleinen Topf pflanzen, können sie sich nur zu einem winzigen Bäumchen entfalten. Und das Gleiche gilt für uns Menschen. Die Armen sind Bonsai-Menschen, weil wir ihnen eine angemessene Grundlage verweigern, einen angemessenen Raum, um das Menschsein überhaupt in allen Facetten leben zu können.

Wenn man Menschen die reelle Chance nimmt, erfolgreich zu sein, dann wird sich ihr wahres Potenzial niemals entfalten können. Sobald man aber den Menschen, die wir in Bonsai-Bedingungen gepresst haben, minimal bessere Umstände bietet, wird man sehen, dass sie ihr Leben vollständig verändern können.

Mikrokredite sind eine Möglichkeit, dieses Potenzial freizusetzen. Die weltweite Bewegung der Vergabe von Mikrokrediten an die Ärmsten der Armen hat dies unzweifelhaft belegt. Es sind nicht die Armen, die von uns lernen müssen, sondern wir müssen von den Armen lernen. Sie können uns sagen, was zu tun ist, damit sich ihre Lebensumstände ändern und sie sich nicht länger mit einem Bonsai-Leben zufrieden geben müssen. Die Ärmsten können die mutigsten Unternehmer sein, wenn wir ihnen nur das einfache Recht auf einen Kredit zugestehen.

Dieser wunderbare Bildband, den meine guten Freunde Hans Reitz, Roger Richter und Peter Spiegel verwirklicht haben, macht die Menschen, die bis heute noch immer in Armut leben, in ihrer tief bewegenden Würde sichtbar. Durch dieses Buch können andere die Tragik sehen, die durch Armut erzeugt wird. „Die Armen" haben Namen, Pläne und ihre Erfolgsgeschichten sind erstaunlich. Ich bin sicher, dass dieser Bildband wesentlich dazu beitragen wird, die Vorstellungen grundlegend zu verändern, die immer noch zu viele Menschen mit Armut verbinden. Je schneller immer mehr Menschen das Bonsai-Bild verstehen, desto eher wird das Armuts-Museum, von dem ich träume, möglich werden. Dieses Museum wird dann der einzige Ort sein, an dem man Armut noch finden kann, und die Fotos in diesem Buch werden historische Dokumente sein, die Zeugnis ablegen von einer Zeit, als Armut noch existierte.

Professor Muhammad Yunus, Bangladesch

FOREWORD BY THE NOBEL PEACE PRIZE LAUREATE PROFESSOR MUHAMMAD YUNUS

Poor people are completely different from our perception of them. In order to change the situation of the poor, we have to first view "the poor". I have always argued that poverty is not created by the poor, it is created by the institutions and policies that we have established. Poverty continues to exist in part because we have accepted as unchangeable many conditions that create poverty in the first place.

I describe the poor as bonsai people because they are like bonsai trees. There is nothing wrong in the seeds of bonsai trees, they have within them all the potential to grow into a beautiful tree. It is because we put them in a small pot, that it grows only into a tiny tree. The same is true for us humans. The poor people are bonsai people because we deny them the proper base, the proper space to develop into fully developed human beings.

When one robs people of a fair chance to succeed, then their true potential is never unleashed. As soon as the people we have pressed into such miniature Bonsai conditions are given only minimally better conditions we see that they can completely transform their own lives.

Microcredit is one way to unleash this potential. The worldwide microcredit movement for the poorest has demonstrated this beyond any doubt. It is not the poor who need to learn from us but rather we must learn from the poorest. We can learn from them what needs to be done to change their living environment so that they do not need to eke out any longer a Bonsai existence. The poorest can be the most courageous entrepreneurs if we can only provide them with the simple right to loans.

This magnificent book of photographs that my good friends Hans Reitz, Roger Richter and Peter Spiegel have produced makes the people who are still living in poverty today visible in their deeply moving dignity. Through this book, others can experience the tragedy that poverty begets. "The poor" have names, they have plans and they have astonishing success stories. I am sure that this book of photographs will contribute to fundamentally changing the perception that too many people have of "the poor". The sooner more people understand the Bonsai story, the sooner the Poverty Museum that I dream of creating will be possible. The museum will be the only place where one would be able to find poverty, and the photos in this book will be historical documents testifying to the times when poverty existed.

Professor Muhammad Yunus, Bangladesh

VORWORT DES HERAUSGEBERS
HANS REITZ

Die Würde des Menschen – den meisten von uns fällt es schwer zu beschreiben, was genau damit gemeint ist. Doch begegnet sie uns, erkennen wir sie unmittelbar: an ihrem ganz eigenen, stillen Glanz.

Ich hatte das Glück, diesen Glanz häufig zu sehen. Besonders intensiv durfte ich ihn wahrnehmen auf meinen Reisen in Indien und Bangladesch. Dort traf ich Menschen, die – unter für uns unvorstellbar schwierigen Bedingungen – ganz offensichtlich das Wesen des Menschseins für sich wie einen inneren Schatz bewahrten. Sich aus eigener Kraft von buchstäblich lebensbedrohender Armut befreien zu können, war wohl das Geheimnis ihres Schatzes.

Mit Professor Yunus lernte ich einen Menschen kennen, der sich ganz dem Kampf für diese Befreiung, der unermüdlichen Arbeit für die Würde jedes Menschen verschrieben hatte. Wie nur, so fragte ich mich, kann ein einzelner Mensch so viel Großes leisten. Die Antwort fand ich schnell:

Er kann es nicht. Nicht Sie, nicht ich und auch nicht der Nobelpreisträger Yunus können es. Hinter jeder großen Idee steht ein großer Mensch. Hinter diesem Menschen jedoch stehen unzählige andere, die aus Ideen Leben schaffen. In diesem Fall besseres Leben für Hunderttausende. Hinter Muhammad Yunus steht die Grameen Family – eine Kraft, die nach meiner festen Überzeugung das Gesicht unserer Welt nachhaltig zum Besseren verändern wird. Die, um mit den Worten meines Freundes Muhammad Yunus zu sprechen, „die Armut für immer ins Museum verbannt".

Die Grameen Family inspirierte mich zur Idee dieses Buches. Und auch ich bin vielen Menschen zu Dank verpflichtet, die aus der Idee des Buches das werden ließen, was Sie heute in Händen halten. Besonders erwähnen möchte ich Peter Spiegel, dessen Texte uns die Idee der Grameen Family und die Geschichten hinter den Menschen auf so wunderbare Weise vermitteln. Und natürlich gilt mein Dank meinem langjährigen Weggefährten Roger Richter, dessen Fotografien in meinen Augen genau das einfangen, worum es hier geht: den stillen Glanz der Würde.

Die Frage bleibt, wie es um unsere eigene Würde bestellt ist. Ich persönlich finde die Antwort darauf in den Gesichtern dieser Menschen: Unsere Würde ist untrennbar verbunden mit der Würde aller Menschen dieser Welt. Und aus ihr wächst die Kraft, die Welt zu verändern. The Power of Dignity.

Hans Reitz, Mumbai, im Oktober 2008

FOREWORD BY THE EDITOR
HANS REITZ

The dignity of people – most of us find it difficult to describe exactly what is meant by this. But when we meet it, we immediately recognise it by its very special quiet glowing radiance.

Fortunately, I was able to see this glow frequently. I was privileged to observe this, intensely, during my trips to India and Bangladesh. I met people there who, under what we view as unbelievably difficult conditions, have quite obviously captured, like an inner treasure, the true nature of humanness. Being able to free themselves by their own strength from literally life-threatening poverty, is no doubt the secret of their treasure.

In Professor Yunus, I met a person who has devoted himself entirely to the battle of this liberation, tirelessly working for the dignity of every person. I asked myself, how can a single person accomplish so much of significance? I very quickly discovered the answer:

He can't. Nor you, nor I, and also not the Nobel Prize winner Yunus can do it. Behind every great idea is a great person. Behind this person, however, stand numerous others who bring ideas into life. In this case, a better life for hundreds of thousands. Behind Muhammad Yunus stands the Grameen family – a power that I am firmly convinced will lastingly change the face of our world for the better. Which, in the words of my friend, Muhammad Yunus, "will banish poverty into a museum forever."

The Grameen family inspired me with the idea of this book. And I am also obliged to thank the many people who have made the book you are holding in your hands today possible. I would especially like to mention Peter Spiegel whose words convey to us in such a wonderful way the ideas of the Grameen family and the stories behind the people. And, naturally, my thanks go to my fellow traveller of many years' standing, Roger Richter, whose photographs, in my eyes, capture exactly what this is all about: the quiet glow of dignity.

The question remains, what of our own dignity? I personally find the answer in the faces of these people: our dignity is inseparably connected with the dignity of all the people in the world. The strength to change the world grows out of it.

Hans Reitz, Mumbai, October 2008

❖ **DIE GESCHICHTE BEGINNT** ... in Chittagong, der großen Hafenstadt von Bangladesch. Dort lehrte Muhammad Yunus als Professor der Ökonomie – eine Ökonomie, die die Reichen noch reicher machte und den Ärmsten allenfalls Arbeiten ließ wie das Ausschlachten der ausrangierten Tanker der Weltwirtschaft.

❖ **THE STORY BEGINS** ... in Chittagong, the large harbour in Bangladesh. Muhammad Yunus was Professor of Economics there – economics that made the wealthy even wealthier and let the poor, at best, work at the cannibalisation of discarded tankers of the world economy.

✣ **GESICHTER DER GLOBALISIERUNG.** Bellal Hussain, links, und Muhammad Shahjahan, beide zwischen 45 und 50 Jahre alt, trieb es etwa Mitte der 1990er-Jahre aus dem Norden Bangladeschs in die Wirtschaftsmetropole Chittagong im Süden. Sie arbeiten als Abwracker der Schiffsleichen – ein langes, hartes Arbeitsleben. Der Stundenlohn von 15 Taka (15 Euro-Cent) reicht gerade, um die Familie im Norden einmal in zwei Monaten zu besuchen.

✣ **FACES OF GLOBALISATION.** Bellal Hussain, left, and Muhammad Shahjahan, both aged between 45 and 50, were driven in the middle of the 1990s from northern Bangladesh to the economic capital in the south, Chittagong. They work as scrap breakers on ship hulls – a long hard working life. The hourly wages of 15 Taka (15 euro cents) is just enough to allow a visit to the family in the north once every two months.

❀ **LOKALISIERUNG DER ARMUT — UND IHRER LÖSUNG.**
Aufnahme am Ort des ersten Zweigbüros der Grameen Bank. Als Muhammad Yunus Ende der 1970er-Jahre seine Universität in Chittagong verließ, um den Ursachen der Armut auf den Grund zu gehen, führte ihn sein Weg in das nahegelegene Dorf Jobra. Dort befragte er die Ärmsten der Frauen. Sie erklärten ihm, sie bräuchten Kredite im Gegenwert von weniger als einem Euro, um unabhängig von den Kredithaien arbeiten zu können.
SOLEMA KHATUN, heute 70 Jahre alt, war eine der ersten Grameen-Kreditnehmerinnen. Ihr erster Kredit betrug umgerechnet 25 Euro, um in Selbstständigkeit Bambusstühle fertigen zu können. Heute arbeitet sie mit einem Kredit von umgerechnet 1.300 Euro und hat längst die Armutsgrenze hinter sich gelassen.

❀ **LOCATION OF POVERTY — AND ITS SOLUTION.**
Photographed on location of the first branch office of the Grameen Bank. When Muhammad Yunus left the University of Chittagong at the end of the 1970s to thoroughly investigate the causes of poverty, his path led him to the nearby village, Jobra. There he questioned the poorest women. They explained to him how they needed a loan equivalent to less than one euro in order to work independently from the loan sharks.
SOLEMA KHATUN, today 70 years old, was one of the first Grameen borrowers. Her first loan amounted to about 25 euros, to make bamboo chairs in self-employment. She works today with a loan of 1,300 euros and has long left the poverty level behind her.

✤ **DER BOHRENDE SCHMERZ SOLCHER BILDER.** Yunus hielt es irgendwann nicht mehr aus. Jeden Tag sah er auf dem Weg zum Campus solche Bilder und schlimmere. Auf diesem Bild sind zwei Geschwistergruppen, zwischen 4 und 17 Jahre alt, die sich zusammengetan haben, um nachts Papierabfälle zu sammeln und zu verkaufen. Der Erlös reicht, wenn es gut geht, zum Vegetieren auf der Straße lebenslanger Armut.

✤ **THE PIERCING PAIN OF SUCH PHOTOGRAPHS.** Yunus at some point could not stand it anymore. He saw such scenes or worse every day on his way to the campus. In this photograph there are two groups of siblings aged between 4 and 17 who have joined together to collect paper trash at night to sell. Their proceeds, when things go well, are enough for a miserable existence on the street in lifelong poverty.

❁ **DAS STERBEN VOR DEM TOR.** Wenn Yunus Mitte der 1970er-Jahre aus dem Tor 2 der Universität von Chittagong heraustrat, sah er auf dieses Gebäude. Jeden Tag lagen dort Verhungernde und Verhungerte. Direkt gegenüber liegt die Jonata Bank. Als Yunus die Banker fragte, ob sie bereit seien, den Ärmsten kleine Kredite für den Ausstieg aus dem Teufelskreis der Armut zu geben, wurde dieses Ansinnen brüsk abgelehnt. Wo früher so viele arme Menschen starben, sitzt heute der Schuhputzer und Schuster Muhammad Auib Ali. Er verdient 2 Euro am Tag. Seine Frau ist Grameen-Kreditnehmerin. Sie arbeitet inzwischen mit einem 160-Euro-Grameen-Kredit.

❁ **DYING IN FRONT OF THE DOOR.** In the middle of the 1970s when Yunus stepped out of Gate 2 of the University of Chittagong, he saw this building. Every day the hungry and starving lay there. Directly across from them is the Jonata Bank. When Yunus asked the bankers if they would be prepared to give the poorest a small loan so they could leave the vicious circle of poverty, the suggestion was brusquely refused. Where so many people used to die, today the cobbler and shoeshine man sits, Muhammad Auib Ali. He earns 2 euros a day. His wife is a Grameen borrower. She works in the meantime with a 160-euro Grameen loan.

❀ **SUMANA BARUA,** heute 53 Jahre alt, war eine jener Frauen, die in der allerersten Experimentierphase von Yunus privat einen Kredit erhielten. Von den Allerärmsten stieg sie inzwischen in die Mittelschicht Bangladeschs auf, ihre Tochter absolvierte das College, zwei ihrer drei Söhne arbeiten erfolgreich als Kaufleute in Korea und Kanada.

❀ **SUMANA BARUA,** today 53 years old, was one of the women in the very first experimental stage who received a private loan from Yunus. From one of the poorest, she has risen in the meantime to the middle class in Bangladesh, her daughter graduated from college, and two of her sons work successfully as businessmen in Korea and Canada.

❀ Das inzwischen verfallene Wohnhaus von **MUHAMMAD YUNUS,** als dieser als Professor an der Universität Chittagong lehrte.

❀ The residence of **MUHAMMAD YUNUS** when he taught as professor at the University of Chittagong, now dilapidated.

❖ **IM ERSTEN STOCK DIESES HAUSES** in der Bokshir-Hat-Gasse in Chittagong lebte die Familie Yunus. Darunter befand sich der Juwelierladen des Vaters.

❖ **THE YUNUS FAMILY LIVED ON THE FIRST FLOOR** of this house in the Bokshir Hat Lane in Chittagong. Beneath it was his father's jewellery shop.

❖ **DAS ERSTE GRAMEEN OFFICE** in Jobra von 1976 bis 1978. Heute beherbergt es eine Schreinerei und einen Gemüseladen.

❖ **THE FIRST GRAMEEN OFFICE** in Jobra from 1976 to 1978. Today it accommodates a carpenter's workshop and a greengrocer.

WAS IST ARMUT? WAS IST BEFREIUNG AUS DER ARMUT?

Für jeden zweiten Mitbewohner unserer gemeinsamen globalen Heimat namens Erde ist Armut tägliche Lebensrealität. Und doch ist Armut den Vorstellungen vieler Menschen weit entrückt. Uns in der westlichen Welt erreicht sie allenfalls noch schemenhaft, in schnellen Bildern auf Bildschirmen oder in Magazinen – ohne jeden Impuls, bei diesem Phänomen innezuhalten und wirklich nachzudenken. Und auch auf der sprachlichen Ebene erreichen uns nur Schemen: Armut begegnet uns in Slogans, die mit Spendenaufrufen verknüpft sind, in Appellen, die an unser schlechtes Gewissen rühren wollen. Ist dies Armut?

In wohlhabenden Ländern und Regionen bräuchte es schon heute häufig ein „Museum der Armut" – um jene Details sichtbar zu machen, die uns erst ein Verstehen erschließen können.

Dieser Bildband zeigt uns wesentlich mehr als das Vertraute. Wir sehen hier nicht einfach „Arme" – wir sehen hier Menschen: Menschen mit Namen, mit starken Gesichtern, mit Geschichten, mit Verwandten, mit Orten, in denen sie leben und mit Gemeinschaften, die sie mitgestalten. Aber vor allem: Die Armen werden hier zu Menschen mit Zukunft, zu Menschen auf dem Weg aus der Armut heraus.

WHAT IS POVERTY? WHAT IS LIBERATION FROM POVERTY?

For every second fellow occupant of our common global home called Earth, poverty is the daily reality of life. And yet, poverty is far removed from the imaginations of many people. It still touches us in the western world as a shadow at most, in quick images on the screen or in magazines – without our retaining and really thinking about any impulses from these phenomena. And on the level of words, too, we recognise only patterns: we encounter poverty in slogans that are connected with calls for donations, appeals that want to appeal to our guilty consciences. Is this poverty?

In prosperous countries, a "Museum of Poverty" is required today to make the details visible so we can begin to develop an understanding.

This book of photographs shows us considerably more than what we are accustomed to seeing. We do not simply see "poverty" here – we see people, people with names, with strong faces, with histories, with relatives, with the places in which they live, with communities that they have created and that they help shape. But especially: the poor here become people with a future, people on the way out of poverty.

✣ **RECYCLING DER ARMUT.** Aleya Begum* aus dem Dorf Kagogepara recycelt Zementsäcke. Zementsäcke bestehen aus sechs Lagen Papier. Nur eine Lage kommt mit Zement in Berührung. Diese Schicht wird für Baustoffverpackungen und Ähnliches recycelt, die anderen fünf Schichten für Tüten der Gemüse-, Obst- und Textilienhändler. Aleya hält eine Schüssel mit Kleister in der Hand.

✣ **RECYCLING POVERTY.** Aleya Begum** from the village of Kagogepara recycles cement bags. Cement bags are made of six layers of paper. Only one layer comes into contact with the cement. This layer is recycled for packaging building materials and the like, the other five layers for bags for vegetables, fruit and fabrics. Aleya is holding a bowl with paste in her hands.

---

* In Bangladesch ist es nicht immer üblich einen Nachnamen zu verwenden. Zum Teil aber drücken diese Zugehörigkeiten aus und wiederholen sich daher häufig.

** In Bangladesh it is not generally common practice to use last names. However, in part they stand for social affiliation and are therefore found repeatedly.

❦ **SYMBIOSE DES ÜBERLEBENS.** Amena Khatun, 42 Jahre alt, ist Mitglied einer Kreditgruppe im Dorf Boligau. Zehn Kreditgruppen von jeweils fünf Personen unterhalten dort ein eigenes Grameen Center. Frau Khatun pflegt unter anderem eine trächtige Kuh und unterhält zwei Hühner, drei Enten und eine Ziege. Von den 30 Euro Einkommen im Monat kann sie leben. Den Grameen-Kredit investierte sie nicht in ihr Geschäft, sondern in die Ausbildung ihrer beiden noch nicht verheirateten Töchter.

❦ **SYMBIOSIS OF SURVIVAL.** Amena Khatun, 42 years old, is a member of a loan group in the village of Boligau. Ten loan groups of five persons each maintain their own Grameen centre here. Mrs Khatun cares for a pregnant cow, as well as two chickens, three ducks and a goat among other things. She can live from her income of 30 euros a month. The Grameen loan is not invested in her business but rather in the education of both of her still unmarried daughters.

In anderen Bildern und Bildbänden begegnen uns „die Armen" immer wieder als Hilfesuchende, als nach Hilfe Rufende. Anders in diesem Bildband: Wer sich auf die Augen der hier fotografierten Menschen einlässt, sieht Überraschendes. Er erfährt eine neue Ästhetik, eine Ästhetik der Würde. Er schaut in Gesichter, die tief gefurcht sind durch ein hartes, ein äußerst hartes Leben – in unerwartet klare, mehr noch: leuchtende Augen. Inmitten der Armut leuchtende Augen – wie kann das sein?

Dies liegt zum einen am Auge des Fotografen: Ein guter Fotograf macht in seiner Arbeit das sichtbar, was er sieht und sichtbar machen will. Will er Elend sichtbar machen um der Demonstration des Elends willen? Oder will er Menschen ihr Gesicht zurückgeben als Menschen in Würde, auch wenn sie allzu offensichtlich in unerträglichem Elend leben?

In other photographs and illustrated books, we encounter "the poor" over and over again as people seeking help, calling for help. In this book of photographs, it is different: whoever looks into the eyes of the people photographed here sees something surprising. We experience a new aesthetic, an aesthetic of dignity. We see – in the faces that are deeply furrowed through a hard, an unbelievably hard life – unexpectedly clear, and yes, even more, shining eyes. In the middle of poverty, shining eyes – how can that be?

For one, this depends on the eye of the photographer: a good photographer brings into his work what he sees and wants to make visible. Does he want to make misery visible as a demonstration of misery? Or does he want to give people their identity back as people of dignity, even when they all too obviously live in unbearable poverty?

Die ungewohnte Intensität der Menschen, die uns hier so nahekommen, liegt in diesem Fall auch an den Augen der Fotografierten: Es sind Menschen, in deren Blick sich das viel beschworene Licht am Ende des Tunnels spiegelt. Es sind Menschen der Grameen Family; Arme, die nicht mit Almosen abgespeist werden, sondern – „normaler" Sichtweise diametral entgegengesetzt – von jenen, die sie unterstützen, als selbstständige Unternehmer gesehen werden.

Dieser Bildband erzählt von fundamentalen Veränderungen – und er wird unser Bild von den Armen verändern. Er erzählt die Geschichte eines Menschen namens Muhammad Yunus, der eines Tages zu lernen begann. Um den sich dann unter dem Namen „Grameen" schrittweise ein – heute weltweit organisiertes – Team formierte. Dieses gesamte Grameen-Team änderte im Laufe seiner Arbeit sein Bild von den Armen fundamental. Und genau dadurch änderte es das Bild dieser Armen von sich selbst, und damit die Realität dieser Armen.

The unusual intensity of the people who come so close to us here in this case also lies in the eyes of those photographed: they are people whose expressions reflect the frequently attested light at the end of the tunnel. They are people of the Grameen family; poor who are not fobbed off with alms but – diametrically opposed to the "normal" point of view – seen by those who support them as self-employed entrepreneurs.

This book of photographs depicts fundamental change – and it will change our view of the poor. It tells the history of a person named Muhammad Yunus who began one day to learn. And who then, under the name Grameen, step by step formed what is today a worldwide organised team. This entire Grameen team fundamentally changed his view of the impoverished in the course of his work. And through this, the way the poor viewed themselves changed, and with it, their reality.

❊ „GRAUE EMINENZ". UNTERNEHMERIN IM HINTERGRUND. Fuloni Rangsha, 55 Jahre, baute mit ihren schrittweise steigenden Grameen-Krediten eine Geflügelfarm auf mit inzwischen rund 400 Hühnern. Ihr Einkommen: 70 Euro im Monat. Da die fünf Kinder alle außer Haus sind, liegt dieses Einkommen bereits oberhalb der Armutsgrenze. Ihr Mann ist der „Direktor" ihrer Farm, die Besitzerin bleibt im Hintergrund. Der Friseurstuhl vor ihrem Haus gehört einem Freund der Familie namens Montu Dus, einem Hindu. Dieser trägt den Stuhl jeden Tag auf dem Kopf zum nahegelegenen Bazar, um dort mitten im Getümmel seinem Geschäft des Haareschneidens nachzugehen. Abends stellt er ihn dann am Haus der Rangshas unter; dort ist er vor Diebstahl besser geschützt.

❊ "GREY EMINENCE", BUSINESSWOMAN IN THE BACKGROUND. Fuloni Rangsha, 55 years old, who with her gradually increasing Grameen loan built up a chicken farm which now has about 400 chickens. Her income: 70 euros a month. Because all of her five children left home this income already lies below the poverty level. Her husband is the "director" of the farm, the owner stays in the background. The hairdresser's chair in front of their house belongs to a friend named Montu Dus, a Hindu. Every day he carries the chair on his head to the bazaar nearby, in order to follow his business of cutting hair there in the middle of the hubbub. In the evening, he then places it again by the Rangsha's house where it is better protected from theft.

❖ **WEBEN FÜR EIN BESSERES LEBEN.** Amina Begum, 22 Jahre, arbeitet in einer Weberei im Dorf Tenguria. Die Weberei mit 100 Webstühlen wurde von Renu Begum aufgebaut. Ihr derzeitiger Kredit von Grameen beläuft sich auf 2.000 Euro, investiert in den Ausbau ihrer Weberei sowie in den Aufbau einer Kuhfarm. Ferner gehört ihr noch ein Shop im Bazar von Bollar, in dem sie Baumwolle verkauft. Ihr erster Kredit im Jahre 1985 betrug noch 20 Euro. Damals lebte die heutige Webereibesitzerin Renu Begum bei ihren Schwiegereltern und besaß buchstäblich nichts. Heute liegt ihr Nettogewinn bei 200 Euro im Monat. Zwei ihrer Söhne sowie ihr Mann arbeiten in ihrem Unternehmen, zwei weitere Söhne studieren an der Universität. Renu Begum ist eine von derzeit 8 Millionen Selbstständigen, die dank Grameen heute vielen weiteren Millionen Menschen Arbeit geben.

❖ **WEAVING FOR A BETTER LIFE.** Amina Begum, 22 years old, works in a weaving mill in the village of Tenguria. The weaving mill with 100 looms was built up by Renu Begum. Her current loan from Grameen amounts to 2,000 euros invested in the extension of her weaving mill, as well as the construction of a cattle farm. Furthermore, she also has a shop in the Bollar bazaar where she sells cotton. The present owner of the weaving mill used to live with her parents-in-law and owned literally nothing. Today, her net monthly profit is 200 euros. Two of her sons, as well as her husband, work in the business, two other sons study at the university. Renu Begum is one of currently eight million self-employed people who thank Grameen today, and who give work to many millions more.

✤ **EIN GROSSES RAD DREHEN.** Muhammad Shohaq ist 4 Jahre alt. Er spielt auf dem Gelände der Weberei seiner Großmutter im Dorf Tenguria. Auf den großen Rädern im Hintergrund werden Baumwollfäden aufgezogen, um daraus Saris zu produzieren. Die Weberei mit 30 Webstühlen und 42 Angestellten gehört Mohammad Jakir Hossain, dem Sohn der 60-jährigen Grameen-Kreditnehmerin Jorina Begum. Sie investierte in dessen Unternehmen. Die Arbeitnehmer verdienen mit der Herstellung von 3 bis 4 Saris am Tag rund 2 Euro. Das ist das Doppelte dessen, was die Vereinten Nationen als Grenze zur absoluten Armut definieren. Auch ihr Lebensrad dreht sich somit ein gutes Stück schneller aus der Armut heraus als früher.

✤ **TURNING A LARGE WHEEL.** Muhammad Shohaq is 4 years old. He plays on the property of his grandmother's weaving mill in the village of Tenguria. On the large wheels in the background, cotton threads are wound from which saris are produced. The weaving mill with 30 looms and 42 employees belongs to Mohammad Jakir Hossain, the son of the 60-year-old Grameen borrower, Jorina Begum. She invested in this business. The employees earn about 2 euros a day with the production of three to four saris. This is twice as much as what the United Nations defines as absolute poverty. Therefore, the wheel of life is turning a great deal faster out of poverty than earlier.

VISION 2030
DIE WELT IST BEFREIT VON ARMUT!

Springen wir einige Zeit in die Zukunft. Dhaka, Bangladesch. Irgendein Tag so etwa um das Jahr 2030, gut 50 Jahre nach dem Start des ersten Kleinkreditprojektes von Muhammad Yunus. Sitz der Weltbank ist mittlerweile die Hauptstadt Bangladeschs. Oloka Begum, seit 2022 Präsidentin der Weltbank, stellt den aktuellen Weltarmutsbericht vor. Sie tritt vor die Weltpresse, die zu diesem Ereignis mit Tausenden von Vertretern angereist ist, und verkündet mit unübersehbarem Stolz: „Dies ist der letzte Weltarmutsbericht in der Menschheitsgeschichte! Wir haben es endlich geschafft: Die Welt ist befreit von Armut!"

Das letzte Mal, dass so viele Staatsoberhäupter zusammentrafen, war im Jahr 2000 – als die Vereinten Nationen zum Millenniumsgipfel nach New York geladen hatten: Nahezu alle Mächtigen der Welt kamen damals zusammen, um den Beginn eines neuen Jahrtausends zu begehen. Kofi Annan, der damalige Generalsekretär der Vereinten Nationen, setzte alles daran, den Nationen ein klares Versprechen abzuringen. Ziel war die weltweite Überwindung der Armut. Die Nationen sollten sich verbindlich verpflichten, bis zum Jahr 2015 wesentliche Teilziele zu erreichen; es ging um ein bislang ungekanntes Ausmaß konkreter Selbstverpflichtungen der Staaten.

VISION 2030
THE WORLD IS FREE FROM POVERTY!

Let us jump sometime into the future. Dhaka, Bangladesh. Let us say in the year 2030, one day a good 50 years after the start of the first microcredit project from Muhammad Yunus. Meanwhile, the headquarters of the World Bank are situated in the capital city of Bangladesh. Oloka Begum, President of the World Bank since 2022, presents the current report on poverty. She appears before the members of the world press, who have travelled by the thousands to this event, and announces with obvious pride: "This is the last report on world poverty in the history of mankind! We have finally succeeded: the world is free from poverty!"

The last time that so many heads of state came together was in the year 2000, when the United Nations invited them to New York for the Millennium Summit: almost all of the most influential people in the world came together then to celebrate the beginning of the new millennium. Kofi Annan, Secretary-General of the United Nations back then, set everything on wresting a clear promise from the nations. The goal was the worldwide defeat of poverty. The nations should bindingly commit themselves to achieving substantial partial objectives by the year 2015; it was an extent unknown until then of specific self-commitment of the nations.

❈ **AUS DEM TEUFELSKREIS DER ARMUT HERAUSTRETEN.** Sonia Akter aus dem Dorf Bagdi, 13 Jahre, hilft etwa zwei Stunden pro Tag außerhalb der Schulzeiten ihrer Mutter und Grameen-Kreditnehmerin Parvin Begum bei der Herstellung von Baby-Hängestühlen aus Jute. Der Bambuskreis hält das Jutenetz. Die Herstellung eines Baby-Hängestuhls dauert etwa eine Stunde und bringt auf dem Markt 1,50 Euro, an einem Baby-Hängebettchen arbeiten sie etwa drei Stunden und erzielen dafür 4 bis 5 Euro. Sonia mag die Arbeit, weil sie unmittelbar spürt, wie ihre Familie und damit auch sie selbst jeden Monat ein kleines Stück mehr Wohlstand erlangen.

❈ **STEPPING OUT OF THE VICIOUS CIRCLE OF POVERTY.** Sonia Akter from the village of Bagdi, 13 years old, helps her mother and Grameen borrower, Parvin Begum, for about two hours a day after school in the production of hanging babies' chairs made of jute. The bamboo circle holds the jute net. The construction of a hanging babies' chair takes about an hour and pays 1.50 euros at the market. For a hanging babies' bed, she works for about three hours and receives four to five euros. Sonia likes the work because she can see how her family, and therefore herself, gain a little bit more prosperity each month.

❋ **12 UHR MITTAGS** – Siesta in Bagdi.
❋ **NOON SIESTA** in Bagdi.

037

Erinnern wir uns an die Versprechen der Staatsoberhäupter – festgehalten in den so genannten „Millenniumentwicklungszielen", den „Millennium Development Goals". Im Jahr 2015 sollte Folgendes erreicht sein:

- Die Zahl der „absolut Armen" sollte halbiert sein. Als „absolut arm" definierten die Vereinten Nationen Menschen, deren Einkommen unterhalb von einem US-Dollar pro Tag lag, was seinerzeit noch auf mehr als eine Milliarde Menschen zutraf.

- Die Zahl der Menschen, die keinen Zugang zu sauberem Wasser hatten – was gleichfalls auf eine Milliarde Menschen zutraf –, sollte halbiert sein.

- Alle Kinder der Welt sollten zumindest Zugang zum Besuch eines vollen Grundschulprogramms haben. Der Zugang sollte für beide Geschlechter in gleicher Weise sichergestellt sein.

- Die Kindersterblichkeit sollte auf ein Drittel des Standes von 2000 gesenkt sein.

- Der Trend bei epidemischen Krankheiten wie HIV/AIDS oder Malaria sollte gewendet sein.

- Der Trend beim Verlust von Umweltressourcen sollte gleichfalls gewendet sein.

- Und schließlich nahm man sich substanzielle Verbesserungen für die Zusammenarbeit auf globaler Ebene vor, um weltweit – für alle Menschen und Nationen – bessere Verhältnisse zu schaffen: Auf wirtschaftlicher Ebene strebte man einen wirksamen Schutz vor Ausbeutung, Verschuldung und Abhängigkeit an, auf politischer Ebene verantwortliche und effektive Regierungen.

Let us remind ourselves of the promises made by the heads of states recorded in the so-called "Millennium Development Goals". By the year 2015, the following should be accomplished:

- The number of "absolute poor" should be halved. The United Nations defines as "absolute poor" people whose income lies below one US dollar a day, which in those days still applied to more than a billion people.

- The number of people with no access to clean water, which likewise affected a billion people, should be halved.

- All the children in the world should at least have access to attendance of a complete elementary school programme. The access should be equally available for both genders.

- The infant mortality rate should sink to a third of the level of 2000.

- The trend toward epidemic diseases such as HIV/AIDS or malaria should be turned around.

- The trend toward the loss of environmental resources should likewise be turned around.

- And finally, one should plan substantial improvement of cooperation on a global level in order to create better conditions worldwide for all people and nations: on an economic level striving for effective protection against exploitation, indebtedness and, on a political level, dependency on responsible and effective government.

✣ **ANALPHABETISMUS WAR GESTERN.** Die beiden Schulmädchen Rotna, 6 Jahre, und Zakia, 8 Jahre, kommen aus dem Bambusdorf Golnogor. Dort leben 100 Familien überwiegend von der Bambusflechterei; davon sind 60 Familien Kreditnehmer bei der Grameen Bank. Eine der vielen sozialen Nebenwirkungen des Grameen-Kreditsystems für die Armen: Obwohl nahezu alle Kreditnehmer selbst zunächst noch Analphabeten waren, ist der Analphabetismus bei ihren Kindern vollständig getilgt.

✣ **ILLITERACY WAS YESTERDAY.** The two schoolgirls, Rotna, age 6, and Zakia, age 8, come from the bamboo village of Golnogor. 100 families live there predominantly from plaiting bamboo; 60 of these families are borrowers from the Grameen Bank. One of the many social side effects of the Grameen loan systems for the poor: although almost all borrowers themselves were illiterates, illiteracy among children has been completely eliminated.

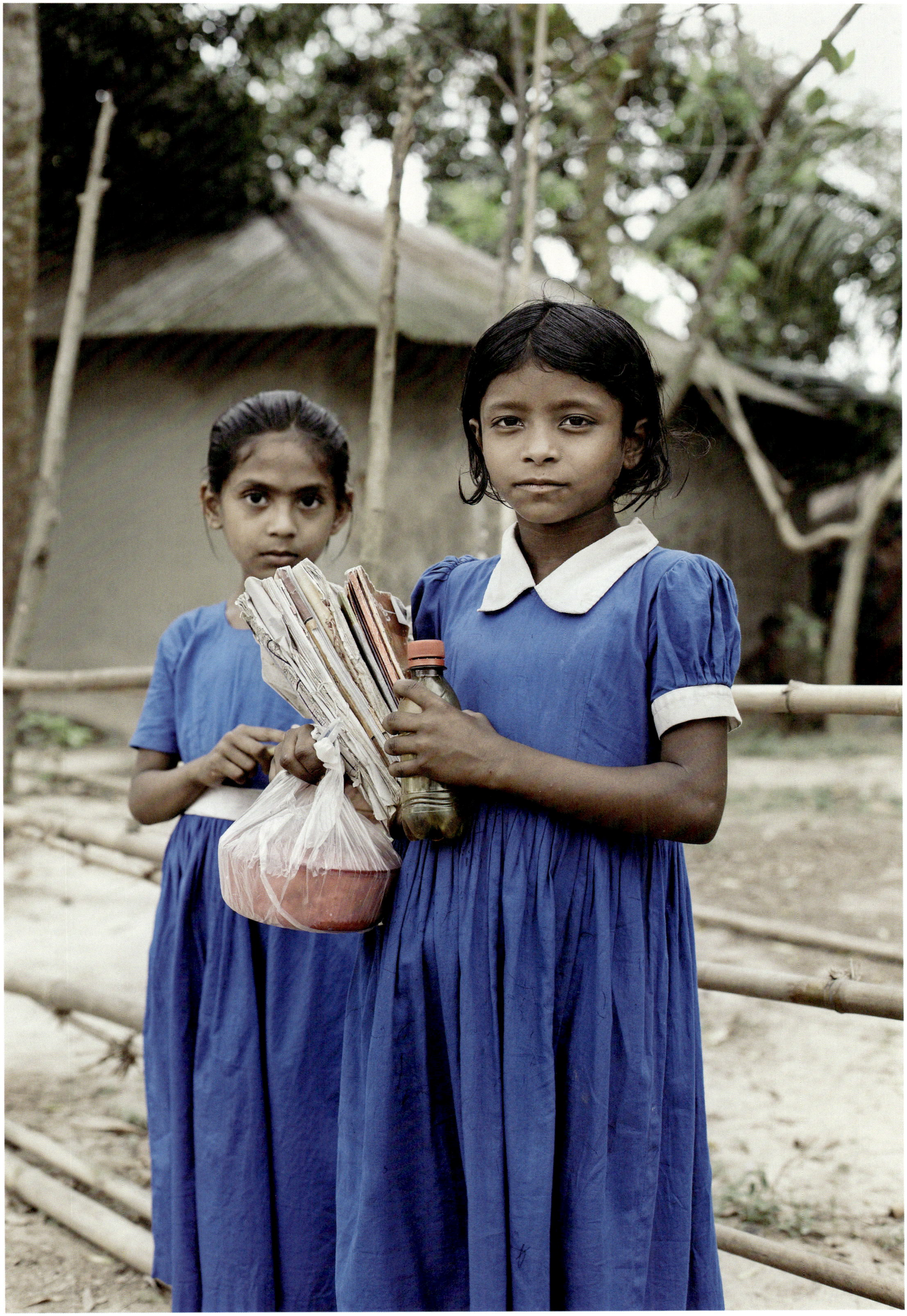

Wir wissen heute, an diesem Tag irgendwann um das Jahr 2030, als der letzte Weltarmutsbericht der Menschheitsgeschichte vorgestellt wird: Mit Ausnahme des letzten Punktes waren die Millenniumsziele im Jahr 2015 im Wesentlichen erreicht – wenn auch auf anderem Wege, als man sich das im Jahr 2000 vorgestellt hatte.

Dieser heutige Tag ist ein Tag der großen Freude der gesamten Weltgemeinschaft. Kein einziges Staatsoberhaupt hat es sich nehmen lassen, persönlich nach Dhaka anzureisen. Doch Weltbankchefin Begum hat sich mit ihrer Forderung durchgesetzt, zu diesem Gipfeltreffen auch die wahren Helden der Armutsüberwindung als gleichwertige Gipfelteilnehmer einzuladen. So ist nun jedem Staatschef bzw. jeder Staatschefin eine ausgewählte Persönlichkeit seines bzw. ihres Landes zur Seite gestellt, die sich um die Überwindung der Armut im jeweiligen Land besonders verdient gemacht hat – ein Pionier der Armutsüberwindung. Und während auf Seiten der Staatschefs noch immer drei Viertel Männer sind, ist das Verhältnis auf Seiten der Pioniere exakt umgekehrt: Drei Viertel sind Frauen.

We know today – on this day sometime in the year 2030 – as the last report about world poverty in human history is presented that, with the exception of the final points, the millennium goals were essentially reached in the year 2015, although in a different way than the one we had imagined in the year 2000.

This today is a day of great happiness for the entire international community. Not a single head of state refused to personally travel to Dhaka. But the World Bank President Begum had imposed her demand that the real heroes of the defeat of poverty should be invited as equal participants of this summit meeting. So now each head of state is supported by an elected personality from his or her country who had made a special contribution to eliminating poverty in each country – a pioneer in the fight against poverty. And while three-quarters of the heads of state are still men, the ratio on the side of the pioneers in the defeat of poverty is exactly the opposite: three-quarters of these pioneers are women.

❖ **BLICK IN EINE BESSERE ZUKUNFT.** Der 8-jährige Nasmul, ebenfalls aus dem Dorf Golnogor, sitzt auf Bambusstangen. Aus seinen Augen spricht deutlich Zuversicht – anders als bei den Generationen vor ihm.

❖ **VIEW OF A BETTER FUTURE.** The 8-year-old Nasmul from the village of Golnogor sits on bamboo stalks. His eyes speak of a clear confidence – different than those in the generation before him.

041

※ „SALUTE!" STRAMMSTEHEN VOR SICH SELBST.

Amena Khatun, die uns schon auf Seite 24 begegnete, hebt die rechte Hand zum Gruß der Grameen-Kreditnehmerfamilie. Jedes Treffen in jedem Grameen Center beginnt mit diesem Gruß: dem Aufstehen aller Anwesenden und einem lauten „Salute", während die Hand zackig sich zur Schläfe erhebt. Wir kennen diesen Gruß aus militärischen Traditionen, doch bei Grameen hat er eine völlig andere Bedeutung: Das Strammstehen vor Befehlsgebern ist hier gerade nicht gemeint. Die Frauen in Bangladesch blickten traditionell stets zu Boden, wenn sie sich in Gegenwart von Fremden oder von Männern außerhalb ihrer engsten Familie befanden. Der Grameen-Gruß „Salute" ist die täglich neue Erinnerung an den aufrechten Gang und den offenen Blick – auf Augenhöhe mit allen anderen Menschen.

※ "SALUTE!" TO STAND TO ATTENTION BEFORE YOURSELF.

Amena Khatun, who we have already met on page 24, lifts her right hand in the greeting of the Grameen loan family. Every meeting in each Grameen centre begins with this greeting: everyone present stands and with a loud "Salute!", they smartly raise their hands to their temples. We know this greeting from military traditions but at Grameen it has a completely different meaning: standing to attention in front of a commander is not what is meant here. The women of Bangladesh traditionally always look at the floor when they find themselves in the presence of strangers or of men outside their closest family. The Grameen greeting, "Salute!" is the daily reminder of the upright posture and open gaze – at eye level – with all other people.

❖ **AM ANFANG WAR DIE EIGENE UNTERSCHRIFT.** Monjura Khatun, 25 Jahre, aus dem Dorf Baligoan, trägt ihren Namen in das Kreditheft ein. Jeder Kreditnehmer und jede Kreditnehmerin muss lernen, zumindest den eigenen Namen zu schreiben, bevor er oder sie einen Kredit von Grameen erhalten kann. Der eigene Name und die eigene Unterschrift im Kreditbuch symbolisieren den Schritt in eine andere Welt, sie sind die Signatur der eigenen Identität und der neu gewonnenen Selbstständigkeit.

❖ **IN THE BEGINNING, THERE WAS HER OWN SIGNATURE.** Monjura Khatun, 25 years old from the village of Baligoan, writes her name in the loan book. Each borrower, male or female, must learn to write at least their own name before he or she can receive a loan from Grameen. Their own name and their own signatures in the loan books symbolise a step into another world; they are the signatures of their own identity and their newly gained independence.

044

❂ **SCHWEIN HABEN.** Aunu Radha Ransha, 32 Jahre, Christin aus dem Dorf Gul Para, kaufte sich von ihrem 40-Euro-Kredit ein Schwein und zwei Ziegen. Sie arbeitet ferner auf dem Feld im Reisanbau und als Fischerin. Auf dem Bild zeigt sie ihr Fischernetz. Insgesamt kommt sie inzwischen auf ein Einkommen von 40 Euro im Monat. Ihr Mann ergänzt das Familieneinkommen als Tagelöhner. Ihre drei Kinder besuchen die Schule. Das wurde erst durch die Erweiterung ihrer Tätigkeiten um die Nebenselbstständigkeit mit Schwein und Ziegen möglich.

❂ **LUCK WITH A PIG.** Aunu Radha Ransha, age 32, a Christian from the village of Gul Para, bought from her 40 euros loan a pig and two goats. In addition, she works in the field raising rice, and also as a fisherwoman. Here she is holding a fishing net. Altogether, she earns an income of 40 euros a month. Her husband contributes to the family income as a day labourer. Their three children attend school. This became possible through the extension of her occupation with the additional self-employment with the pig and the goats.

❂ Grameen-Kreditbuch.
❂ Grameen loan book.

❂ Ihre Einkommensergänzung.
❂ Her income supplement.

Auch ein anderes Vorhaben ist termingerecht vollendet. Oloka Begum wollte unbedingt das seit einiger Zeit im Bau befindliche „Weltmuseum der Armut" fertiggestellt sehen, wenn sie diesen Weltarmutsbericht vorstellt. Die Eröffnung des Museums sollte der Höhepunkt dieses historischen Gipfeltreffens sein.

Im Vorblick auf diesen denkwürdigen Wendepunkt – das weltweite Ende der Armut – gab es schon seit längerer Zeit auf verschiedenen Kontinenten Initiativen zum Bau von Museen der Armut. Man bezog sich dabei jeweils auf die Vision von Muhammad Yunus. Lange vor der Jahrtausendwende hatte er gesagt: „Ich stelle mir ein Museum der Armut vor. Irgendwann werden die Menschen in Museen gehen müssen, um zu verstehen, was Armut einmal war und wie sie aussah, und sie werden entsetzt sein und sich wundern, dass wir nicht viel früher etwas dagegen unternommen haben." Alle Initiativen zum Bau von Museen der Armut waren sich einig: Das erste Museum sollte von niemand anderem als Muhammad Yunus selbst eröffnet werden. Und einig war man sich auch: Das „Weltmuseum der Armut" sollte seinen Sitz in Dhaka haben.

Another plan was also finished according to schedule. Oloka Begum insisted that the "World Museum of Poverty", which had been in construction for some time, should be completed when she presented the report on world poverty. The opening of the museum should be the highlight of this historical meeting.

As a preview of this historical turning point – the end of poverty worldwide – initiatives in various continents for the construction of "Museums of Poverty" have existed for a long time. For each one reference was always made to the vision of Muhammad Yunus. Long before the turn of the millennium, he said: "I imagine a Museum of Poverty. At some point, people will have to visit a museum in order to understand what poverty once was and how it looked. They will be appalled, and will wonder why we did not do something about it much earlier." Every initiative for the construction of the "Museums of Poverty" agreed: the first such museum should be opened by no other than Muhammad Yunus himself. And they were also in agreement: the "World Museum of Poverty" should have its headquarters in Dhaka.

❖ **RELIGION UND KASTEN SPIELEN KEINE ROLLE.** Der 3-jährige Gopinath Pal im Hindu-Dorf Chapire ist von niedriger Kastenherkunft. Traditionell zwingt eine solche Herkunft die Menschen in lebenslange Armut: Töpfern gilt im Hinduismus als eine Arbeit der Armen und wird so bezahlt, dass man der Armut nicht entfliehen kann. Der Grameen-Kredit ermöglicht indes den Familien in Chapire das Entkommen aus der Armut: der Mehrwert ihrer Arbeit verbleibt bei ihnen selbst.

❖ **RELIGION AND CASTE DO NOT PLAY A ROLE.** The 3-year-old Gopinath Pal in the Hindu village of Chapire is from a lower caste heritage. Traditionally, such a background forced people into lifelong poverty: pottery making is considered in Hinduism as work for the poor and is paid so little than one cannot escape poverty. The Grameen loan enables the families in Chapire to escape from poverty because the profit from their work stays with them.

047

❋ „SEHR KLEIN, ABER STABIL UND MEIN."

Solema Khatun, 70 Jahre alt, konnte sich mittels eines speziellen Grameen-Baudarlehens irgendwann endlich ein eigenes kleines Häuschen leisten. Das Haus im Dorf Fateka ist nicht viel größer als das Bett, auf dem sie sitzt, und dieses dient daher zugleich auch als „Kleiderschrank". Dennoch bedeutet das eigene Heim einen großen Schritt im Vergleich zum vorherigen Leben.

❋ "VERY SMALL BUT STABLE AND MINE."

Solema Khatun, 70 years old, was finally able at some point to afford her own small house with the funds from a special Grameen construction loan. The house in the village of Fateka is not much larger than the bed on which she sits and it serves, therefore, as a "clothes closet" at the same time. Nevertheless, her own home represents a large step in comparison to her previous life.

049

050

�֍ **GRAMEEN BEI DEN ADIBASHI.** Shantora Rema, 40 Jahre, aus dem Dorf Telungia, gehört der ethnischen Minderheit der Adibashi an. Grameen ist überall im Lande verbreitet und kennt ethnische Grenzen ebenso wenig wie religiöse. Frau Rema ist Näherin und stellt Babykleidung her. Mit ihrem jüngsten Kredit in Höhe von 120 Euro kaufte sie sich Hühner und eine Kuh, um so zum einen die Ernährung ihrer Familie zu verbessern und zum anderen Zusatzeinkünfte zu generieren. Sie kommt inzwischen auf ein Monatseinkommen von 60 Euro, gemäß Bangladesch-Niveau das Sechsfache der Grenze absoluter Armut. An der Hauswand trocknet Kuhdung. Dieser wird als Brennmaterial verwendet.

�֍ **GRAMEEN BY THE ADIBASHI.** Shantora Rema, 40 years old, from the village of Telungia, belongs to the ethnic minority of the Adibashi. Grameen is spread out everywhere in the country and knows no ethnic nor religious borders. Mrs Rema is a seamstress and makes babies' clothing. With her latest loan in the amount of 120 euros, she bought some chickens and a cow to improve the diet of her family on the one hand, and to generate additional income on the other. Since then, she has a monthly income of 60 euros, which seen from the Bangladeshi viewpoint is six times the limit of absolute poverty. Cow manure is drying on the wall of the house. This is used as fuel.

Oloka Begum lässt es sich nicht nehmen, vor dem Hauptredner – Muhammad Yunus – noch ein paar Worte an die versammelte Weltprominenz und an die Weltgemeinschaft zu richten. Mit Stolz, doch ohne eine Spur von Überheblichkeit, beginnt sie mit ihrer eigenen Lebensgeschichte:

„Meine Mutter war eine der Ersten, die von den frühen Mitarbeitern der Grameen Bank angesprochen wurde, ob sie nicht versuchen wolle, sich mit einem kleinen Kredit aus dem immer gleichen Teufelskreis der Abhängigkeit und hoffnungslosen Armut herauszuarbeiten. Wie oft erzählte sie mir, was an diesem Tag in ihr vorging. Sie hatte noch nie in ihrem Leben eigenes Geld in der Hand gehalten. Von Wirtschaft verstand sie nicht mehr, als dass sie tagein, tagaus und meist bis an den Rand der Erschöpfung arbeiten musste. Doch gleichgültig, wie fleißig sie war, das von ihr erarbeitete Geld, das man ihrem Mann aushändigte, reichte nie aus, die Lebenssituation ihrer Familie zu verbessern. Spätestens mit der nächsten Naturkatastrophe und Hungersnot war die Situation ihrer Familie wieder verzweifelt: Kinder starben, alles mühselig Erreichte war erneut unwiederbringlich verloren.

Oloka Begum could not resist addressing a few words to the assembled world prominents and world communities in front of the main speaker, Muhammad Yunus. With composed pride, though without a trace of a sense of superiority, she began with her own life story:

"My mother was one of the first asked by an employee of the Grameen Bank, whether she would like to try, with a small loan, to work her way out of the continuous vicious circle of dependence and hopeless poverty. How often she told me what she felt inside her on that day. She had never in her life held her own money in her hands. She did not understand anything about economy other than that she had to work day-in and day-out until she was on the verge of exhaustion. But no matter how diligent she was, the money that her husband received was not enough to improve the living conditions of the family. And when the next natural disaster and famine occurred, the situation of the family would once again become desperate! Children died, everything laboriously achieved was irretrievably lost again.

052

❖ **LANDNAHME DURCH KREDIT.** Momota ist 30 Jahre alt und lebt im Dorf Kalimazane. Mit ihrem gegenwärtigen Kredit von 150 Euro hat sie von einem Landbesitzer für eine Jahrespacht von 100 Euro Land übernommen, um es zu bewirtschaften. Mit den restlichen 50 Euro konnte sie sich Samen, Düngemittel und Werkzeuge leisten sowie die Bewässerung organisieren und gar Hilfskräfte bezahlen, die sie zur Erntezeit braucht. Für die Düngung baut sie Dhumcha an (im Hintergrund des Fotos zu sehen). Den Samen dieser Pflanze bringt sie dann auf den Feldern aus, was für eine natürliche Düngung sorgt. – Inzwischen hat sich die Familie selbst ein erstes Stück Land gekauft und darauf ein Haus gebaut. Bald soll es auch reichen, die Landwirtschaft auf eigenem Grund zu betreiben.

❖ **LAND SETTLEMENT THROUGH LOANS.** Momota is 30 years old and lives in the village of Kalimazane. With her current loan of 150 euros she has leased land from a landowner for an annual lease of 100 euros in order to work on it. With the remaining 50 euros she was able to afford seeds, fertiliser and tools, as well as organising the irrigation and even to pay help that she needs during the harvest season. To fertilise, she grows Dhumcha (seen in the background of the photo). The seeds of this plant are then spread on the fields as a natural fertiliser. In the meantime, the family have bought themselves their first piece of land and built a house on it. Soon there should be enough to farm on their own land.

‚Das Leben sieht für mich keine Chance vor.' Immer wieder schoss meiner Mutter dieser Gedanke durch den Kopf. Mehr als ein Jahr brauchte sie, um ‚Ja' zu sagen und in einer Grameen-Kreditgruppe mitzumachen. Und erst allmählich konnte sie Vertrauen fassen, wich die existenzielle Unsicherheit. Dann wurde die Unternehmerin, die in ihr steckte, immer mehr sichtbar, für sie selbst wie für das ganze Dorf. Sobald sie wirtschaftlich den ersten Boden unter den Füßen spürte, sparte meine Mutter jeden Taka für ihre größte Hoffnung an, die plötzlich wie ein völlig anderes, neues Leben vor ihren Augen stand. Diese Hoffnung hatte einen Namen: Oloka. Ich – ihre älteste Tochter – sollte die bestmögliche Bildung erhalten. Unter größten eigenen Entbehrungen sparte sie darauf hin. Später nahm die Grameen Bank spezielle Bildungskredite in ihr Programm auf, die mir tatsächlich ermöglichten, als Tochter einer Analphabetin eine der bekanntesten Elitehochschulen zu besuchen.

Der eiserne Lebenstraum meiner Mutter – und wie sie mit mir immer wieder darüber sprach – weckte auch in mir einen Lebenstraum. Schon mit Studienbeginn stand mir mein Traumberuf vor Augen: Ich wollte die erste Nicht-Amerikanerin und die erste Frau sein, die an die Spitze der Weltbank kommt, um diese aus der Perspektive der Armen umgestalten zu können. Die Türen waren damals noch verschlossen für einen derart verrückten Traum. Viele Veränderungen, auf die ich keinen Einfluss hatte, öffneten sie dann im Laufe der Zeit.

'Life doesn't intend for me to have a chance.' This idea went through my mother's head over and over again. She needed more than a year to say 'yes' and to take part in a Grameen loan group. Only gradually could she gain trust in this existential uncertainty. Then the entrepreneur that was in her became more and more visible, not just to herself, but also to the entire village. As soon as she felt economically sure of the ground under her feet, my mother saved every Taka for her greatest hope, which suddenly appeared before her like a completely different new life. This hope had a name: Oloka. I, her oldest daughter, should have the best possible education. With great personal deprivation, this is what she saved for. Later the Grameen Bank added the special education loan to their programme that actually made it possible for me, the daughter of an illiterate, to attend one of the best-known elite universities.

My mother's resolute life's dream – and how she spoke again and again to me about it – awoke a life's dream in me, too. Even as my studies began, my dream job stood clearly before me: I wanted to be the first non-American and the first woman to rise to the top of the World Bank, so that I could reorganise it from the perspective of the poor. The doors were still closed then for such a crazy dream. Many changes, upon which I had no influence, opened them in the course of time.

Die Weltbank war zwar schon in den 1990er-Jahren unter James Wolfensohn offen für die Kleinkreditidee. Wolfensohn tat viel, um seinen Apparat für die neuen Chancen zu sensibilisieren. Aber erst nach 2015 reichte die Offenheit innerhalb dieser Weltorganisation dafür aus, um die notwendigen radikalen Umstellungen zu vollziehen – von einer typischen klassischen Beraterorganisation von westlichen Elitehochschulabsolventen zu einem echten Sozialunternehmen.

Irgendwann erschien dann auch der Gedanke schlüssig, eine Weltbank, die vor allem für die Entwicklung der Ärmsten da sein sollte, in eine Metropole eines Entwicklungslandes zu verpflanzen. Und ein noch größeres Wunder vollzog sich eines Tages, als Amerika nicht länger auf dem ungeschriebenen Recht bestand, nach dem nur Amerikaner die Weltbank führen dürften. Die Erkenntnis setzte sich durch, dass in einer vernetzten Welt Führung nur noch funktioniert, wenn sie sich als Dienerin einer Welt im Gleichgewicht versteht.

Nun, im Jahr 2030, da zumindest die schlimmsten Auswüchse an Armut wohl endgültig Geschichte sind, möchte ich – jemand, für den diese Geschichte noch ein wesentlicher Teil seines persönlichen Lebenswegs war – kurz innehalten. Es ist wichtig, zu verstehen, was die Menschheit an dieser Stelle hinter sich lässt und was sie vor sich hat.

The World Bank, under the presidency of James Wolfensohn, was already open to the idea of microcredits in the 1990s. Wolfensohn did a lot to sensitise his apparatus for the new chances. But only after 2015 was there sufficient openness within this world organisation to carry out the necessary radical conversions – from a typical classical advisory organisation of western elite university graduates to a real social enterprise.

At some point, the idea arose to transplant the World Bank, which should be there especially for the development of the poorest people, to the capital city of a developing country. And an even greater wonder took place one day when America no longer insisted on the unwritten right by which only Americans were allowed to run the World Bank. The insight was accepted that a linked world leadership could only function when it is understood to be a servant of a truly balanced world.

So, in the year 2030, when at least the worst excesses of poverty have become history, as someone for whom this story is still an essential part of her personal life's path, I would like to briefly pause. It is important to understand what humanity at this point has left behind, and what lies ahead.

❧ **BILDUNGSKREDIT — DAS KATAPULT NACH OBEN.** Die 45-jährige Lalbanu aus Kalimazane ist ebenfalls in der Landwirtschaft tätig. Doch ihr ganzer Stolz ist der Bildungskredit für ihren Sohn, den ihr ein neues Kreditprogramm von Grameen ermöglichte. Es ist ein Kredit von 770 Euro; angesichts der Lebensverhältnisse der Grameen-Kreditnehmerinnen, die ausnahmslos alle aus der absoluten Armut kommen, klingt dies astronomisch hoch. Doch die Erfahrung zeigt: Die Grameen-Kinder verdienen mit einem Hochschulstudium derart viel mehr als sie ohne dieses verdient hätten, dass die Rückzahlung in der Regel absolut kein Problem darstellt.

❧ **EDUCATION LOAN — THE CATAPULT UPWARDS.** The 45-year-old Lalbanu from Kalimazane is also active in farming. However, her greatest pride is the education loan for her son, made possible by a new loan programme from Grameen. It is a loan of 770 euros; in the face of the Grameen borrowers, who all without exception come from absolute poverty, this sounds astronomically high but experience shows that with a college education the Grameen children earn much more than they would have without it, so the repayment usually does not present a problem.

055

056

✣ **RENTE FÜR EINE BESSERE ALTERSSICHERHEIT.** Shuvashini Rangdi, 35 Jahre, lebt in West Utrail. Sie gehört ebenfalls zur Minderheit der christlichen Adibashi; sie sitzt vor ihrem Haus, das ein auf die Wand aufgetragenes Tigergemälde ziert. In der Hochsaison verdient sie mit Töpfern inzwischen 20 Euro. Mit den 60 Euro Kredit kaufte sie Töpferutensilien, mit denen sie ihre Wertschöpfung deutlich steigern konnte. Seit einiger Zeit zahlt sie 1 Euro pro Monat in ein Rentenprogramm ein, das Grameen anbietet. Die drohende Altersarmut war lange Zeit ein Hauptgrund, so viele Kinder wie möglich in die Welt zu setzen – was dann selbst zu einer Ursache für Armut wurde.

✣ **PENSION FOR MORE SECURITY IN OLD AGE.** Shuvashini Rangdi, 35 years old, lives in West Utrail. She also belongs to the minority of the Christian Adibashi; she sits in front of her house that is decorated with a painting of a tiger on the wall. In the busiest time, she earns about 20 euros making pottery. With a 60 euros loan, she bought pottery utensils with which she can increase her value considerably. For some time now, she pays one euro each month into a pension plan that Grameen offers. The threat of poverty in old age was one of the main reasons for a long time for bringing as many children as possible into the world – which then itself became one of the reasons for poverty.

✣ **MIT NEBENEINKÜNFTEN ZUM EIGENEN HAUS.** Gul Para: Shujanti Rangsha, 28 Jahre und gleichfalls aus dem christlichen Adibashi-Stamm, sitzt vor ihrem Besitz, der sie mit Stolz erfüllt: ein eigenes Haus. Zusammen mit ihrem Mann, der als Schreiner arbeitet, verdient sie 40 Euro im Monat. Von ihrem ersten Kredit bei Grameen über 50 Euro, den sie erst vor wenigen Wochen erhielt, kaufte sie sich unter anderem ein Schwein, das trächtig ist. Jedes Ferkel wird ihr einen Ertrag von 10 bis 20 Euro bringen.

✣ **WITH ADDITIONAL INCOME, HER OWN HOUSE.** Gul Para: Shujanti Rangsha, 28 years old and also from the Christian Adibashi group, sits in front of her possession that fills her with pride: her own house. Together with her husband who works as a carpenter, she earns 40 euros each month. From her first loan from Grameen for 50 euros, which she received just a few weeks ago, she bought a pregnant pig, among other things. Each piglet will yield a revenue of 10 to 20 euros.

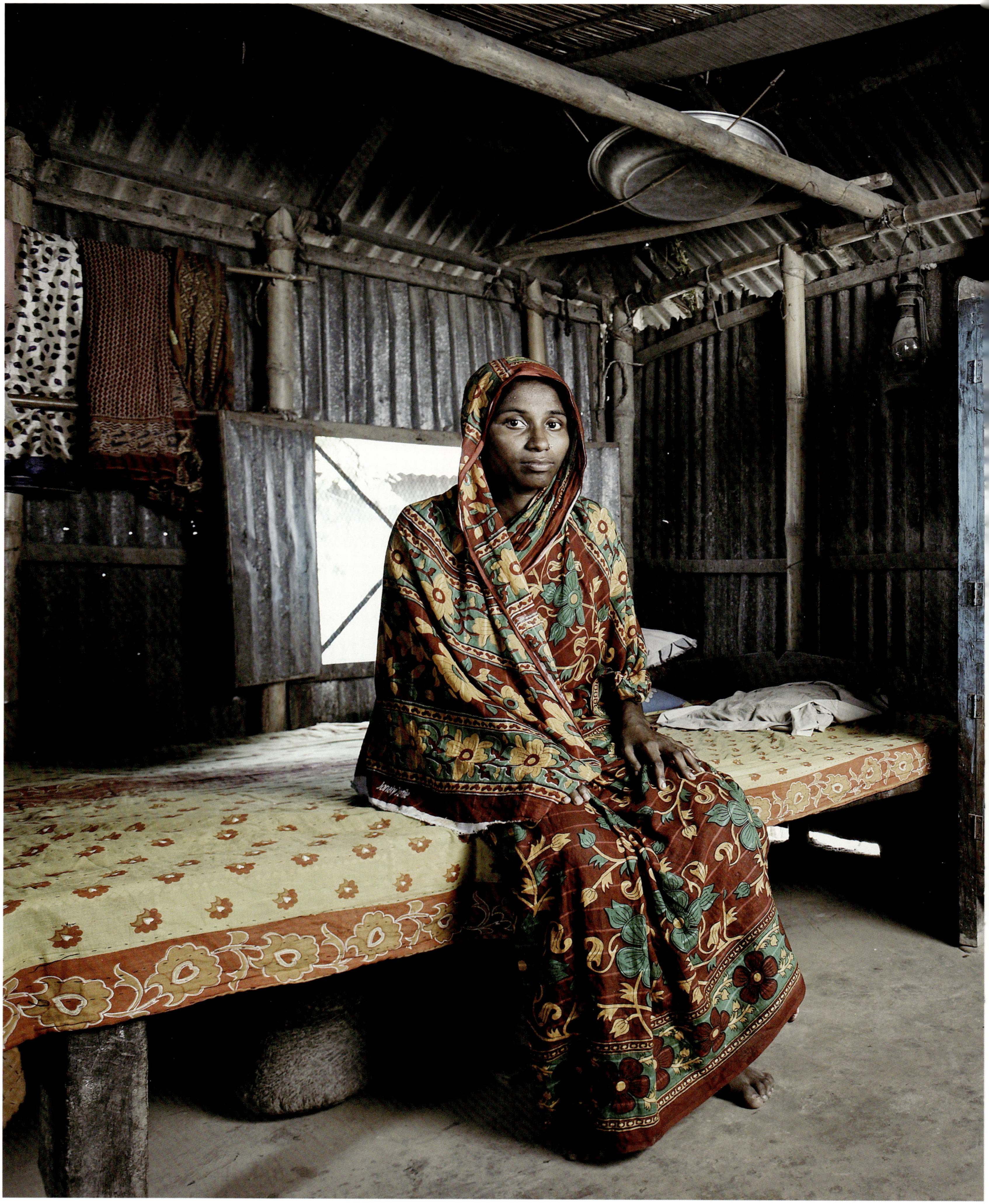

✣ **INVESTITION IN EXPANSION.** Suriya Akhter, 23 Jahre, sitzt in ihrem Haus im Dorf Baghai Kande auf der gleichnamigen Insel. In der blauen Tonne verwahrt sie Reis, um ihn vor Mäusen und dem Monsun zu schützen. Mit dem ersten Kredit kaufte sie eine Kuh, mit dem zweiten und dritten investierte sie in den Lebensmittelladen ihres Mannes, der seither immer größer wird. Ihr Gesamteinkommen liegt bei 50 Euro im Monat, von denen sie 30 Euro zum Leben brauchen. Der Rest fließt in die permanente Erweiterung des Sortiments in ihrem Laden.

✣ **INVESTMENT IN EXPANSION.** Suriya Akhter, 23 years old, sits in her house in the village of Baghai Kande on the island of the same name. In the blue bin she stores rice to protect it from the mice and from the monsoon. With her first loan, she bought a cow, with the second and the third she invested in her husband's grocery store that since then has grown and grown. Their entire income each month is 50 euros, from which they need 30 euros to live. The rest flows into the permanent expansion of the range of goods in their store.

✣ **OHNE MUTTER.** Afroza Begum, heute 13 Jahre alt, verlor ihre Mutter bereits im Alter von 8 Jahren. Ein solches Schicksal ist in Bangladesch nicht selten; die Folgen der Armut raffen noch immer viele Menschen viel zu früh hinweg. Afroza besucht die Schule und hilft im Haushalt mit.

✣ **WITHOUT A MOTHER.** Afroza Begum, 13 years old now, lost her mother when she was only 8 years old. Such a fate is common in Bangladesh; the results of poverty still carry off too many people too soon. Afroza attends school and helps with the household.

✣ **EIER.** Eine Kreditnehmerin mit Hühnerfarm aus dem Dorf Dhakkin Salna zeigt ihr Produkt: Eier. Mit 30 Euro Kredit hat sie begonnen. Vor 10 Jahren hatte sie 50 Hühner, heute besitzt sie 1.000.

✣ **EGGS.** A borrower with a chicken farm from the village of Dhakkin Salna shows her product: eggs. She started with a 30 euros loan. Ten years ago she had 50 chickens and today she owns 1,000.

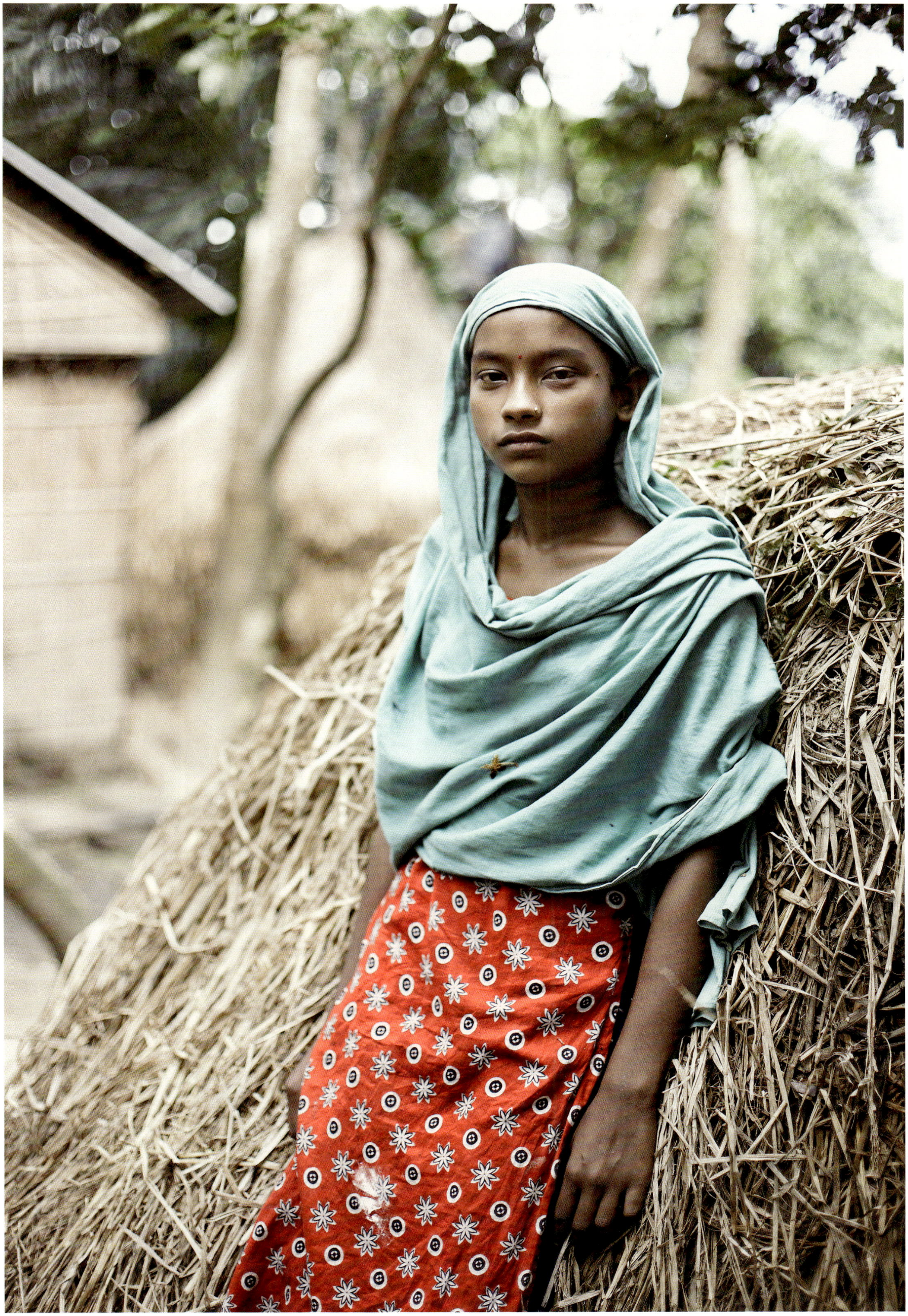

064

✺ **MILCH.** Dank des neuen Grameen-Unternehmens Grameen Danone im nahegelegenen Städtchen Bogra blüht in der Region schrittweise eine Milchindustrie auf. Hier eine Milchsammelstelle im Dorf Nimgachi von Grameen Fisheries und Livestock Foundation. Vier Dörfer tragen hier ihre Milchausbeute zusammen.

✺ **MILK.** Thanks to the new Grameen Danone business in the neighbouring town, Bogra, the milk industry in the area is gradually flourishing. Here is a milk collection point in the village of Nimgachi of Grameen Fisheries and Livestock Foundation. Four villages bring their milk yields together here.

✺ **FISCH.** Ein weiteres Grundnahrungsmittel und damit auch einen Produktionsschwerpunkt in Bangladesch stellen Fische dar. Hier im Dorf Nimgachi wird die Fischzucht unter anderem durch künstliche Befruchtung vorangetrieben.

✺ **FISH.** An additional basic foodstuff and also a production priority in Bangladesh is fish. Here in the village of Nimgachi, fish farming is driven forward with artificial insemination.

✤ **DER FÄHRMANN ZUM ANDEREN UFER.** Moti Mia, 25 Jahre, bietet mit seinem Boot die Dienstleistung der Überfahrt über den Fluss beim Dorf Kalimazane an. Die Überfahrt kostet 2 Taka pro Person, also 2 Euro-Cent für Dorffremde. Er verdient damit pro Tag etwa 2 Euro. Die Bewohner aus dem Dorf bezahlen ihre Überfahrten mit Reis. Diesmal fahren Arbeiter und Schulkinder mit ihm, denn die Schule liegt auf der anderen Flussseite.

✤ **FERRY ACROSS THE RIVER.** Moti Mia, 25 years old, offers his services for crossing the river in his boat near the village of Kalimazane. The crossing costs 2 Taka per person, that is 2 euro cents for strangers to the village. He earns about 2 euros a day this way. The village residents pay for the crossing with rice. This time workers and schoolchildren are travelling with him since the school lies on the other side of the river.

067

✤ **TASLIMA AKTER,** 28 Jahre, ist eine der wenigen Senior-Center-Managerinnen. Sie bearbeitet einen neuen Kredit für Hawarum, 55 Jahre, die seit 19 Jahren Kreditnehmerin bei Grameen ist. Sie führt ein Lebensmittelgeschäft und eine Teestube mit drei Angestellten.

✤ **TASLIMA AKTER,** 28 years old, is one of the few senior centre managers. She is working on a new loan for Hawarun, 55 years old, who has been a borrower from Grameen for 19 years. She manages a grocery store and a tea shop with three employees.

✤ **DAS GRAMEEN OFFICE IM DISTRIKT SADIPUR.**
Die Leitung der Distriktbüros ist ein Bereich, in dem die Männer dominieren. Im Vordergrund Mohammed Momen Miea, Mohammed Sadrul Amin rechts dahinter.

✤ **THE GRAMEEN OFFICE IN SADIPUR BRANCH.**
The manager of the branch office in an area in which men dominate. Mohammed Momen Miea is in the foreground and Mohammed Sadrul Amin is in the background on the right.

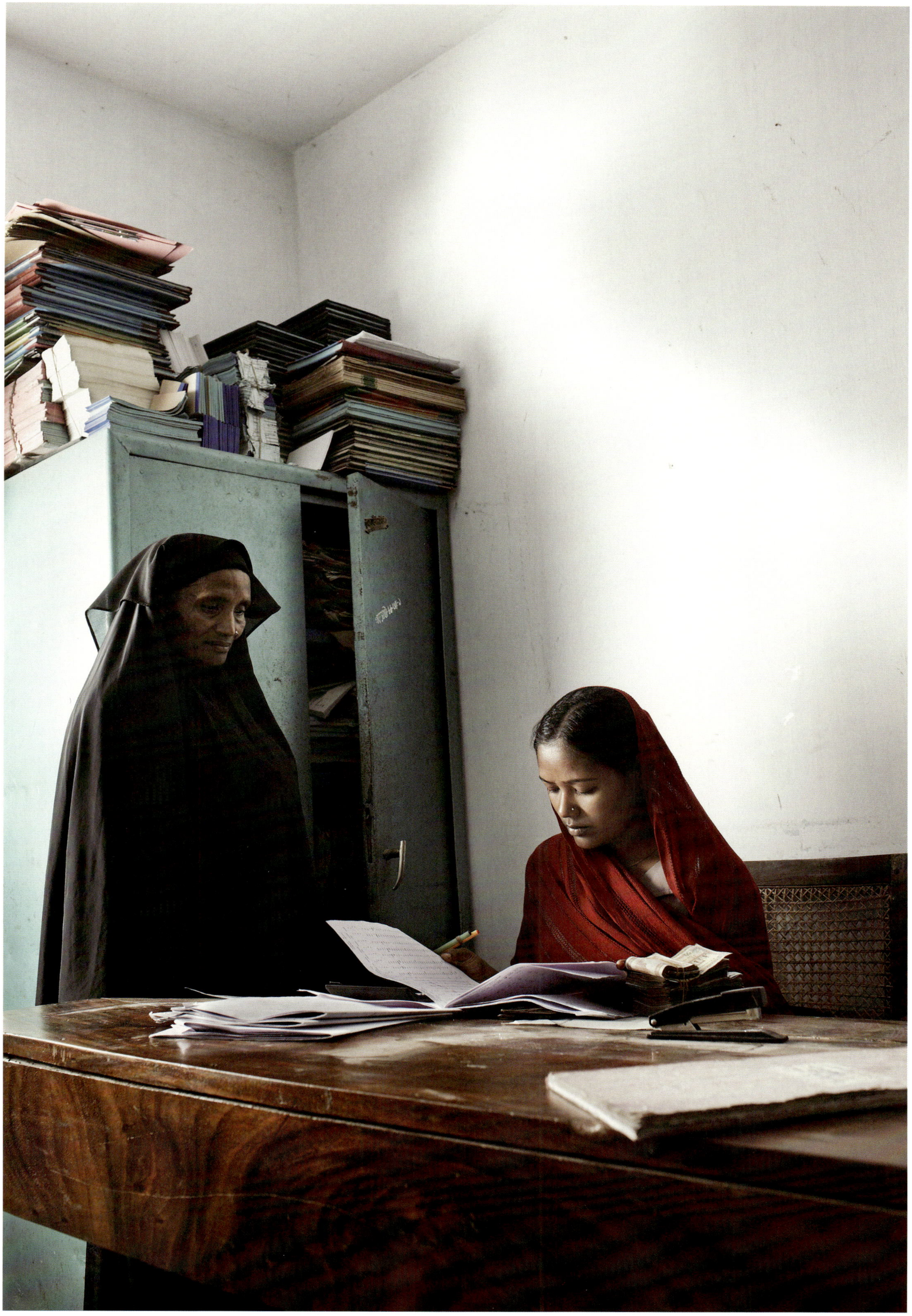

❋ **GRUNDSTEINLEGUNG** für eine weitere Grameen-Zweigstelle. Am Rande des Dorfes West Utrail gibt es im Monsun Anlass zum Feiern bei der Grundsteinlegung für eine neue Grameen-Zweigstelle.

❋ **LAYING THE FOUNDATION STONE** for a further Grameen branch. On the edge of the village of West Utrail there is reason to celebrate in the monsoon with the laying of the foundation stone for a new Grameen branch location.

❖ **ALLGEGENWÄRTIG IM LAND: DAS GRAMEEN-LOGO.** Hassena Akhter, 43 Jahre, steht mit Stolz vor dem Eingang der Grameen-Zweigstelle in Para Tuli, das sie seit eineinhalb Jahren leitet. Sie hat zwei Töchter und einen Sohn, alle drei studieren in Dhaka am College beziehungsweise an der Universität. Über dem Eingang prangt das im Land allgegenwärtige Grameen-Logo. Es zeigt einen nach oben gerichteten Pfeil. Das grüne Quadrat in der Mitte symbolisiert die Landesfarbe Bangladeschs, der Pfeil umfasst dieses in der Farbe Rot, die für revolutionär Neues, für eine große Reform steht; das Weiß dazwischen steht für Transparenz, Korruptionsfreiheit und Fairness sowie eine serviceorientierte Unternehmensführung.

❖ **OMNIPRESENT IN THE COUNTRY: THE GRAMEEN LOGO.** Hassena Akhter, 43 years old, is proudly standing in front of the entrance to the branch office in Para Tuli that she has managed for one and a half years. She has two daughters and a son, all three study in Dhaka at the college or university. The omnipresent Grameen logo is emblazoned over the entrance. It shows an upward directed arrow. The green square in the middle symbolises the colour of the countryside of Bangladesh, the arrow embraces this in the colour red that stands for the great reform, for revolutionary newness; the white between stands for transparency, freedom from corruption and fairness, as well as a service-oriented enterprise management.

Political failure of the state
as a chronic infection
PHILIPS

❖ **DIGITALE REVOLUTION MITTEN IN DER PROVINZ.** Misrat Jahan, 21 Jahre, studiert Sozialwesen. Sie sitzt hier in Rampal im Computer-Trainingszentrum von Akash. Akash ist der Sohn von Jahana Begum, die ihren ersten Kredit für eine Nähstube erhielt. Heute unterhalten sie das Computer-Trainingszentrum mit zwei Lehrern und 400 Kunden. Seit 1988 erhielten sie 3.000 Euro Kredit, mit dem sie der Landbevölkerung Zugang zu einer völlig neuen Wissens- und Arbeitswelt eröffneten: der Computer- und Internetwelt.

❖ **DIGITAL REVOLUTION IN THE MIDDLE OF THE PROVINCE.** Misrat Jahan, 21 years old, studies social sciences. She is sitting here in the computer training centre of Akash in Rampal. Akash is the son of Jahana Begum who received her first loan for a sewing parlour. Today she runs the computer training centre with the two teachers and 400 clients. Since 1988, she has received 3,000 euros in loans with which she has opened a door into a completely new world of knowledge and work, the computer and Internet worlds.

074

WIR BRAUCHEN ZIELE – ODER: DIE „JETZT ERST RECHT"-HALTUNG

Einer der Klassiker der modernen Psychologie, Alfred Adler, kam bei seinen Studien über den Menschen zu einem Ergebnis, das – damals wie heute – vielerorts auf Skepsis stößt: Nicht irgendwelche Umstände sind die Ursache für die Zustände, in denen wir leben, zumindest nicht langfristig. Auf längere Sicht gibt es nur eine Ursache: die Ziele, von denen wir uns antreiben lassen. Eine kühne These – die auf den folgenden Seiten belegt werden wird. Adler befasste sich mit Menschen mit organischen Funktionsstörungen: Die überwältigende Anzahl dieser Menschen reagierte auf diese mit lebenslangem Leid und Ergebenheit in ihr vermeintliches Schicksal. Eine kleine Minderheit reagierte jedoch mit einem „Jetzt erst recht". Adler nannte dies Überkompensation. Bei den größten Genies der Menschheitsgeschichte konnte er nachweisen: Nicht besondere Vorteile bei den Genen oder bei sonstigen Lebensumständen waren die Ursache für ihre großen Leistungen, sondern das unbändige Ziel, ihre Defizitsituation zu überwinden. Nicht nur bei Genies findet man dieses „Jetzt erst recht"-Prinzip, sondern auch bei den so genannten „Helden des Alltags", von denen es gar nicht wenige gibt.

WE NEED GOALS – OR: THE "NOW MORE THAN EVER" ATTITUDE

One of the leading authorities of modern psychology, Alfred Adler, came to a conclusion during his studies about people – then as today – that met with scepticism in many places. It is not just any cause that results in the conditions in which we live, there is only one cause: the goal by which we let ourselves be driven. A bold thesis which will be verified in the following pages. Adler concerned himself with people who had sub-standard organs: the overwhelming number of these people reacted to their condition with lifelong misery and submission to their supposed fate. A small minority reacted, however, with "now more than ever". Adler called this overcompensation. He could prove this by making reference to the greatest geniuses in the history of mankind: it was not special advantages in the genes or other circumstances in life that was the reason for their major accomplishments, but rather the goal of overcoming their handicap. It is not only amongst the geniuses that one can find this "now more than ever" principle, but also in the so-called "everyday heroes", of which there are many.

❦ **TESTPHASE IN UNBEKANNTEM TERRAIN.** Als man Yunus nach den ersten Erfolgen mit der Kleinkreditidee vorhielt, dies funktioniere nur in seinem Heimatgebiet, da man ihn dort persönlich kenne, entschied er sich für ein neues Testgebiet, in dem er völlig unbekannt war. Dies war die Region um Tangail. Heute befindet sich dort das Zweigstellenbüro für 31 Dörfer mit 84 Grameen-Zentren. Malote Rani Sen, 60 Jahre, lebt in Khilda. Aus dem besonderen Schilf hinter ihr stellt sie hochwertige Matten her, die als Bodenbeläge und auch als Bettdecken genutzt werden. Im Dorf Khilda besitzt bereits jede Familie ihr eigenes Handy.

❦ **TEST PERIOD IN AN UNKNOWN TERRAIN.** When one reproached Yunus after his first success with the microcredit ideas, that this could only function in his home area where they know him, he decided on a new test area where he was totally unknown. This was the area of Tangail. Today there is a branch office there for 31 villages with 84 Grameen centres. Malote Rani Sen, 60 years old, lives in Khilda. From the special reeds behind her, she makes high-quality mats that are used as floor coverings and also as bed covers. In the village of Khilda, every family already owns their own mobile phone.

❂ **BEITRAG ZUM FAMILIENEINKOMMEN IST EHRENSACHE.** Bonkim Sen ist inzwischen 85 Jahre alt. Er lebt zusammen mit seinen zwei Söhnen, deren Frauen und Kindern im Dorf Khilda bei Tangail. Noch immer verdient er sein eigenes Geld durch das Weben von Schilfmatten.

❂ **CONTRIBUTION TO THE FAMILY INCOME IS A MATTER OF HONOUR.** Bonkim Sen is now 85 years old. He lives together with his two sons, their wives and children in the village of Khilda near Tangail. He still earns his own money by weaving reed mats.

Bei der Erfolgsgeschichte von Muhammad Yunus und der Grameen Family können wir dieses besondere menschliche Phänomen in einer neuen Qualität beobachten. Hier geht es nicht nur um die Entscheidung eines Menschen für sich selbst, mit seinem eigenen Leben und seinem Umfeld dergestalt zielorientiert umzugehen. Hier fand vielmehr ein Mensch und dann ein Team von Menschen einen Weg, um viele weitere Menschen auf einen solchen Weg des „Jetzt erst recht" erfolgreich einzuladen. Auch eine andere Besonderheit ist bei Muhammad Yunus festzustellen: Er selbst litt nicht unter jener Armut, zu deren systematischer Überwindung er später so viel beitragen konnte. Die Tatsache, dass Menschen vor seinen Augen verhungerten, reichte bei ihm zu einem sehr starken Impuls, „jetzt erst recht" nach einem Ausweg zu suchen. Bei einer der zahlreichen Hungerkatastrophen in seinem Heimatland Bangladesch wurde es für ihn irgendwann schlicht unerträglich, als junger Professor der Wirtschaftswissenschaften auf dem Weg zu seinen Vorlesungen an der Universität Chittagong täglich an Verhungernden und Verhungerten vorbeizugehen. Die Vorstellung, vor einer jungen Wirtschaftselite darüber zu dozieren, wie diese sich künftig bereichern könnte oder anderen Reichen beim „Noch-reicher-Werden" assistieren könnte, wurde für ihn unerträglich. Er erkannte die erschreckende Unzulänglichkeit seines akademischen Wissens darüber, wie er den Armen aus deren Armut helfen könne, und traf die klare Entscheidung, jetzt genau dies lernen zu wollen. Aus diesem Ziel wuchs mit der Zeit die große Vision vom Ende der Armut in der Welt.

In the success story of Muhammad Yunus and the Grameen family, we can observe this special human phenomenon in a new quality. Here it is not only the decision of a person to handle a situation pertaining to himself, about his own life and his surroundings. Rather, here a person and then a team of people found a way to successfully invite many more people on such a path of "now more than ever". Another characteristic can also be identified in Muhammad Yunus: he himself did not suffer under that poverty to which he later contributed so much to its systematic overpowering. The fact that people were starving before his eyes was enough to give him a very strong impetus, "now more than ever", to search for a solution. In one of the numerous catastrophic famines in his homeland of Bangladesh, it became simply unbearable for him, as a young professor of economics, to walk past the hungry and starving on his daily path to his lectures in the Chittagong University. The idea of lecturing in front of a young economic elite, teaching them how they could enrich themselves in the future or to assist other wealthy people to "become even wealthier", became unbearable for him. He recognised the terrible inadequacy of his academic knowledge about how he could help the poor escape their poverty, and made a clear decision to learn how to achieve this knowledge. From this goal, with time a great vision grew about the end of poverty in the world.

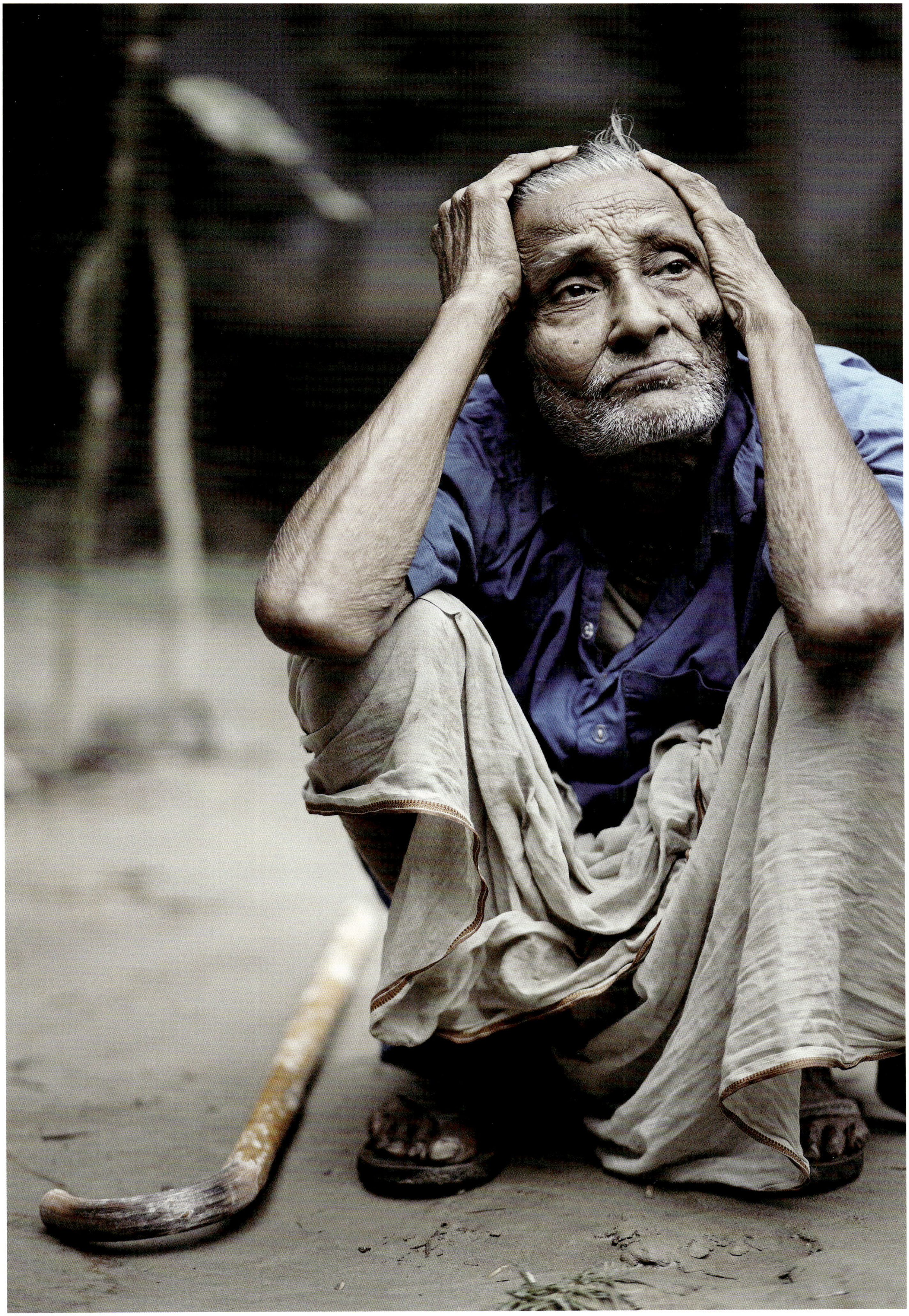

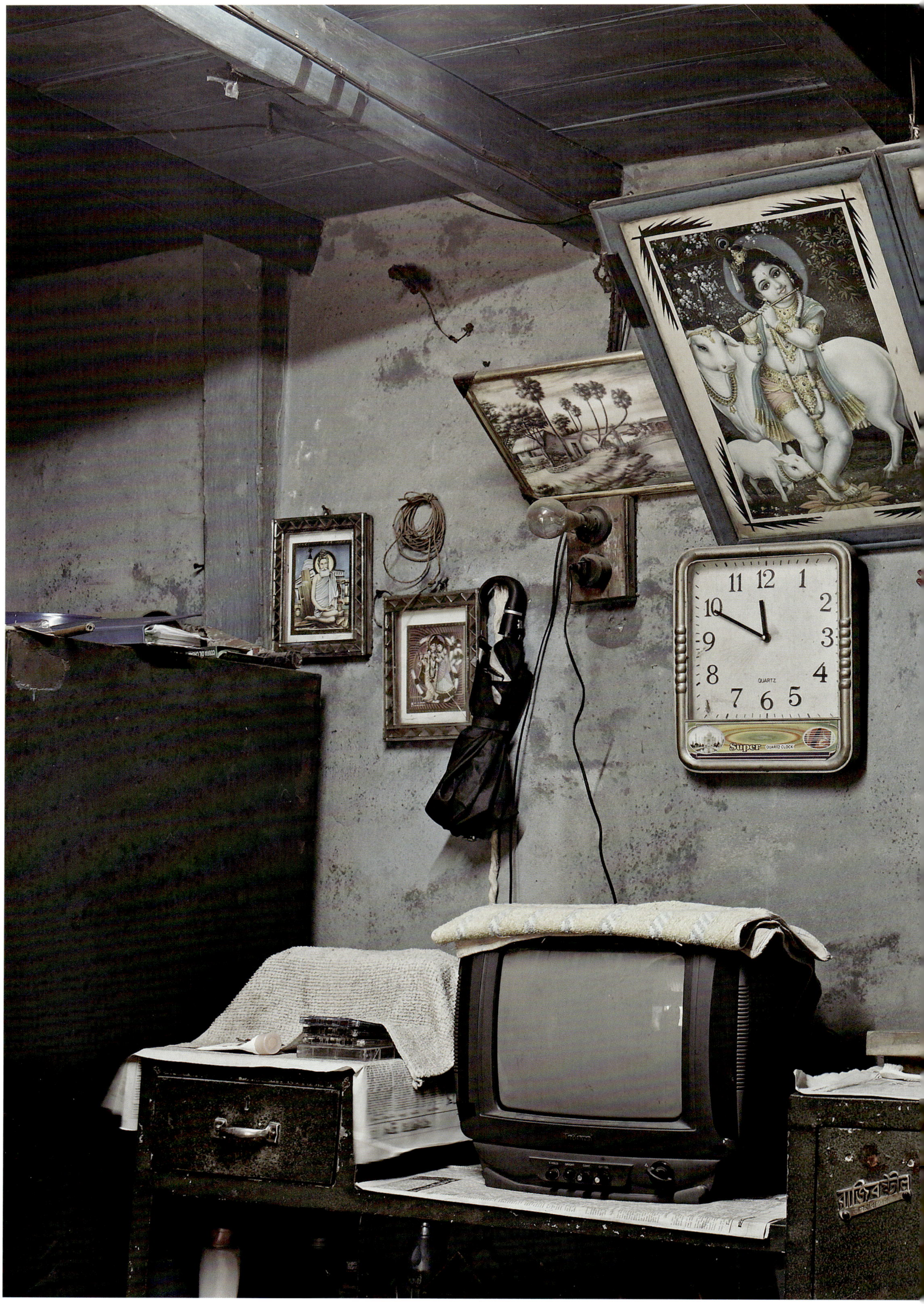
QUARTZ
Super QUARTZ CLOCK

✤ **REQUISITEN EINES BESCHEIDENEN WOHLSTANDS.** Im Haus der Hindu-Frau Mukta Shaha in Bhururia Shaha Para sammeln sich langsam Zeichen von Wohlstand – der im Vergleich zu westlichen Standards freilich noch immer äußerste Armut bedeutet. Doch Fernseher, Wanduhr, Rucksack und Hindu-Bilder sind in dieser Region noch keine Selbstverständlichkeiten. Mukta Shaha verdiente sich dies mit dem Aufbau von Jute-Produktion und Sari-Verkauf.

✤ **PROPS FOR A MODEST PROSPERITY.** In the house for the Hindu Mrs Mukta Shaha in Bhururia Shaha Para, the signs of prosperity are slowly gathering – in comparison with western standards, of course, they still indicate extreme poverty. But windows, a wall clock, a backpack and Hindu books are not a matter of course in this region. Mukta Shaha has earned them by setting up production of jute and selling saris.

⊛ **GOLDENES MITGLIED UND INVESTORIN.** Bina Shaha, 72 Jahre und Schwiegermutter von Mukta Shaha, bekam ihren ersten Kredit im Jahr 1990. Dieser lag bei 20 Euro. Sie begann mit Jute-Produktion. Neun Jahre später erhielt sie den Glückwunschbrief von Grameen mit der Ernennung zum „Goldenen Mitglied". Das bedeutet, sie hat die Grenze zur absoluten Armut hinter sich gelassen. Heute investiert sie einen Kredit von 100 Euro in die Geschäfte ihres Sohnes und ihrer Schwiegertochter.

⊛ **GOLDEN MEMBER AND INVESTOR.** Bina Shaha, 72 years old and mother-in-law of Mukta Shaha, received her first loan in 1990. This was 20 euros. She began with jute production. Nine years later she received a greetings letter from Grameen with the nomination for "Golden Member". That means she had left the level of absolute poverty behind her. Today she invests a loan of 100 euros in the business of her son and daughter-in-law.

081

082

✤ **EMPFÄNGERIN DES FRIEDENSNOBELPREISES.** Rohema Begum, 41 Jahre, gehörte der Delegation an, die im Dezember 2006 gemeinsam mit Professor Yunus nach Oslo reiste, um stellvertretend für die Grameen Bank den Friedensnobelpreis entgegenzunehmen.

✤ **RECIPIENT OF THE NOBEL PEACE PRIZE.** Rohema Begum, 41 years old, belonged to the delegation that in December 2006, together with Professor Yunus, travelled to Oslo to receive the Nobel Peace Prize on behalf of the Grameen Bank.

„Nichts in der Welt ist stärker als eine Vision, für die die Zeit gekommen ist", meinte einst Victor Hugo. Irgendwann erhob ein Mann namens Martin Luther King seine Stimme zu „I have a Dream" und verkündete, in nicht allzu ferner Zeit werde die Rassenzugehörigkeit für die Menschen keinerlei Rolle mehr spielen. Irgendwann stand Mahatma Gandhi auf und ließ sich durch nichts davon abbringen, dass wir Menschen lernen müssen und können, Konflikte auf friedlichem Wege zu lösen. Visionen wie diese beseelen seither Millionen von Menschen, die – trotz aller Rückschläge – sich stets wieder neu daran aufrichten und fortschreiten, diese Visionen in immer stärkere Lebensrealität umzusetzen. Sei es in ihrem ganz persönlichen Umfeld, sei es in ihrem privaten Engagement in einer der mittlerweile Millionen von Nichtregierungsorganisationen weltweit. Sei es in der Unternehmenskultur an ihrem Arbeitsplatz, sei es in der Politik oder sei es an einer sonstigen „Baustelle" des Lebens.

"Nothing is more powerful than an idea whose time has come", Victor Hugo once said. At one point, a man named Martin Luther King, Jr. raised his voice with "I have a dream", and announced that in the not too distant future, belonging to a particular race would no longer play a role for people. At one point, Mahatma Gandhi stood up and did not let himself be dissuaded by anyone that we humans must and can learn to peacefully resolve conflicts. Since then, visions such as these have inspired millions of people, who in spite of setbacks, always stand up again and stride forward to put these visions into practice in constantly stronger realities of life. It can be within their personal surroundings. It can be in their private commitment, in the meantime, to millions of NGOs (nongovernmental organisations) worldwide. It can be in the company culture at their workplace. It can be in politics. It can be in a so-called "construction site" of life.

✤ **IM „NOBELPREISTRÄGER-LADEN"** von Chandon Tola. Frau Begum betreibt gemeinsam mit ihrem Mann Mohammed Bossir im Dorf Chandon Tola einen Lebensmittelmarkt, der gleichzeitig das „Dorfkino" ist – dank des Fernsehers. Frau Begum hat als „Telefonlady" begonnen, die Handyminuten an die Dorfbewohner verkaufte. Sie ist seit 19 Jahren Kreditnehmerin bei Grameen.

✤ **THE "NOBEL PRIZE WINNER SHOP"** from Chandon Tola. Mrs Begum, together with her husband, Mohammed Bossir, runs a grocery store in the village of Chandon Tola, which is also the village cinema – thanks to a TV. Mrs Begum started as a "telephone lady" who sold mobile phone minutes to the village residents. She has been a Grameen borrower for 19 years.

Wann ist die Zeit gekommen für die Vision, die Muhammad Yunus kraftvoll in die Welt hinausgetragen hat? Wann nehmen wir seine Idee auf, die Armut nicht vereinzelt durch die eine oder andere staatliche oder private Aktion zu mildern, sondern sie als historisches Phänomen systemisch zu überwinden? Wann wird aus dieser Vision, die zunächst nur die Vision eines Menschen und dann die Vision einer wachsenden Zahl von Menschen war, eine Vision, die uns kollektiv elektrisiert? Armut muss – nach Yunus – zu etwas werden, das mit unserem Menschenbild vollkommen unvereinbar ist. Der Historiker Ian Semple meinte einmal, künftige Generationen würden auf unsere Zeit mit völligem Unverständnis zurückblicken. Denn uns hätten längst alle Mittel zur Verfügung gestanden, damit niemand mehr verhungern oder in lebenslanger tiefster Entwürdigung hätte verharren müssen. Dieser Historiker meinte, man würde unsere Zeit später als die ungerechteste der gesamten Menschheitsgeschichte brandmarken: Die Kluft zwischen den Gestaltungsmöglichkeiten und dem tatsächlichen Handeln sei niemals zuvor so groß gewesen wie zu unserer Zeit. Yunus wird ihm sicher zustimmen.

When is the time for the vision that Muhammad Yunus powerfully carried out into the world? When do we take up his mission, not to individually alleviate poverty through one or another government or private action, but rather to systematically overcome it as an historical phenomenon? When will this vision, at first only the vision of one person and then the vision of a growing number of people, become a vision to electrify us collectively? Poverty, according to Yunus, must become something absolutely incompatible with our conception of man. The historian, Ian Semple, once said that future generations will look back on our time with a complete lack of understanding. This because we have had for many years every remedy available in order that no one should need to starve, or to persist in lifelong deepest degradation. This historian meant that people will later denounce our time as the least fair in the entire history of mankind. The fissure between organisational possibilities and our actual behaviour was never as great as during our time. Yunus would surely agree with him.

❦ **WEBEN FÜR BESONDERE ANLÄSSE.** Im Weberdorf Gonokbari werden hochwertige Saris angefertigt für Hochzeiten und andere besondere Anlässe. Mit der traditionellen Webtechnik dauert deren Fertigung eine Woche. Das Mädchen im Hintergrund, Yasmin, ist 12 Jahre alt und Tochter einer Grameen-Kreditnehmerin.

❦ **WEAVING FOR A SPECIAL OCCASION.** In the weaver's village, Gonokbari, high-quality saris are made for weddings and other special occasions. With the traditional weaving techniques, their production lasts a week. The girl in the background, Yasmin, is 12 years old and the daughter of a Grameen borrower.

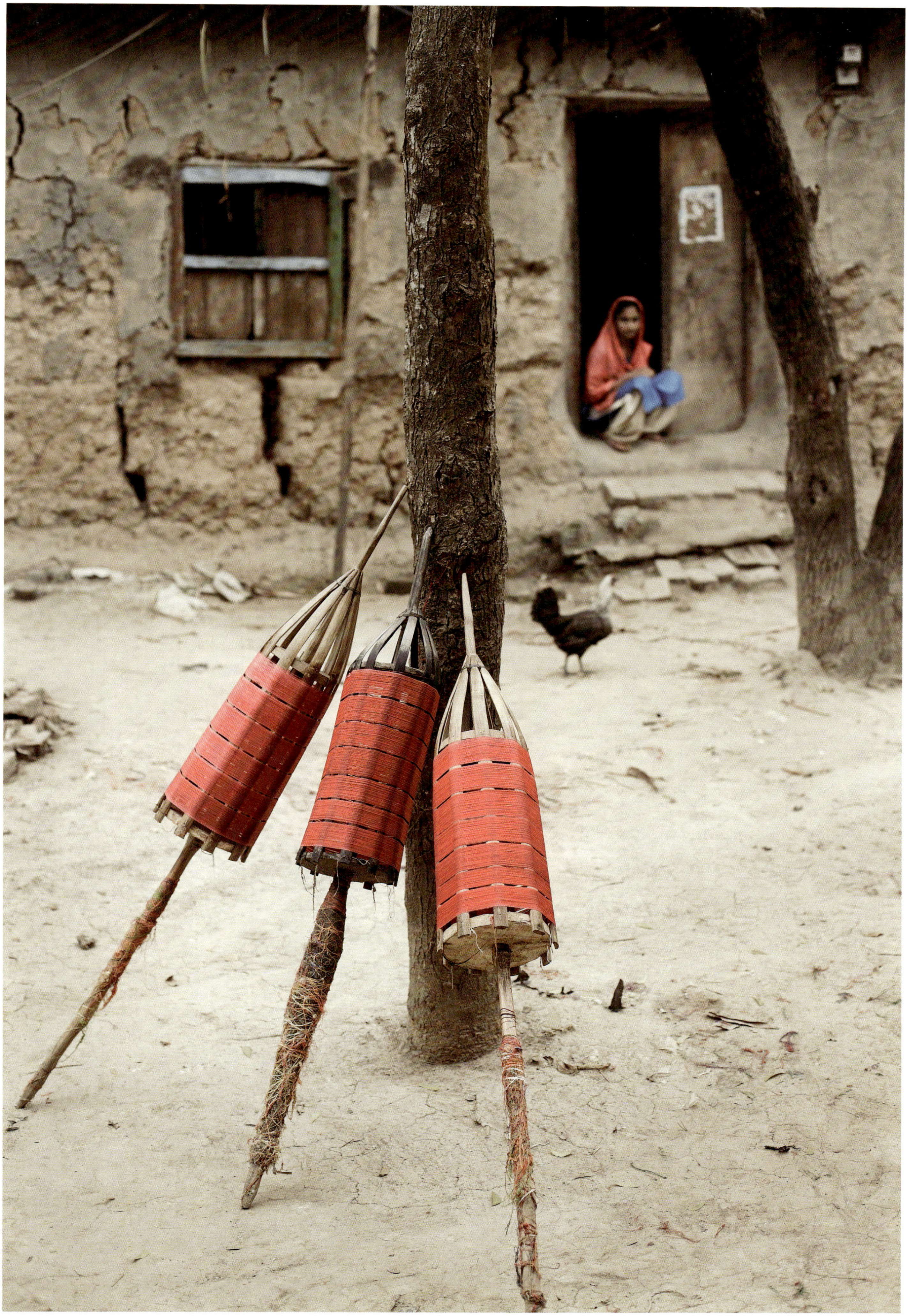

❂ **MANCHMAL IST DAS LEBEN SÜSS.** Kreditnehmerin Kanchon Rani, 35 Jahre, aus dem Dorf Nayapurbazar, stellt Süßspeisen her, die aus Zucker, Butter, Mehl und Wasser bestehen.

❂ **SOMETIMES LIFE IS SWEET.** Borrower Kanchon Rani, 35 years old, from the village of Nayapurbazar, makes sweets from sugar, butter, flour and water.

Woran liegt es, dass wir beim Thema Armut noch nicht zu einer kollektiv hinlänglich wirksamen Vision ihrer Verbannung aus unserer Welt gefunden haben? Warum stehen wir nicht mit ähnlich zäher Nachhaltigkeit auf wie bei Umweltfragen – zu einem entschiedenen „Schluss mit der Armut, spätestens bis 2030"? Warum schläft unser Gewissen so schnell wieder ein, nachdem wir vielleicht wieder einmal etwas Geld an eine der Hilfsorganisationen gespendet haben oder bei einer Talkshow oder einer Vortragsveranstaltung einer Forderung applaudiert haben, die Regierung möge doch etwas mehr Geld in sinnvolle Entwicklungshilfe stecken? Was macht uns so untätig, so hoffnungs- und visionslos in Bezug auf den Sieg über die Armut?

Ganz sicher ist eine der Ursachen, dass wir viel zu wenig über Alternativen zum traditionellen Charity-Denken und -Handeln wissen. Wir haben uns noch viel zu wenig damit befasst, wie viel mehr erreicht werden kann im Kampf gegen die Armut, wenn wir anderen Konzepten folgen. Dabei wäre dieses Defizit so leicht zu beheben. Es reicht, zwei soziale Revolutionen zu betrachten, die beide von Muhammad Yunus und seinem Team, der Grameen Family, ausgingen. Dann wird deutlich: Armut ist mit vergleichsweise sehr wenig Geldmitteln in relativ kurzer Zeit höchst effizient und nachhaltig zu besiegen.

Dank der Verleihung des Friedensnobelpreises an Muhammad Yunus im Jahr 2006 für die erste soziale Revolution – die Vergabe von Kleinstkrediten an die Ärmsten – erhöhte sich deren Bekanntheitsgrad schlagartig. Das Wissen darüber ist zwar noch immer recht oberflächlich, selbst bei jenen, die seine Ideen aufgreifen und in ihre sozialen Projekte zu integrieren suchen. Doch der Damm des Nichtwissens und Nichtverstehens bröckelt spürbar.

Yunus erhielt den Nobelpreis 32 Jahre, nachdem er mit seinen Innovationen begonnen hatte. Bis zum Jahr 2006 führte er diese längst weit über ein neuartiges „Banking für die Ärmsten" hinaus. Er arbeitete schon seit mehreren Jahren und mit großem Erfolg am Konzept eines kompletten ergänzenden Wirtschaftssektors für den umfassenden Ausweg aus der Armut. Er gab diesem Konzept den Namen „Social Business" und nutzte seine neue Popularität zum Start einer weltweiten Kampagne für die damit verbundenen, sehr viel weiter reichenden Innovationen.

What causes this, why have we not found for the theme of poverty a collectively adequate and effective vision about its banishment from our world? Why do we not stand with similar tough perseverance, like we do regarding environmental questions, for a decisive "end to poverty, at the latest by 2030"? Why does our conscience go back to sleep again so quickly after we have donated some money to a relief organisation, or have applauded an appeal during a talk show or a lecture event where the government should invest somewhat more money in worthy development help? What makes us so inactive, so hopeless and visionless in relation to the victory over poverty?

Certainly, one of the reasons is that we know only too little about the alternatives to the traditional charity mentality. We have concerned ourselves far too little with how much more could be accomplished in the battle against poverty while we follow other concepts. It would be so easy to remove this deficit. It is enough to closely examine how two social revolutions started, both from Muhammad Yunus and his team – the Grameen family. It then becomes obvious: poverty can be effectively and lastingly defeated with comparatively few funds in a relatively short time.

Thanks to the bestowal of the Nobel Peace Prize on Muhammad Yunus in 2006 for the first social revolution – the allocation of microcredits for the poorest – his degree of fame has suddenly risen. Understanding of this, however, is still rather superficial, even by those who picked up his ideas and who tried to integrate them into their own social projects. But the dam of not knowing and not understanding is noticeably crumbling away.

Yunus received the Nobel Prize 32 years after he had begun his innovations. By 2006, he had led this far beyond to a new type of "banking for the poorest". He had already worked for many years and with great success on the concept of a completely additional economic field for the full way out of poverty. He gave this project the name "Social Business", and used his new popularity to start a worldwide campaign for the affiliated and very extensive innovations.

❀ **SOLARSTROM BRINGT SONNE INS LEBEN DER ARMEN.** Jorina, 27 Jahre, lehnt mit ihrer 5-jährigen Tochter Monsheda im Dorf Votoliya an einer Bambusstange der besonderen Art: Am oberen Ende der Stange sind Solarzellen auf die Sonne ausgerichtet. Die Solaranlage versorgt das Haus mit so viel Strom, dass es reicht für eine Solarlampe sowie ein wenig Technik, die das Leben erleichtert oder verschönert. In diesem Haus ist es beispielsweise ein Fernseher, dessen Antennenmast außerdem für die Aufhängung einer Stange zum Wäschetrocknen dient.

❀ **SOLAR ENERGY BRINGS SUNSHINE INTO THE LIVES OF THE POOR.** Jorina, 27 years old, with her 5-year-old daughter Monsheda, in the village of Votoliya, is leaning on a special type of bamboo pole. On the top of the pole, solar cells are directed at the sun. The solar installation produces enough electricity for the house with a solar lamp, as well as a little technical equipment to make life easier or more pleasant. In this house, for instance, there is a TV, and the mast is also used to hang a pole for drying laundry.

089

❖ **ZUKUNFTSBERUF SOLARINGENIEURIN.** Jobayda Khatun, 25 Jahre, lässt sich gerade im Grameen Technologiezentrum im Dorf Mawna zur Ingenieurin für die Installation und Reparatur von Solaranlagen ausbilden. Die Lebensdauer von Solaranlagen lässt sich durch elementares Ingenieurswissen leicht verdoppeln bis verdreifachen. Nach Abbezahlung des Kredits für ein Solar Home System steht der Strom dann nicht für fünf, sondern für mehr als fünfzehn Jahre nahezu kostenlos zur Verfügung.

❖ **FUTURE PROFESSION AS A SOLAR ENGINEER.** Jobayda Khatun, 25 years old, is currently training in the Grameen Technology Centre in the village of Mawna to become an engineer for the installation and repair of solar installations. The lifespan of the solar installations can easily be doubled or even tripled through elementary engineering knowledge. After paying off the loan for a solar home system, the electricity is not just available almost for free for more than five years but rather for more than fifteen years.

Nun vergeben nicht alle Kleinkreditorganisationen so konsequent wie die Grameen Bank ausschließlich Kleinkredite an absolut arme Menschen, die über keinerlei Sicherheiten verfügen. Viele Kleinkreditorganisationen wagen sich nicht in dieses aus ihrer Sicht riskante Spektrum der Allerärmsten vor und vergeben daher kleine Kredite an zwar durchaus sehr arme Menschen, die aber deutlich oberhalb der Grenze absoluter Armut leben. Auch funktionieren noch längst nicht alle Kleinkreditsysteme so stabil und erfolgreich wie die Grameen Bank. Daher bedeutet die Zahl von einer halben Milliarde Menschen, die in den Genuss der Wirkungen von Kleinkrediten gekommen sind, nicht, dass bereits die Hälfte der absolut Armen der Welt auf dem Weg aus der Armutsfalle wäre.

Now, not all of these institutions give microcredits as consistently as the Grameen Bank exclusively to the absolutely poor who have no guarantee at their disposal. Many microcredit organisations do not venture into this, from their point of view, risky spectrum of the poorest, and therefore give microcredit to definitely poor people but who live clearly above the border of absolute poverty. In addition, not every microcredit system by far functions as stably and successfully as the Grameen Bank. That is why the number of half a billion people who benefit as a result of microcredits does not show that half of the absolutely poor of the world are already on the way out of poverty.

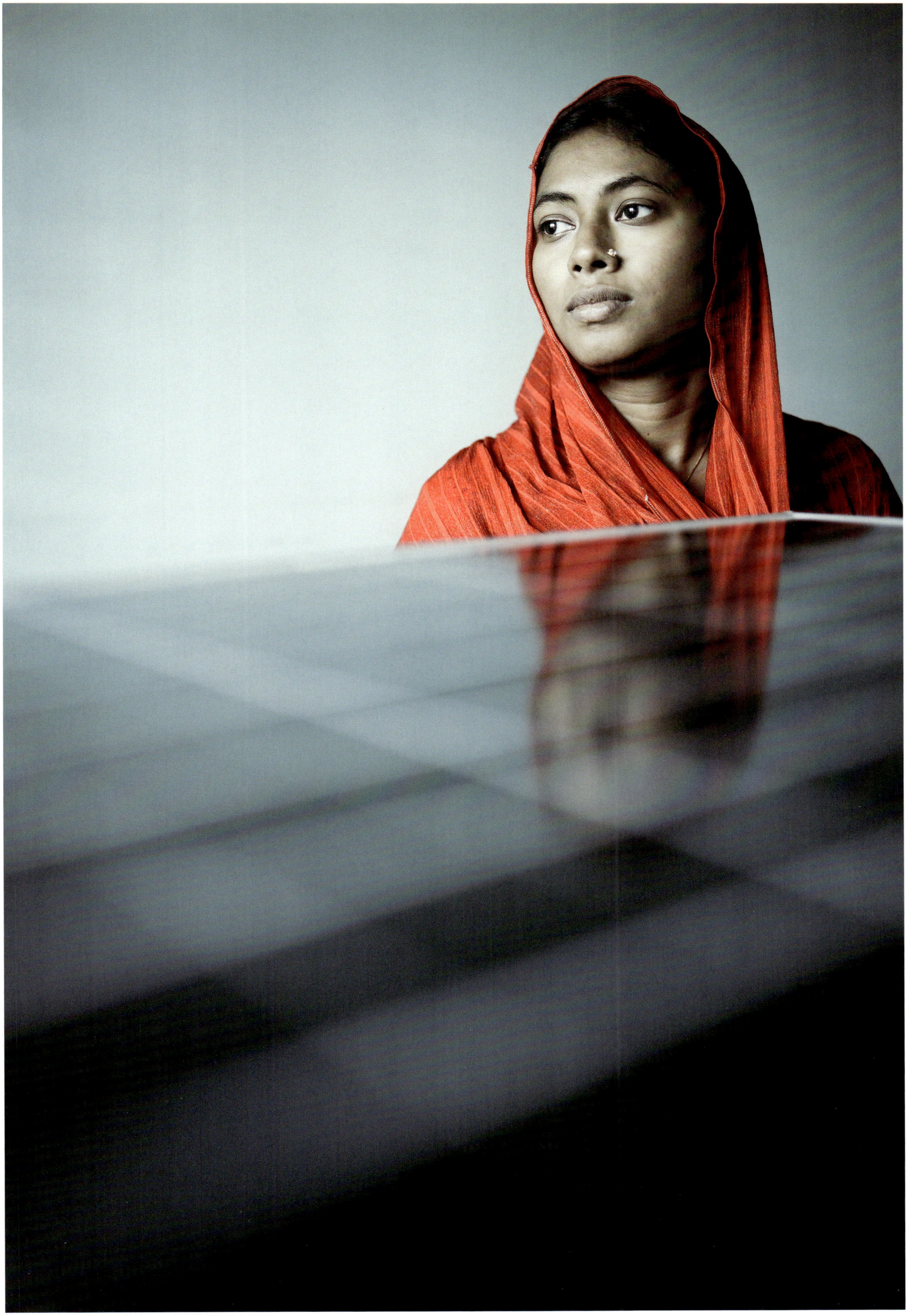

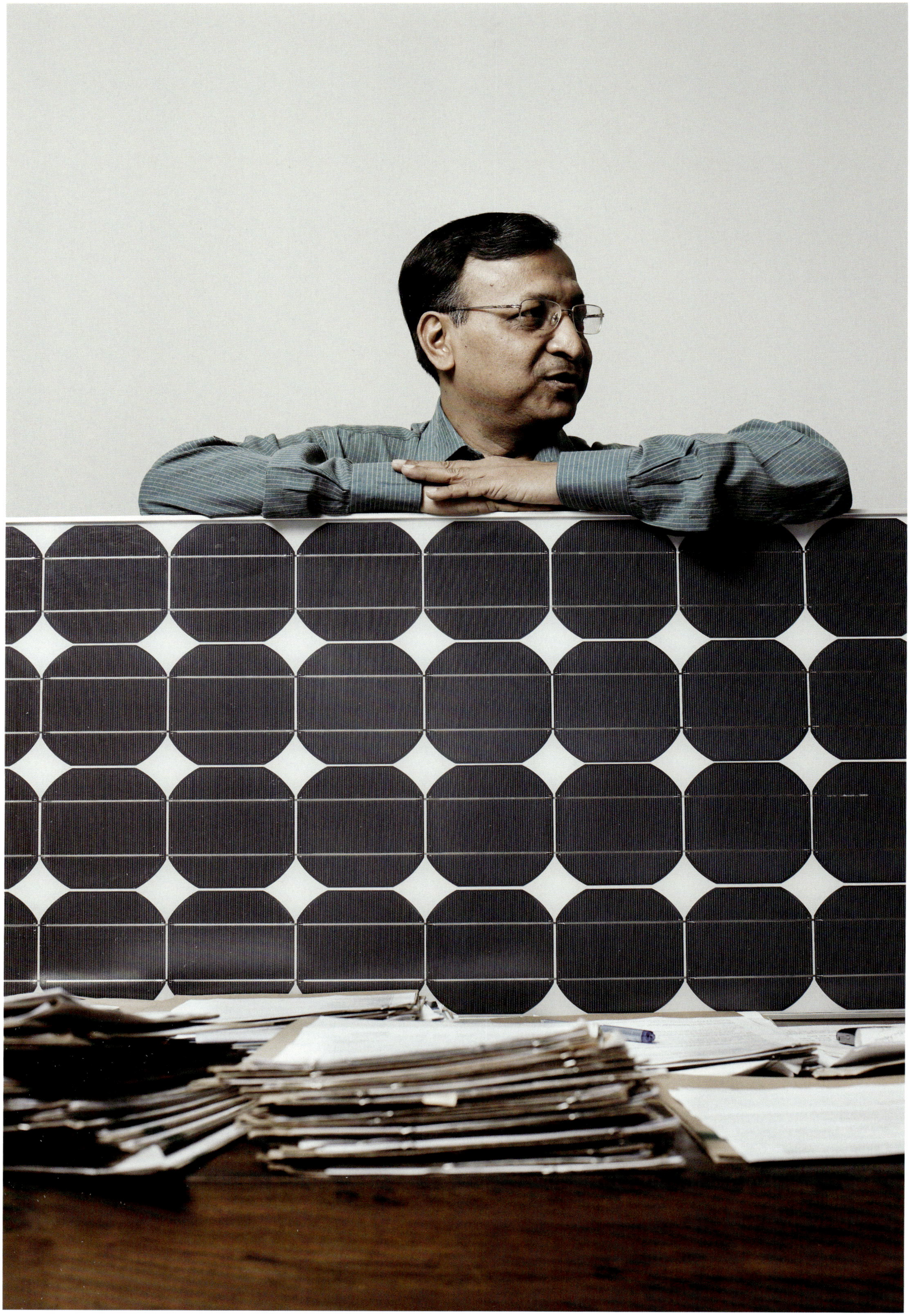

✤ **ALTERNATIVER NOBELPREIS FÜR DIPAL C. BARUA.** Ein Jahr nach dem Friedensnobelpreis für Prof. Muhammad Yunus und die Grameen Bank erhielt ein einzelnes Grameen-Unternehmen, Grameen Shakti, und dessen Leiter Dipal C. Barua den Alternativen Nobelpreis.

✤ **ALTERNATIVE NOBEL PRIZE FOR DIPAL C. BARUA.** A year after the Nobel Peace Prize for Professor Muhammad Yunus and the Grameen Bank, a single Grameen business, Grameen Shakti and its director, Dipal C. Barua received the Alternative Nobel Prize.

Dennoch: Die Chancen haben sich enorm verbessert. Nach der Entscheidung des Nobelpreiskomitees interessieren sich völlig neue Akteure für das Thema Kleinkredite. Für die erste soziale Revolution besteht die Hauptaufgabe nun darin: Die Geheimnisse der erfolgreichsten Kleinkreditorganisationen wie beispielsweise Grameen müssen in alle bestehenden anderen Kleinkreditsysteme Eingang finden. Das Kleinkreditwunder muss schnellstens flächendeckend in allen Armutsregionen der Welt stattfinden.

Dafür ist es unumgänglich und somit unser aller Aufgabe, dass die Kleinkreditbewegung so groß, so stark, so allgegenwärtig wird, wie es inzwischen die Umweltbewegung geworden ist: Fast täglich erfahren wir aus den Nachrichten von den noch nicht gelösten oder noch nicht entdeckten Umweltproblemen wie auch von den kleineren und größeren Fortschritten in den Gesetzgebungen, bei Erfindungen und bei praktischen Initiativen.

Nevertheless, the chances have greatly improved. Since the decision of the Nobel Prize committee, completely new players have become interested in the microcredit theme. For the first social revolution, the main task is now to include the secrets of the most successful microcredit organisations, such as Grameen, into all other existing microcredit systems. The microcredit wonder must rapidly take place covering the needs in every poor area of the world.

Therefore, it is imperative, and consequently the task for every one of us, that the microcredit movement becomes as large, strong and omnipresent as the environmental movement has become. Almost daily we learn in the news about the environmental problems that have not been solved or not even discovered, as well as both smaller and larger improvements in legislation, about inventions and practical initiatives.

✦ **SOLARLICHT IN DER APOTHEKE** – und beim Nachbarn. Das ist Muhammad Ruhul Amin, 20 Jahre, aus dem Dorf Kalihati. Sein Vater führte Solarstrom im Familienhaus ein. Heute sorgt auf dem Dach seiner Apotheke eine Solaranlage für genügend Strom – nicht nur für ihn selbst: Eine Solarlampe, die mit dem Strom der Solaranlage auf seinem Dach versorgt wird, vermietet er für 4 Euro im Monat an einen Laden in der Nachbarschaft. Das Energie-Sharing macht inzwischen Schule.

✦ **SOLAR LIGHT IN THE PHARMACY** – and for the neighbours. Muhammad Ruhul Amin, 20 years old from the village of Kalihati. His father introduced solar electricity into the family home. Today, the solar installation on the roof of his pharmacy provides enough electricity – not only for his own needs: he rents a solar lamp that is supplied with electricity from the solar installation on his roof, for 4 euros each month to a store in the neighbourhood. Energy-sharing is catching one in the meantime.

✦ **20 WATT** beschleunigen die Entwicklung erheblich. Der Schneider Saidul Islam im Dorf Vutholia Bazar kann seinen Laden nun auch nach Sonnenuntergang weiterführen. Die 20 Watt von der Solaranlage auf dem Dach bringen ihm einen erheblichen ökonomischen Vorteil.

✦ **20 WATTS** speeds up the development considerably. The tailor Saidul Islam in the village of Vutholia Bazaar can now continue to work in his shop after sunset. The 20 watts from the solar installation on the roof brings him a considerable economic advantage.

097

860

Für jeden verantwortungsvollen Bürger, Unternehmer, Politiker, Lehrer, Konsumenten, Journalisten usw. muss es genauso selbstverständlich werden, über die Fortschritte im weltweiten Kampf gegen die Armut, insbesondere durch das so erfolgreiche Instrument der Kleinkredite, informiert zu sein. Jeder sollte sich fragen, was er zu dieser globalen Bewegung beitragen kann. Je mehr Menschen über das Konzept der Kleinkredite informiert sind, desto schneller wird sich diese Idee samt aller Unterstützungsmöglichkeiten um die ganze Welt verbreiten. Und je mehr sich bei jedem einzelnen Menschen Schritt für Schritt das Verständnis für die wirklichen Erfolgsgründe von Kleinkreditsystemen vertieft, desto schneller kann die Menschheit auch in diesem Feld die Spreu vom Weizen trennen und sich auf die Förderung der besten Konzepte und Projekte konzentrieren. Die bereits beschriebenen erzielten Erfolge können dann in wenigen Jahren zum großen weltweiten Durchbruch führen. Einer der wunderbaren Aspekte der Kleinkreditidee ist: Zu deren erfolgreicher globaler Durchsetzung müssen kaum staatliche Gesetze geändert werden, und ebenso wenig muss auf langwierige internationale Verhandlungen gewartet werden. Die Kleinkreditidee hat bereits heute gezeigt: Dies ist ein Feld, in dem engagierte Menschen den globalen Durchbruch ganz allein schaffen können. Über die Erfolgsgeheimnisse der Kleinkreditidee erfahren wir im nächsten Teil mehr.

For every responsible citizen, employer, politician, teacher, consumer, journalist, etc., it must become equally as natural to be informed about the progress in the worldwide battle against poverty, especially through the so successful instrument of microcredits. Everyone should ask himself what he can contribute to this worldwide movement. The more people who are informed about the concept of microcredits, the faster this idea, along with all the support possibilities, will spread throughout the world. And the more that each individual person deepens his or her understanding, step by step, of the actual reasons for the success of the microcredit systems, the faster mankind can also separate the wheat from the chaff in this field and concentrate on the demands of the best concepts and projects. The successes already described can then in a few years lead to a great worldwide breakthrough. One of the wonderful aspects of the microcredit idea is that for their successful implementation worldwide, almost no governmental laws need to be changed, and there would equally be little waiting for long-drawn-out international negotiations. The microcredit idea has already shown us today that this is an area in which committed people can accomplish a global breakthrough completely on their own. We will learn more about the secrets of success of the microcredit idea in the next section.

✣ **MODERNES UND SICHERES KOCHEN.** Jorina, 27 Jahre, aus dem Dorf Votoliya ist stolze Besitzerin einer für sie höchst wertvollen Innovation: eine Kochanlage mit Kamin, die überdies wesentlich weniger Brennstoff braucht. Unter dem Dach lagert das Brennmaterial: Holzstäbe mit getrocknetem Kuhdung.

✣ **MORE MODERN AND SAFER COOKING.** Jorina, 27 years old from the village of Votoliya, is the proud owner of a very valuable innovation for her: a cooking facility with a fireplace that in addition needs considerably less fuel. The fuel is stored under the roof: wooden poles with dried cow manure.

❖ **WARME MAHLZEITEN DANK BIOGASANLAGE.** Fatima, 40 Jahre, kommt, noch mit der Burka bekleidet, gerade in ihr Dorf Ghatail Thana Para zurück, um den neugierigen Gästen die Biogasanlage ihres Bruders Muhammad Habibur Rahaman vorzuführen. In diesen Behälter wird jeden Morgen der Hühnermist von der eigenen Hühnerfarm eingeführt. Durch einen chemischen Prozess entsteht das Gas, das durch einen dünnen Schlauch zum Gaskocher in die Küche geführt wird. Drei warme Mahlzeiten am Tag können damit gekocht werden.

❖ **A WARM MEAL, THANKS TO A BIO-GAS INSTALLATION.** Fatima, 40 years old, comes back to her village of Ghatail Thana Para and still dressed in the burka to show curious guests the bio-gas installation of her brother, Muhammad Habibur Rahaman. Chicken manure from their own chicken farm is inserted each morning into these containers. Through a chemical process, gas results which is directed through a thin tube to a gas stove in the kitchen. Three warm meals can be cooked daily this way.

YUNUS' ZWEITE SOZIALE REVOLUTION: SOCIAL BUSINESS

Es mag den Leser vielleicht überraschen: Trotz all der bereits realisierten und der gar nicht so schwer umsetzbaren weiteren Potenziale der Kleinkreditbewegung wertet das Grameen-Team diese dennoch als die letztlich kleinere soziale Revolution. Die zweite soziale Revolution – „Social Business" – soll nach Yunus noch unvergleichlich mehr Schwung in die globale Überwindung der Armut bringen. Im übernächsten Teil erfahren wir darüber mehr.

So viel sei zum jetzigen Zeitpunkt festgehalten: Die Vision einer Welt, die von Armut befreit ist, ist absolut realistisch. Die Zeit für diese Vision ist jetzt gekommen. Das Einzige, was wir dafür tun müssen, ist, die Innovationen der ersten und der zweiten sozialen Revolution besser zu verstehen. Wer diese verinnerlicht hat, kann sich deren Faszination und überzeugenden Wirksamkeit nicht entziehen. Alles Weitere ergibt sich dann aus der Dynamik und der dadurch freigesetzten neuen Kreativität.

YUNUS' SECOND SOCIAL REVOLUTION: SOCIAL BUSINESS

Perhaps it will surprise the reader that in spite of all that has been accomplished and the not so very difficult to imagine further potential of the microcredit movement, the Grameen team has rated this as the smaller social revolution. The second social revolution – "Social Business" – should, according to Yunus, bring incomparably more momentum into the global fight against poverty. We will learn more about this in the section after next.

So much is recorded at this point in time: the vision of a world free from poverty is absolutely realistic. The time for this vision is now. The only thing that we must do is to better understand the innovation of the first and second revolutions. Those who understand this, cannot ignore their fascination and convincing effectiveness. Everything else comes out of the dynamism and the new creativity thus released.

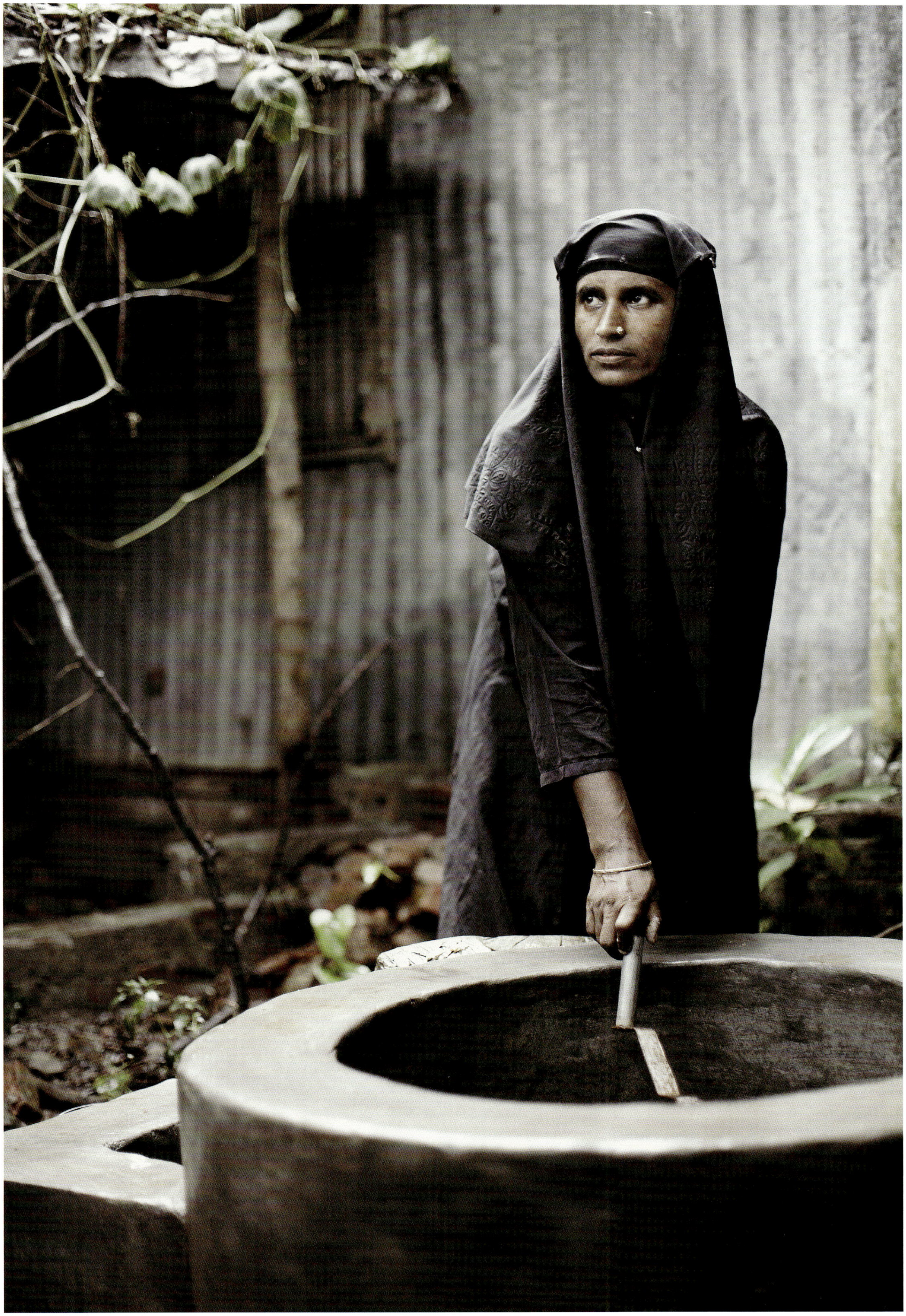

❖ **SPARSAME KOST AUCH FÜR DIE KÜHE.** Ein Bauer führt seine magere Kuh durch die Reisfelder im Dorf Raigong. Die Kuh darf lediglich die wenigen Grasstengel auf den Pfaden zwischen den Feldern fressen.

❖ **FRUGAL FARE FOR THE COWS, TOO.** A farmer leads his cow through the rice fields in the Raigong village. The cow is only allowed to eat the few stems of grass on the paths between the fields.

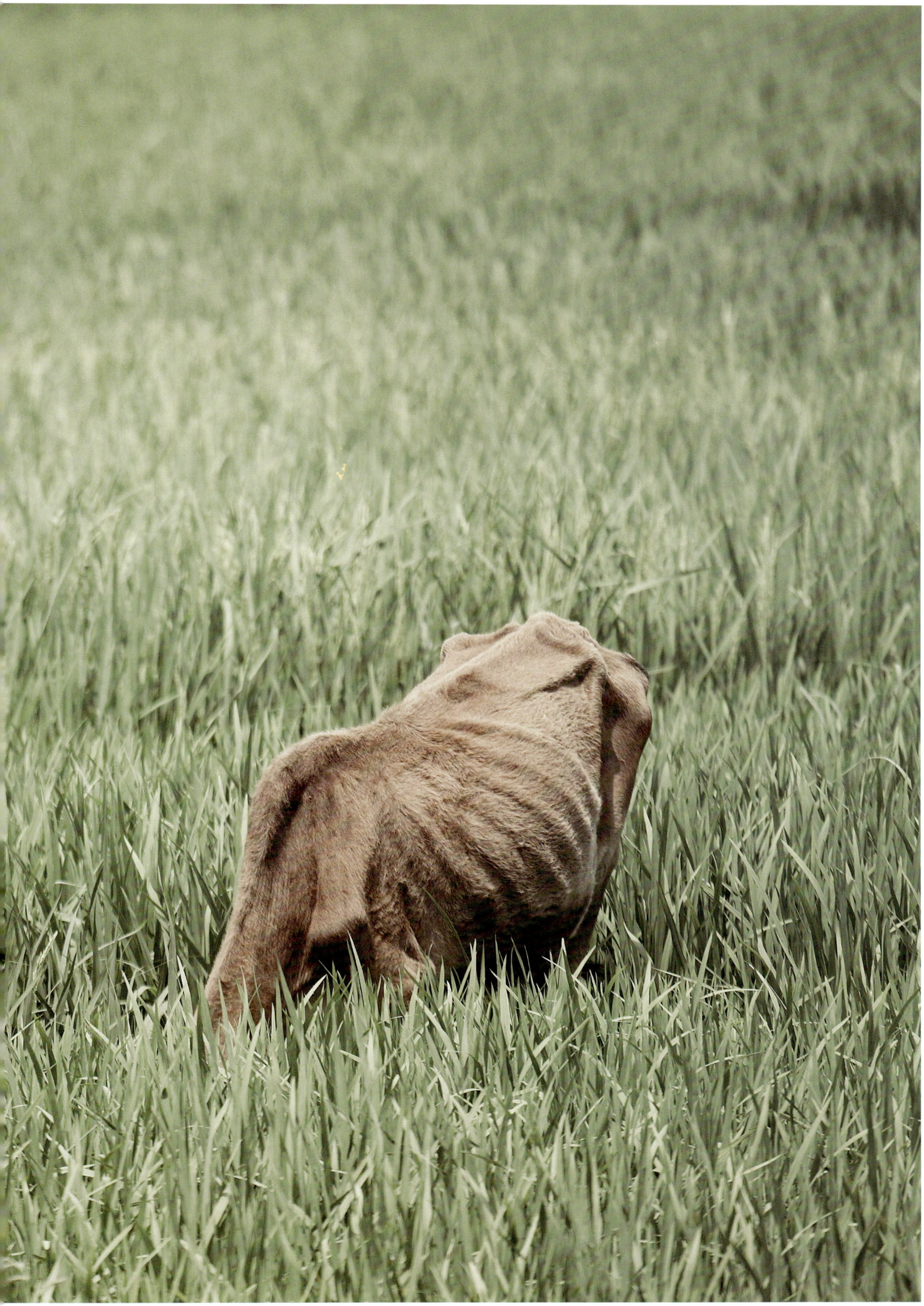

104

✤ **GRAMEEN DANONE** liefert Jogurt für die Armen. Die Ende 2006 eingeweihte Fabrik des ersten Social Joint Ventures – Grameen Danone – liefert nicht nur gesunde und bezahlbare Nahrung für die Ärmsten. Sie ist gleichzeitig Symbol und Auftakt für die zweite soziale Revolution, die Yunus mit seiner Philosophie der Sozialunternehmen einleiten möchte.

✤ **GRAMEEN DANONE** delivers yogurt to the poor. The factory inaugurated at the end of 2006 as the first Social Joint Venture – Grameen Danone – does not just deliver healthy and reasonably priced food for the poor. It is a symbol at the same time and the start of the second social revolution that Yunus with his philosophy of social business would like to introduce.

DER ANFANG – ODER: WIE KANN SO WENIG SO VIEL VERÄNDERN?

Ein Tag im Jahr 1974 im Dorf Jobra, nahe Chittagong, der großen Hafenstadt in Bangladesch. Yunus hat genug von der Hilflosigkeit seines Professorendaseins. Er ist es leid, mit all seinen Wirtschaftstheorien nichts gegen das Massensterben draußen in den Straßen der Stadt unternehmen zu können. „Ich spürte nur noch einen Wunsch: Ich wollte mich aus dem Staub machen, alle Lehrbücher hinwerfen und das Hochschulleben aufgeben. Ich wollte die Wirklichkeit verstehen, die das Leben eines Armen ausmacht, und die wahre Ökonomie entdecken, also die des wirklichen Lebens", berichtet er später über diese Zeit. „Ich beschloss, wieder Student zu werden. Jobra sollte mir als Universität dienen, und die Einwohner sollten meine Professoren sein."

THE BEGINNING – OR: HOW CAN SO LITTLE CHANGE SO MUCH?

One day in 1974 in the village of Jobra, near Chittagong, the large port in Bangladesh. Yunus had had enough of the helplessness of his professorial existence. He was distressed about not being able to do anything with all his economic theories against the widespread deaths out on the streets of the city. "I only felt one wish: I wanted to get away, to throw out all the textbooks and to abandon university life. I wanted to understand the reality that constitutes the life of a poor person and to discover the true economy, in other words real life," he later reported about this period. "I decided to become a student again. Jobra would serve me as a university and the residents should be my professors."

✤ **DIE ERNÄHRUNGSREVOLUTION.** Das Mädchen Saleha Aktar aus dem Dorf Dublagari hält einen Jogurtbecher von Grameen Danone in ihrer Hand. Ein Becher kostet 5 Taka, also 5 Euro-Cent. Dieser Jogurt enthält alle lebenswichtigen Nährstoffe – Nahrungsbestandteile, die in der Ernährung der Armen oft fehlen.

✤ **THE NUTRITIONAL REVOLUTION.** Saleha Aktar from the village of Dublagari holds a yogurt container from Grameen Danone in her hand. A container of yogurt costs 5 Taka, that is 5 euro cents. This yogurt contains all the essential nutrients and food components that are often missing in the diet of the poor.

Gemeinsam mit seinem Professorenkollegen und einigen Studenten setzt er seinen Entschluss in die Tat um. Sie machen Ernst damit, fortan mittellose Analphabeten als ihre neuen Professoren anzusehen. Von wem sonst sollten sie lernen, was diesen Menschen, die nie die kleine Welt ihres Dorfes verlassen hatten, wirklich fehlte?

„Gehört Ihnen dieser Bambus hier?", fragt Yunus eine 21 Jahre alte Muslimin, die er nur hinter einem Vorhang sprechen kann, weil es die strikten religiösen Regeln so verlangen, zu dieser Zeit, an diesem Ort.

„Ja", gibt die Frau zur Antwort.

„Wie beschaffen Sie sich den?"

„Ich kaufe ihn."

„Wie viel bezahlen Sie dafür?"

„5 Taka." (Was dem aktuellen Gegenwert von 5 Euro-Cent entspricht.)

„Haben Sie diese 5 Taka?"

„Nein, ich leihe sie mir von den Paikari."

„Von den Zwischenhändlern? Was handeln Sie mit denen aus?"

„Am Ende des Tages muss ich ihnen meine Bambushocker verkaufen, um das Darlehen zurückzuzahlen. Was übrig bleibt, ist mein Gewinn."

„Wie viel bringt Ihnen das ein?"

„5 Taka und 50 Paisa."

„Sie machen also einen Gewinn von 50 Paisa."

Sie bestätigt dies mit Kopfnicken. Ihr Gewinn liegt somit umgerechnet bei 0,5 Cent.

Yunus fragt weiter: „Können Sie sich das Geld denn nicht anderswo leihen und das Material selbst kaufen?"

„Schon, aber der Geldverleiher würde noch viel mehr von mir verlangen. Die Leute, die sich mit ihnen abgeben, werden nur noch ärmer."

„Wie viel nimmt der Geldverleiher?"

„Das hängt davon ab. Manchmal verlangt er zehn Prozent pro Woche. Einer meiner Nachbarn muss sogar zehn Prozent pro Tag zahlen."

Together with his professor colleagues and some students, he put his decision into action. They treated it seriously, and henceforth looked on the penniless illiterates as their new professors. From whom else should they learn what these people, who had never left the little world of their village, really lacked?

"Does this bamboo here belong to you?" Yunus asked a 21-year-old Muslim woman, with whom he could only speak from behind a curtain as the strict religious rules demanded at that time, in that place.

"Yes," the woman answered.

"How do you get it for yourself?"

"I buy it."

"How much do you pay for it?"

"Five taka".
(This currently corresponds to 5 euro cents)

"Do you have this five taka?"

"No, I borrow it from the Paikari."

"From the middlemen? What arrangement did you make with them?"

"At the end of the day, I must sell them my bamboo stool to pay back the loan. What is left is my profit."

"How much do you earn?"

"Five taka and 50 paisa."

"So you make a profit of 50 paisa."

She confirmed this with a nod of her head. Her profit, therefore, is about 0,5 cents when converted.

Yunus continued to question: *"Can't you borrow the money somewhere else and buy the materials yourself?"*

"Of course, but the moneylender would demand even more from me. The people who deal with him become even poorer."

"How much does the moneylender take?"

"That depends. Sometimes he demands ten per cent per week. One of my neighbours must even pay him ten per cent per day."

The small team around Yunus checked again: the middlemen or rather the moneylender demand from the poor an annual interest rate of more than 14,000 per cent when they "only" demand ten per cent interest per week. Does anyone know how an entrepreneur could function with such an interest rate? Where is the protest from all the economists of the world? Where can the analysis of this simple and scandalous connection, which is obviously causal for the conditions of poverty all around the globe, be found on the business pages of the international press? No one has even the slightest chance under such conditions to economically stand on his own two feet. Trade associations warn about the widespread demise of businesses in their land when their government raises the taxes only marginally. However, silence prevails regarding an economic scandal that robs thousandfold more people of their existence and is many hundredfold more drastic. How can alms help in such a situation? "The people are not to blame for their poverty; it obviously lies in the system in which one lets them live." Yunus would never tire of making this clear during thousands of lectures to his audiences around the world.

Several days later, Yunus sent one of his students, Maimuna, back to Jobra to inquire about what was needed there so that they themselves could obtain the raw materials for their work. Maimuna returned with a list of names of 42 village residents and at the end of the list was the sum of 856 Takas that all of them together needed in order to be free from the vicious circle of profiteering. That is the equivalent of 27 US dollars!

The only irrefutable evidence that the economic freedom of these people actually hangs on a so incredibly absurd small amount, so Yunus thought, can be brought about by giving these people exactly this amount of loan. He required a repayment from them as soon as they were in a position to do so. And they paid it back, punctually and without problems.

Yunus was inconsolable: how could he, how could the entire world, have missed such a simple connection for so long? He recalled the many prejudices about the poor that are passed on in such a matter of fact way: they should not under any circumstances receive loans, as they are incapable of handling money, let alone being able to save or even to invest. They cannot look ahead and think independently. They cannot work together, and so on. He had also thought so for a long time.

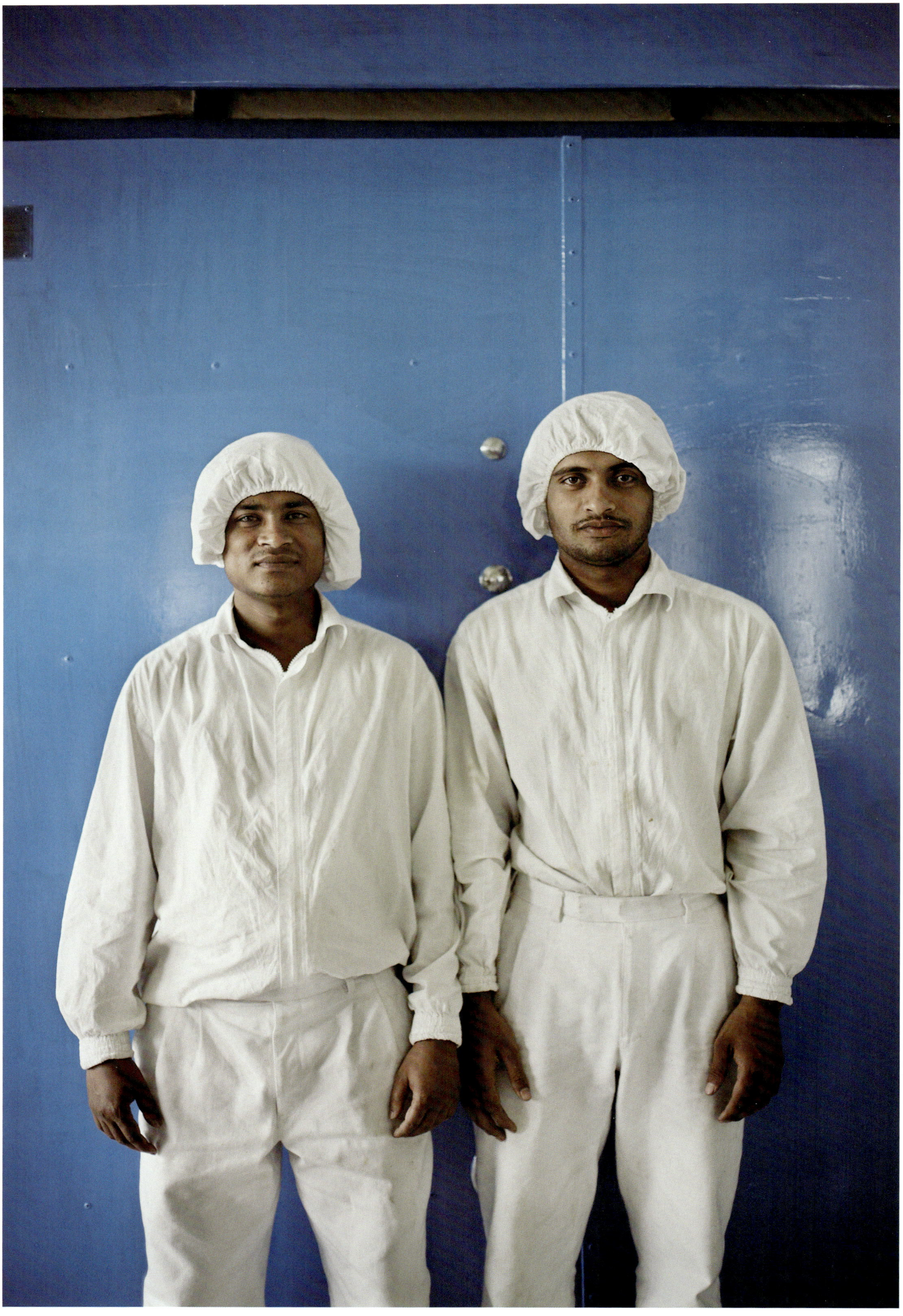

✣ **STANDARDERFÜLLUNG WIE IN EINEM MODERNEN INDUSTRIELAND.** Die Arbeiter Abdul Rashid, 25 Jahre, und Mosiur Rahman, 22 Jahre, arbeiten in der Grameen-Danone-Fabrikanlage in Bogra – ebenso wie alle anderen Mitarbeiter – nach höchsten westlichen Umwelt- und Sicherheitsstandards.

✣ **FULFILLING THE STANDARDS AS IN A MODERN INDUSTRIAL COUNTRY.** The workers Abdul Rashid, 25 years old, and Mosiur Rahman, 22 years old, work in the Grameen Danone factory installation in Bogra – just like all the other employees, to the highest western ecological and security standards.

❂ **STAPELWEISE GESUNDHEIT.** Die Arbeiterin Salma Akter, 25 Jahre, vor einem Stapel von Kisten mit dem gesunden und leckeren Jogurt.

❂ **PILES OF HEALTH.** The worker Salma Akter, 25 years old, in front of a pile of boxes of the healthy and tasty yogurt.

❂ **MOBILER JOGURT-LIEFERSERVICE.** Jogurt-Verkaufslady Shobita Rani mit Motorrikscha-Fahrer Saiful Islam sind unterwegs im Dorf Majhera. Die Verkäuferin erhält 1 Taka Provision pro verkauften Jogurt. Das Risiko trägt nicht sie, sondern Grameen Danone.

❂ **MOBILE YOGURT DELIVERY SERVICE.** Yogurt saleslady Shobita Rani with the motor rickshaw driver, Saiful Islam, in the village of Majhera. The saleslady earns 1 Taka commission per yogurt sold. She does not carry the risk, rather Grameen Danone does.

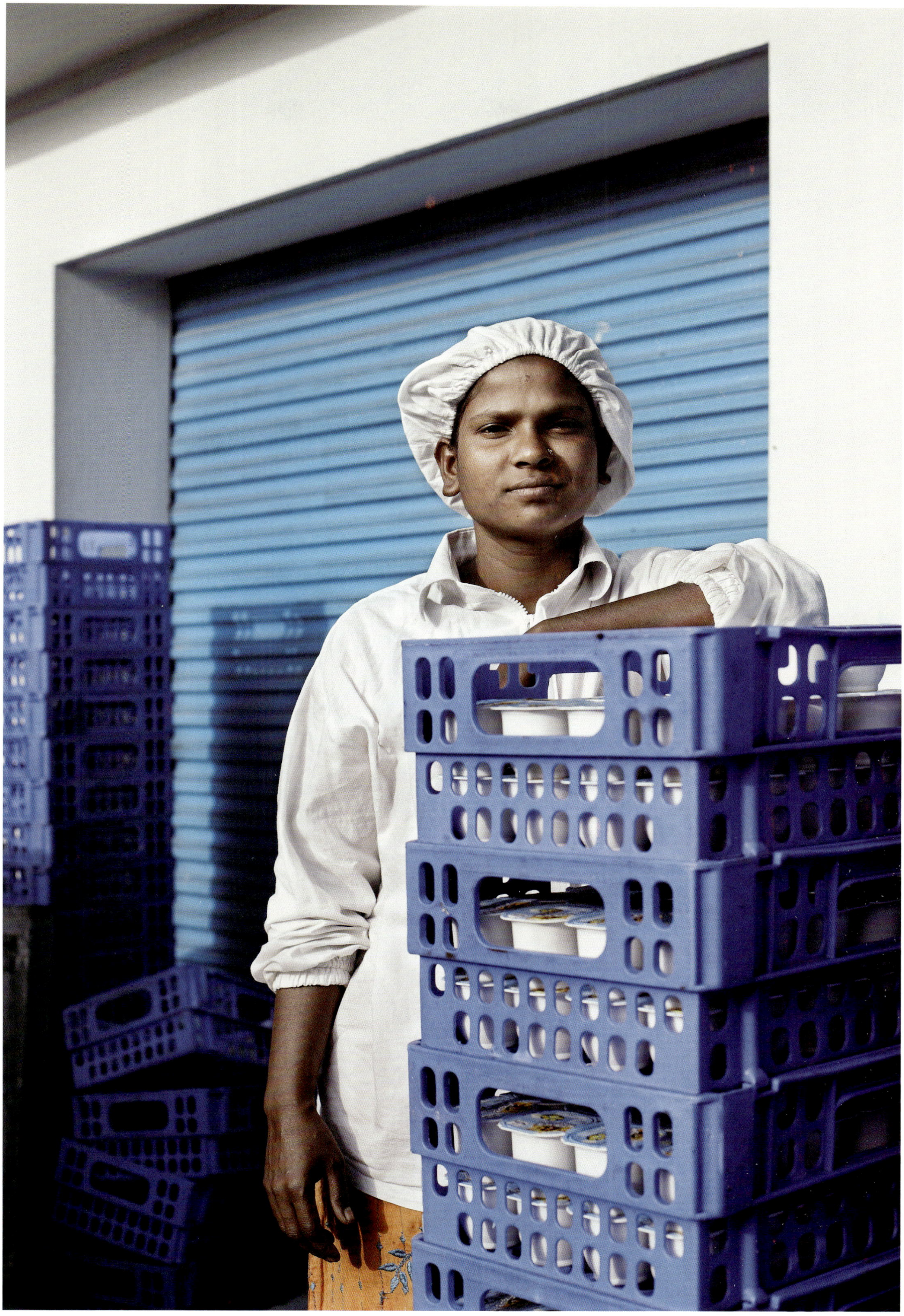

EINE BANK, DIE BEINAHE ALLES ANDERS MACHT

Das Erlebnis von Jobra ließ Yunus und sein Team alles in Frage stellen, was sie bis dahin zu wissen glaubten über die Welt der Armen, über die „bankgeschäftlich Unberührbaren in einem finanziellen Apartheidsystem", wie er seither formuliert, wenn er seine Gesprächspartner aus ihrer desinteressierten Lethargie aufwecken will.

Er versuchte es zunächst mit seiner persönlichen Hausbank. Natürlich kam nichts anderes als das, was man erwarten konnte: Man erklärte ihn für verrückt. Er hakte nach und bot an, dass er persönlich für die erforderlichen Minikredite bürgen würde. Abgelehnt. Also startete er einfach selbst mit der Kreditvergabe von seinem privaten Geld. Nachdem die Experimente mit der Kreditvergabe an die Allerärmsten so überraschend gut funktionierten, sammelte das sich langsam erweiternde Team aus verschiedenen Quellen Geld – nicht zuletzt von ausländischen Stiftungen. In den 1980er- und 1990er-Jahren pendelte sich der Anfangskredit bei der zu der Zeit bereits gegründeten Grameen Bank bei 20 bis 30 Dollar ein.

In den ersten Jahrzehnten des Aufbaus der Grameen Family reagierten die weitaus meisten Menschen überall in der Welt ausgesprochen skeptisch und ungläubig auf das angebliche Wunder der Kleinkredite. Nur wer es selbst ausprobierte, fand die Erfahrung von Grameen bestätigt, nach der es den Armen deutlich weniger schwerfiel, Kredite wieder zurückzuzahlen, als man dies aus der Ferne relativen Wohlstands vermutet. Als das Grameen-Team dann 1983 entschied, aus dem Projekt Grameen eine „richtige" Bank zu machen, wurden sie selbst von vielen Gutmeinenden für endgültig verrückt erklärt. Wie sollte mit den Ärmsten ein Wirtschaftsbetrieb funktionieren? Und wenn er funktionieren sollte – konnte dies dann noch ethisch vertretbar sein? Musste man dann nicht auch wieder ausbeuterische Zinssätze verlangen?

A BANK WHICH DOES ALMOST EVERYTHING DIFFERENTLY

The experience of Jobra made Yunus and his team question everything that they had until then believed about the world of the poor, about the "untouchables of bank transactions in a financial apartheid system", as he described it when trying to awaken his discussion partners out of their indifferent lethargy.

He first tried with his local bank. Naturally nothing came of this, other than what one could expect: they declared him insane. He persisted and offered to personally guarantee the necessary microcredit. Refused. Therefore, he simply started making loans from his private money. After this experiment of granting loans for the very poorest functioned so surprisingly well, his slowly growing team collected money from various sources – not least of all from foreign foundations. In the 1980s and 1990s, the initial loans from the Grameen Bank, which was founded at this time, ranged from 20 to 30 dollars.

In the first decade, during the development of the Grameen family, the reaction of most people worldwide was distinctly sceptical, and with disbelief as to the alleged wonder of microcredits. Only those who tried it out themselves confirmed the Grameen experience that the poor found it clearly less difficult to repay the loans than one would have imagined from the distance of relative wealth. When the Grameen team then decided in 1983 to make a "real" bank out of the Grameen project, they were declared completely crazy, even by their many sympathisers. How could a company with the poorest function? And if it should function, can this then be ethically tenable? Must one not then also demand exploitative interest rates?

❧ **GESUNDHEITSZENTRUM GRAMEEN KALYAN IM DORF AJGANA.**
Im Geburtsraum hält sich gerade der Pathologe Muhammad Abdul Halim auf.

❧ **GRAMEEN KALYAN HEALTH CENTRE IN THE VILLAGE OF AJGANA.**
The pathologist, Muhammad Abdul Halim, is in the delivery room at the moment.

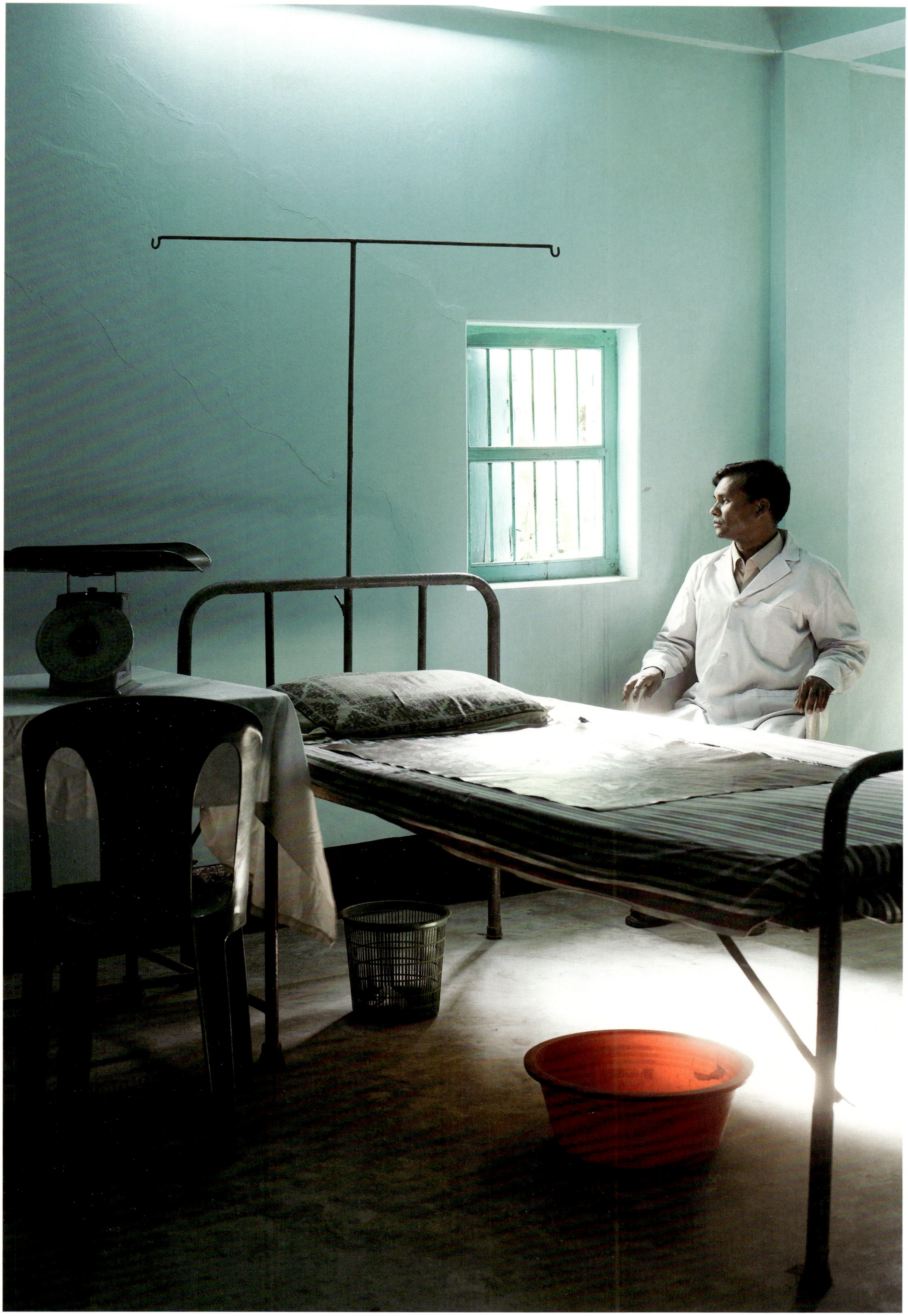

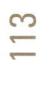

❁ **DAS GESUNDHEITSUNTERNEHMEN FÜR DIE ARMEN.** Shaikh Abdud Daiyan, Managing Director Grameen Kalyan, leitet das neue Gesundheitsunternehmen der Grameen Family von seinem Büro in Dhaka aus.

❁ **THE HEALTH ENTERPRISE FOR THE POOR.** Shaikh Abdud Daiyan, Managing Director of Grameen Kalyan, directs the new health enterprise of the Grameen family from his office in Dhaka.

❁ **MORGEN WIRD SIE WIEDER RICHTIG SEHEN.** In der neu errichteten Augenklinik von Grameen Health Care Services Ltd. in Bogra wartet Lutfun Nessa, 60 Jahre, auf die Operation ihres grauen Stars. Ihre Schwiegertochter Setera Begum sitzt bei ihr und unterstützt sie bei der Vorbereitung auf den großen Tag, der ihr wieder das volle Augenlicht zurückgeben wird. Die Operation wird von ihrem Sohn bezahlt. Sie kostet 60 Euro.

❁ **TOMORROW SHE WILL SEE CLEARLY AGAIN.** In the newly constructed eye care hospital of Grameen Health Care Services Ltd. in Bogra, Lutfun Nessa, 60 years old, waits for her cataract operation. Her daughter-in-law, Setera Begum, sits beside her and supports her in the preparation for the great day when her eyesight returns completely. The operation will be paid for by her son. It costs 60 euros.

গ্রামীণ কল্যাণ
GRAMEEN KALYAN

❀ **WIE EIN VICTORY-ZEICHEN DES GLÜCKS.**

Krankenschwester Sharmin Akhter, 20 Jahre, prüft die Sehkraft des 60-jährigen Mokbul Hussain. In der Freude über die Wiedererlangung seiner alten Sehfähigkeit hebt er seine Finger immer wieder in Richtung der Testzeichen. Es sieht so aus, als forme er sie zum „V", dem Victory-Zeichen.

Er hat den grauen Star besiegt, die Operation vor einem Monat verlief erfolgreich, nachdem die Sehkraft vorher fast vollständig verloren ging. Sie kostete 30 Euro.

❀ **LIKE A VICTORY SIGN OF HAPPINESS.**

The nurse Sharmin Akhter, 20 years old, checks the vision of 60-year-old Mokbul Hussain. With joy for regaining his previous ability to see, he lifts his finger again and again in the direction of the test symbol. It looks as though he is forming them into the "V" for victory symbol.

He has overcome cataracts, the operation ran successfully a month ago after he had almost completely lost his vision. The cost was 30 euros.

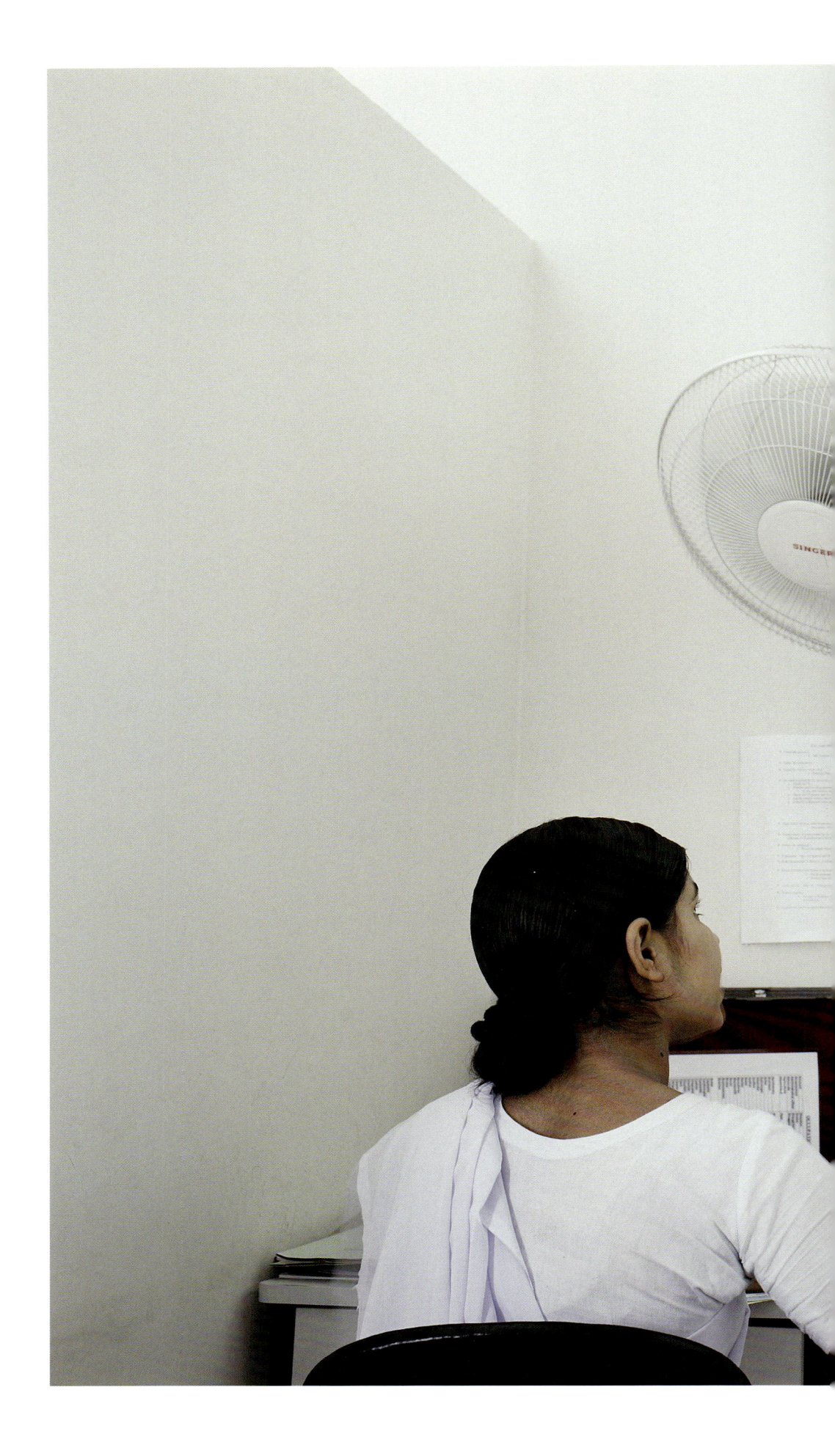

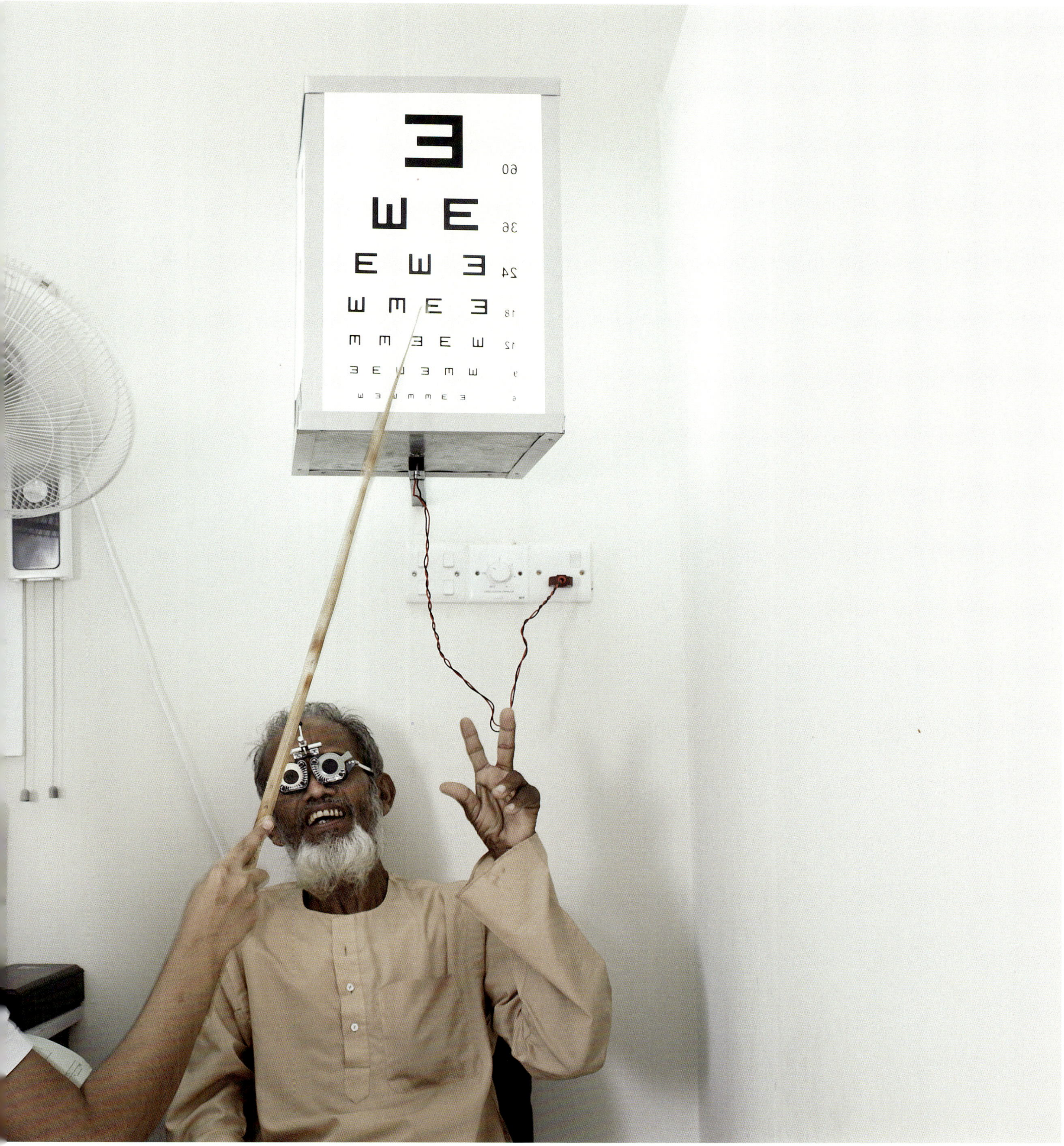

◈ **SINNSTIFTEND ARBEITEN.** Die OP-Schwester Tofy Aktar, 23 Jahre, im alten Augenhospital in Bogra. Sie verdient 50 Euro im Monat.

◈ **INSPIRATIONAL WORK.** The operating room nurse Tofy Aktar, 23 years old, in the hospital for the aged in Bogra. She earns 50 euros a month.

Das Grameen-Team errechnete: Will man mit dem bis dahin entwickelten System der Kreditvergabe vollständig unabhängig als Wirtschaftsbetrieb arbeiten, muss man auf der Basis eines Jahreszinssatzes von 20 Prozent arbeiten. Schon diese Zahl rief vor allem bei einigen westlichen Hilfswerken scharfen Protest hervor. Sie beachteten nicht: Selbst die großen Unternehmen zahlen in Bangladesch Zinsen in derselben Größenordnung, weil die gesamtökonomischen Risiken in diesem Land deutlich höher sind als in gut organisierten westlichen Volkswirtschaften. 20 Prozent Zinsen bedeuten zunächst eine Verbesserung gegenüber den vorherigen 14.000 Prozent um den Faktor 700. Von dieser Differenz hatten die Wucherer und ausbeuterischen Zwischenhändler sehr gut gelebt. Warum sollte es für die Ärmsten ein ökonomisches Problem darstellen, wenn diese Differenz nun – dank der Grameen Bank – in die eigenen Hände gelangte?

The Grameen team calculated that if one were to work with the system developed until now for the allocation of loans entirely independently as a company, one must work on the basis of an annual interest rate of 20 per cent. This figure alone caused sharp protests, especially from some of the western relief organisations. They did not take into account that large companies in Bangladesh pay interest in the same order of magnitude because the overall economical risks in this country are noticeably higher than in well-organised western national economies. Twenty per cent interest means, first of all, an improvement over the previous 14,000 per cent by the factor of 700. The profiteers and the exploiting middlemen lived very well on this difference. Why should it represent an economical problem for the poorest when this difference, thanks to the Grameen Bank, ends up in their own hands?

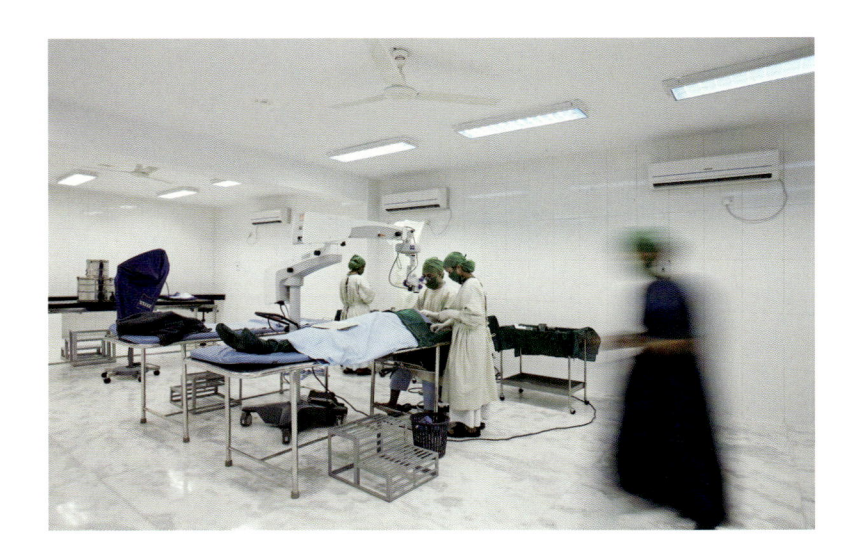

◈ **MODERNER STANDARD NACH INDISCHEM ERFOLGSMODELL.** Der 45-jährige Dr. R. Nabi ist Chefarzt in der Augenklinik von Grameen GC Eye Hospital. Zum Start im Mai 2008 hatte die Klinik drei Ärzte und 18 Arzthelfer bzw. Arzthelferinnen. Alle wurden in einer vorbildlichen Augenklinik in Indien ausgebildet, an der sie auch lernten, wie man eine Augenklinik auf hohem Standard mit optimaler Effizienz führen kann, so dass die Kosten so weit wie möglich gesenkt werden. Die Operation eines grauen Stars dauert 15 Minuten. Inklusive Vor- und Nachbereitungen konnte man zum Start 13 Operationen am Tag durchführen.

◈ **MODERN STANDARD AFTER THE SUCCESSFUL EXAMPLE FROM INDIA.** The 45-year-old Dr R. Nabi is head doctor in the eye clinic of Grameen GC Eye Hospital. At the beginning of May 2008, the clinic had three doctors and 18 helpers. All of them were trained in the exemplary eye clinic in India where they also learned how one can run an eye clinic on a high standard with optimal efficiency so that the costs can be held as low as possible. An operation on a cataract lasts 15 minutes. Including the preparations before and afterwards, in the beginning they could handle 13 operations a day.

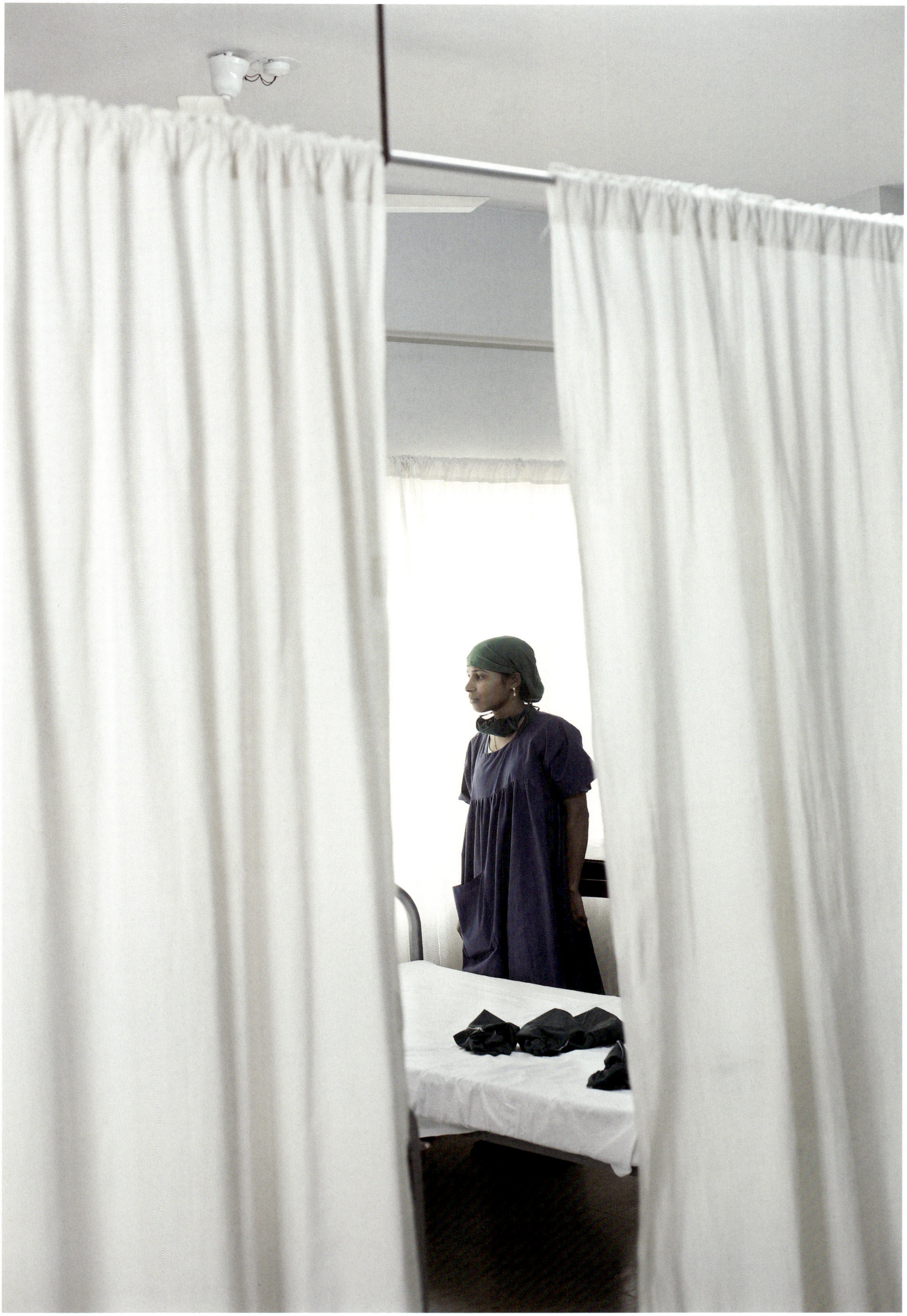

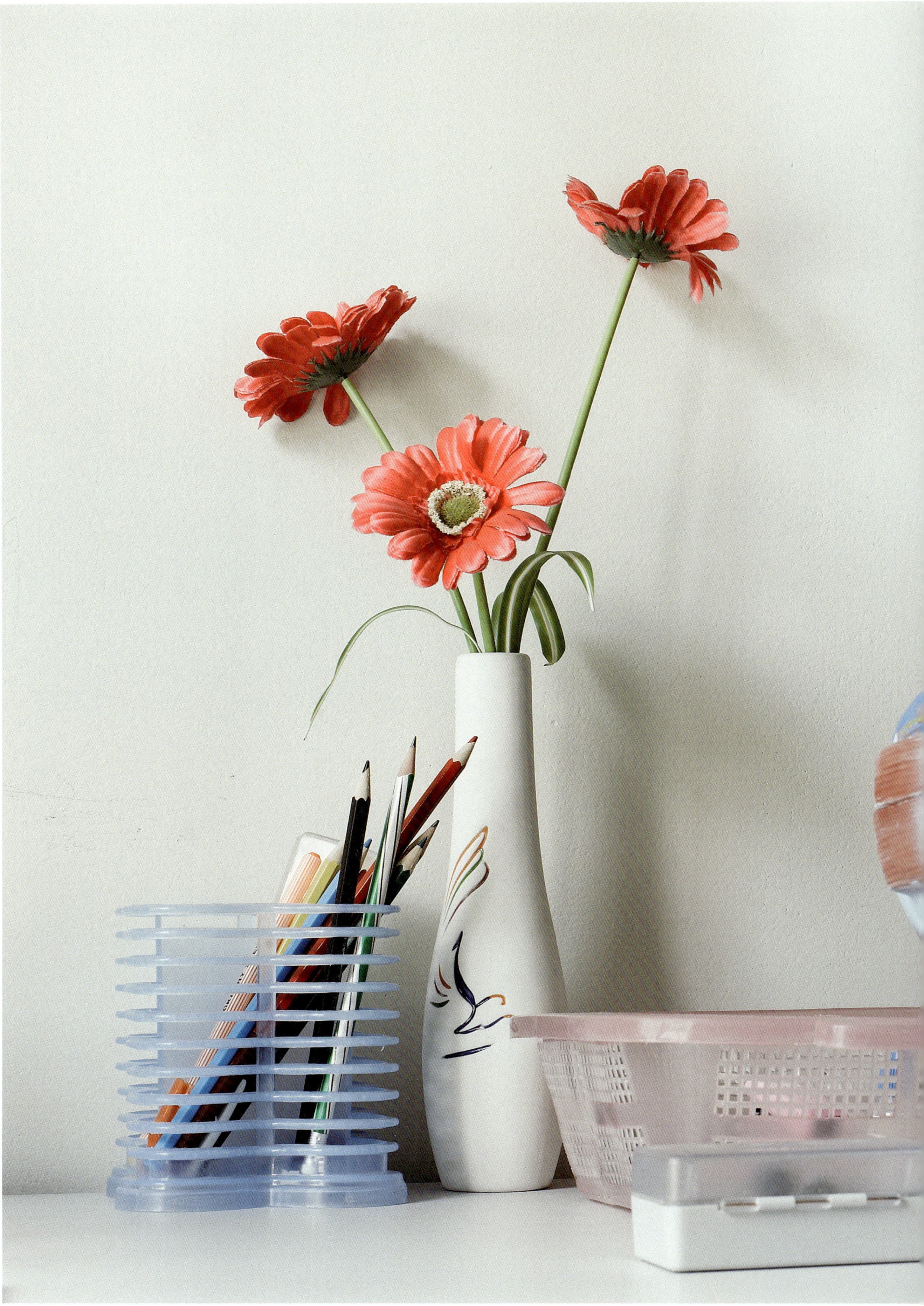

❖ **BLIND FÜR DREIEINHALB JAHRE.** Sahar Banu, 70 Jahre, litt gleichfalls an grauem Star. Dieser war so weit fortgeschritten, dass sie die letzten dreieinhalb Jahre vollständig blind war. In zwei Schritten wurde zunächst das eine, dann das andere Auge operiert. Die insgesamt 60 Euro für beide Operationen brachte ihr Mann auf. Sahar Banus Tochter ist Grameen-Kreditnehmerin. Sie informierte ihre Mutter über die neue Klinik in der Grameen Family.

❖ **BLIND FOR THREE AND A HALF YEARS.** Sahar Banu, 70 years old, also suffered from cataracts. These were so far developed that she was completely blind during the last three and a half years. In two operations, first one eye and then the other one was operated on. The 60 euros for both operations together was paid for by her husband. Sahar Banus' daughter is a Grameen borrower. She told her mother about the new clinic in the Grameen family.

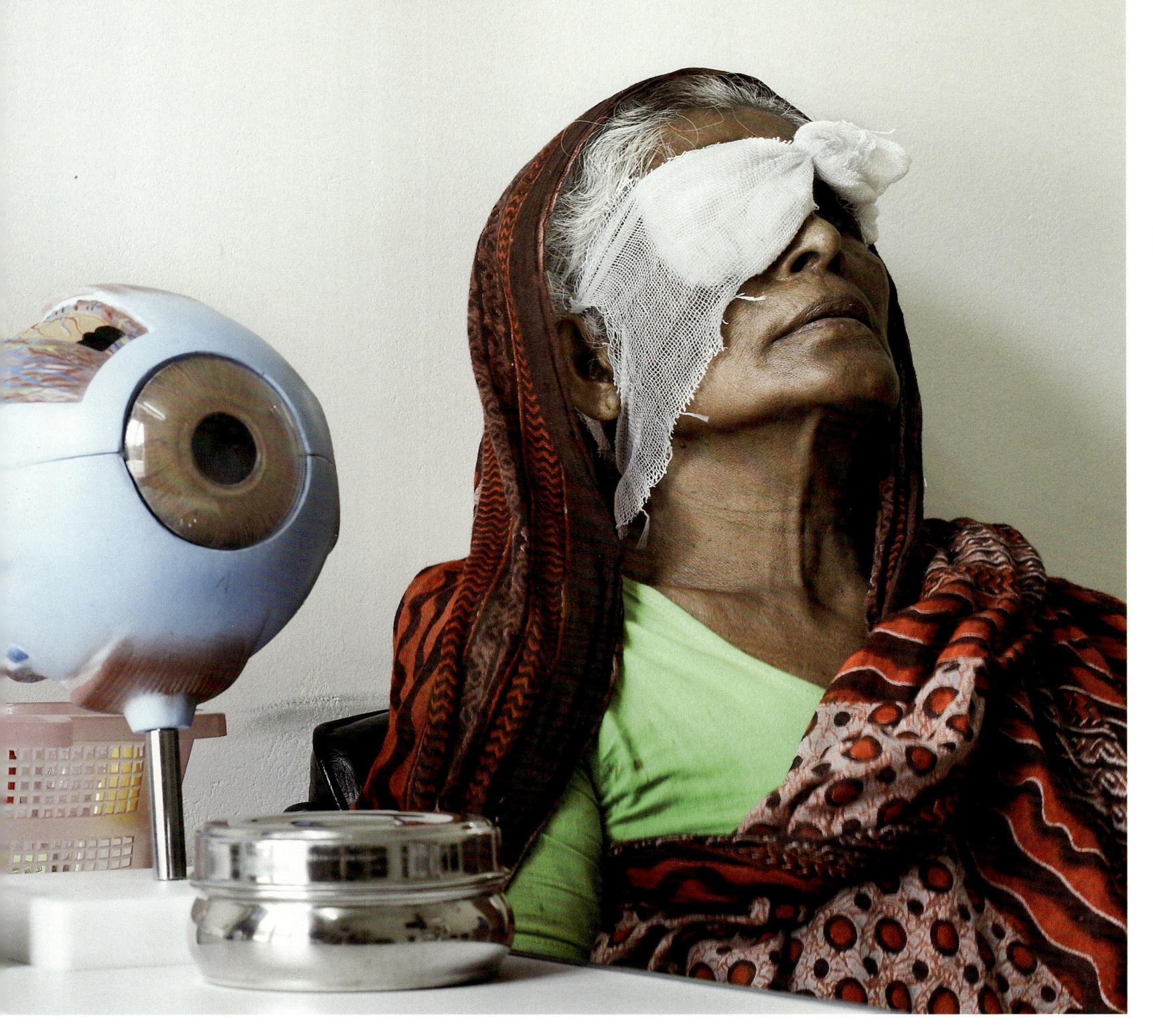

ERFOLGSFAKTOR INVESTIVES DENKEN

Entscheidend für den Erfolg bei der Vergabe von Kleinkrediten ist, ob diese Gelder investiv eingesetzt werden. Wenn sie für Konsum verwendet werden, erwächst daraus für eine arme Familie selbstverständlich ein großes Problem. Wenn das Geld aus einem Kleinkredit investiv eingesetzt wird – wenn man zum Beispiel den Rohstoff, mit dem man seine Wertschöpfung erarbeitet, selbst kaufen kann, oder eine kleine Maschine usw. –, dann stellt die Rückzahlung der Kredite plus Zinsen überhaupt kein Problem dar. Dann wirkt vielmehr – sehr unmittelbar und auf marktwirtschaftliche Weise – die Übereignung dessen, was zuvor an Wucherer und Ausbeuter ging, an die Ärmsten.

Dennoch kann und sollte man die Frage stellen: Was geschieht denn mit den 20 Prozent Zinsen? Das Grameen-Team legte aus einer Vielzahl von Gründen fest, dass mit der Kreditvergabe, im Zusammenhang mit der schrittweisen Zurückzahlung des Kredits, auch immer eine Verpflichtung zum Sparen verbunden ist. Zum einen wird dadurch eine Spardisziplin bei jenen entwickelt, die bis dahin nie die Chance hatten, den Umgang mit Geld zu lernen. Zum zweiten findet aber noch etwas ganz anderes statt: Die Grameen Bank ist eine Genossenschaftsbank. Das bedeutet, sie gehört den Ärmsten selbst. Weder Muhammad Yunus noch die anderen Beteiligten sind „Banker" in dem Sinne, wie wir dies von unseren Banken kennen.

SUCCESS FACTOR THINKING OF INVESTMENT

Decisive for the successful grant of microcredits is whether this money is to be used for investment. When it is used for consumption, a large problem naturally arises for a poor family. When the money from a microcredit is used for investment – for example, for purchasing the raw materials for value creation, or a small machine, etc. – then the repayment of the loan plus interest presents absolutely no problem. The transfer of ownership of what before went to the profiteers and exploiters has much more of an effect – very directly and in a market economy manner – on the poorest.

However, one can and should ask the question: what happens to the 20 per cent interest? The Grameen team set down a multitude of reasons that with the granting of a loan, in connection with the gradual repayment of the loan, one is bound to the obligation to save. First of all, through this a discipline to save is developed by those who until this time had never had the chance to learn how to handle money. Secondly, something still entirely different is happening: the Grameen Bank is a cooperative bank. That means it belongs to the poor themselves. Neither Muhammad Yunus nor the others persons involved are "bankers" in the sense that we all know.

❖ GRAMEEN SHIKKHA AUF TALENTSUCHE IN DEN ARMUTSREGIONEN.

Shimul Sarkar, 17 Jahre, hat gerade ihre Hochschulreife erlangt. Sie verlor ihre Mutter, als sie 6 Jahre alt war. Die Versuche, deren Leben zu retten, ließ die Familie noch mehr verarmen. In ihrer Not beschloss Shimul Sarkar als Kind, besonders gut in der Schule zu sein. Als Grameen Shikkha in ihr Dorf kam, erhielt sie von dort ein Stipendium in Höhe von 5 Euro im Monat. Da sie aufgrund ihrer außergewöhnlichen Leistungen vom Schulgeld befreit ist, investierte sie dieses in die Anschaffung von Schulbüchern. Grameen Shikkha sucht besondere Talente in den Dörfern Bangladeschs, um mit verschiedenen Modellen deren Ausbildung bis zum Hochschulabschluss zu fördern.

❖ GRAMEEN SHIKKHA SEARCHES FOR TALENT IN THE POOR REGIONS.

Shimul Sarkar, 17 years old, has just received her high school graduation. She lost her mother when she was 6 years old. The attempt to save her life left the family even poorer than before. In her distress, Shimul decided as a child to be especially good in school. When Grameen Shikkha came into her village, she received a scholarship for the sum of 5 euros a month. Since she was excused from school fees because of her exceptional performance, she invested this money by purchasing school books. Grameen Shikkha searches for such exceptional talent in the Bangladeshi villages in order to support their education with various models up to university graduation.

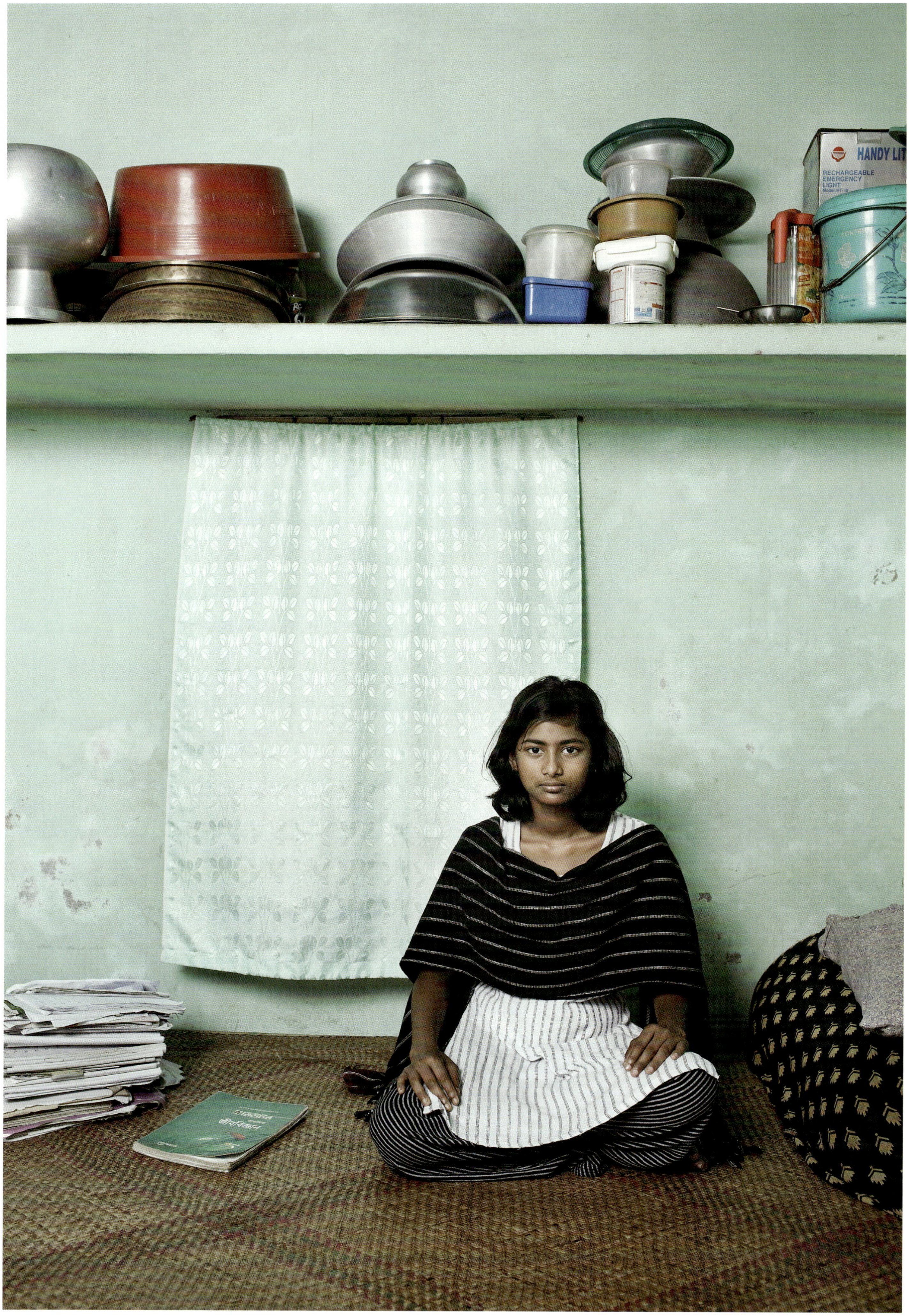
HANDY LIT
RECHARGEABLE
EMERGENCY
LIGHT

Wenn die Bank somit den Ärmsten gehört, bestimmen letztlich sie, wie hoch der Zinssatz sein muss, damit das Gesamtsystem ihrer Bank genau das leisten kann, was es aus ihrer Sicht leisten soll. Der Zinssatz wird auf diese Weise wiederum zu einem investiven Faktor für ihre eigene wirtschaftliche Entwicklung. Sie, die Ärmsten, entscheiden letztlich, wie viel von eventuellen Überschüssen an sie ausgeschüttet werden soll und wie viel in die Weiterentwicklung bestehender oder in die Entwicklung neuer Dienstleistungen zu ihren eigenen Gunsten investiert werden soll. Es ist erstaunlich, wie oft dieser sehr entscheidende Unterschied zwischen der Grameen Bank und den meisten sonstigen Kleinkreditsystemen in Diskussionen nicht bedacht und nicht erwähnt wird.

Wenn „die Bank für die Ärmsten" zugleich auch „die Bank der Ärmsten selbst" ist, verbleibt zur Bewertung ihrer Funktionsfähigkeit im Dienste der Armutsüberwindung vor allem die Frage: Wie stellt sie sicher, dass die Gelder aus ihren Krediten tatsächlich investiv und nicht konsumtiv eingesetzt werden? Dies war die eigentliche kreative Herausforderung an das Grameen-Team, denn dafür gab es keine Vorbilder und keine tauglichen Vorerfahrungen. Man musste selbst an der Praxisfront experimentieren und Erfahrungen sammeln.

Im Zuge der Anwendung eines ethischen Prinzips, das dem Grameen-Team wichtig war, machte man hier zunächst eine sehr bezeichnende Entdeckung: In Bangladesch wie in fast allen Entwicklungsländern der Welt sind es traditionell immer die Männer, denen von außenstehenden Partnern und Organisationen Verantwortung übertragen wird. Das gilt auch für die „Verantwortungs-Währung" namens Geld. Bevor die Grameen Bank mit einer radikal anderen Geschäftspolitik antrat, waren auch in Bangladesch weitaus weniger als ein Prozent aller Kreditnehmer weiblichen Geschlechts. Das Grameen-Team wollte sich hier zunächst nur in Richtung einer Balance bewegen und begann aus diesem Motiv heraus, mit der Kreditvergabe an Frauen zu experimentieren.

Therefore, when the bank belongs to the poorest, they must determine in the end how high the interest rate must be so that the entire system of their bank can provide exactly what it should provide from their point of view. In this way the interest rate becomes an investment factor for their economic development. They, the poorest, decide now how much of the eventual profits should be paid out to them and how much should be invested in the further development of existing or new services to their own advantage. It is astonishing how often these decisive differences between the Grameen Bank and most of the other microcredit systems are not considered and not mentioned in discussions.

When "the bank for the poorest" is, at the same time, "the bank of the poorest themselves", the question above all remains about the evaluation of their ability to function in the service of overpowering poverty: how do they guarantee that the money from their loans is actually used for investment and not for consumption? This was the real creative challenge for the Grameen team because there were no examples or any suitable previous experience. They needed to experiment for themselves on the front line of practice and gain experience.

In the course of the application of an ethical principle that was important to the Grameen team, initially a very characteristic discovery was made here: in Bangladesh, as in almost all developing countries of the world, it is always the men on whom traditionally responsibility is transferred from outside partners and organisations. That also applies to the "responsibility currency" money. Before the Grameen Bank started with a radically different business policy, in Bangladesh considerably less than one per cent of all recipients of loans were women. The Grameen team wanted to move in the direction of balance and began to experiment with granting loans to women.

❖ **PRAXISAUSBILDUNG IN GRAMEEN-UNTERNEHMEN.** Rotna Shasa, 14 Jahre, wird durch das Grameen Shikkha „Management Programm" gefördert. Dies bedeutet eine schulbegleitende Ausbildung bei Grameen Phone, dem größten Einzelunternehmen in der Grameen Family. Sie lernt hier zu Hause in ihrem kleinen Zimmer in ihrem Dorf Nagirpur. Der Hausrat lagert, sauber geordnet, über ihr auf einem Brett.

❖ **PRACTICAL TRAINING IN GRAMEEN ENTERPRISES.** Rotna Shasa, 14 years old, is supported by the Grameen Shikkha "Management Programme". This means training which accompanies school at Grameen Phone, the largest single enterprise in the Grameen family. Here she is studying at home in her little room in the village of Nagirpur. The household goods are stored, neatly arranged, over her on a shelf.

✤ **STUDENT DANK BEGLEITENDER GESCHÄFTSTÄTIGKEIT.** Muhammad Faruque Hossein, 24 Jahre, studiert islamische Geschichte. Seine Mutter ist seit 17 Jahren Kreditnehmerin bei Grameen. Mutter und Sohn betreiben gemeinsam einen Laden für Telefonie, Internet und Digitalfotografie in ihrem Dorf Durgapur.

✤ **STUDENT THANKS TO ACCOMPANYING BUSINESS ACTIVITY.** Muhammad Faruque Hossein, 24 years old, studies Islamic history. His mother has been a borrower from Grameen for 17 years. Mother and son operate a store together for telephones, Internet and digital photography in the village of Durgapur.

Als man auf diesem Weg mit einer genügend großen Anzahl von Frauen Erfahrungen gesammelt hatte, überprüfte man deren Kreditwürdigkeit durch Vergleiche zu den männlichen Kreditnehmern. Bei den Männern waren es 85 Prozent, die pünktlich zurückzahlten – bei den Frauen 99 Prozent. In genauer Umkehrung der tradierten Erwartungshaltung stellte man bei der näheren Analyse der Gründe für dieses Ergebnis fest: Frauen trafen zu fast 100 Prozent investive Entscheidungen für ihren Umgang mit dem geborgten Geld. Bei Männern war der Anteil, der in Konsumausgaben – vor allem in Statussymbole – floss, deutlich größer. Daher wandelte sich die Kreditnehmerstruktur bei Grameen in wenigen Jahren so stark, dass seither rund 95 Prozent der Kreditnehmer Frauen sind. Sie sichern ihrem eigenen Bankensystem eine stabile Rückzahlungsquote von 98 Prozent. Damit ist ausgerechnet eine Kleinkreditbank für die Ärmsten absolute Weltspitze bei der Rückzahlung der von ihr vergebenen Kredite!

Dies ist bis heute für viele, die erstmals von Grameen hören, einfach nicht nachvollziehbar, und sie fragen sich: Müssen da nicht doch auch erhebliche „Daumenschrauben" im System installiert sein, um zu solchen Zahlen zu kommen? Frauen sind leidensfähiger; vielleicht halten sie einfach mehr Druck aus und können deshalb bessere Rückzahlungsquoten sichern…? Unser Denken ist offensichtlich sehr stark geprägt von unseren Erfahrungen, nach denen wirtschaftlicher Profit für die einen durch wirtschaftlichen und sozialen Druck auf die anderen erzielt wird. Es fällt den meisten von uns noch immer schwer, sich vorzustellen: Ökonomie kann auch ganz anders funktionieren. Zum Beispiel durch Teambildung.

When they had collected a large enough number of experiences with women in this way, their creditworthiness was examined through comparison with the male borrowers. With the men, 85 per cent repaid punctually – with the women, 99 per cent. In an exact reversal of traditional expectations, on closer analysis the reason for this result was determined: almost 100 per cent of the women made decisions to invest the borrowed money. The percentage that flowed into consumer goods, especially for status symbols, was clearly larger with the men. That is why the loan structure at Grameen changed so greatly in just a few years that since then about 95 per cent of the borrowers are women. They guarantee their own bank system a secure 98 per cent repayment rate. In this way, of all banks, a microcredit bank for the poor is the absolute best in the world for the repayment of loans given!

This is, even today, simply not comprehensible for many people. Those who hear about Grameen for the first time ask themselves: are there considerable "thumbscrews" installed in the system in order to arrive at such figures? Women are more capable of suffering; perhaps they can simply withstand more pressure and can, therefore, guarantee better repayment rates … ? Our thinking is obviously very strongly influenced by our experiences through which economic profit for the one is reached through economic and social pressure on the others. It is still difficult for most of us to imagine that the economy can also function entirely differently: for example, through team building.

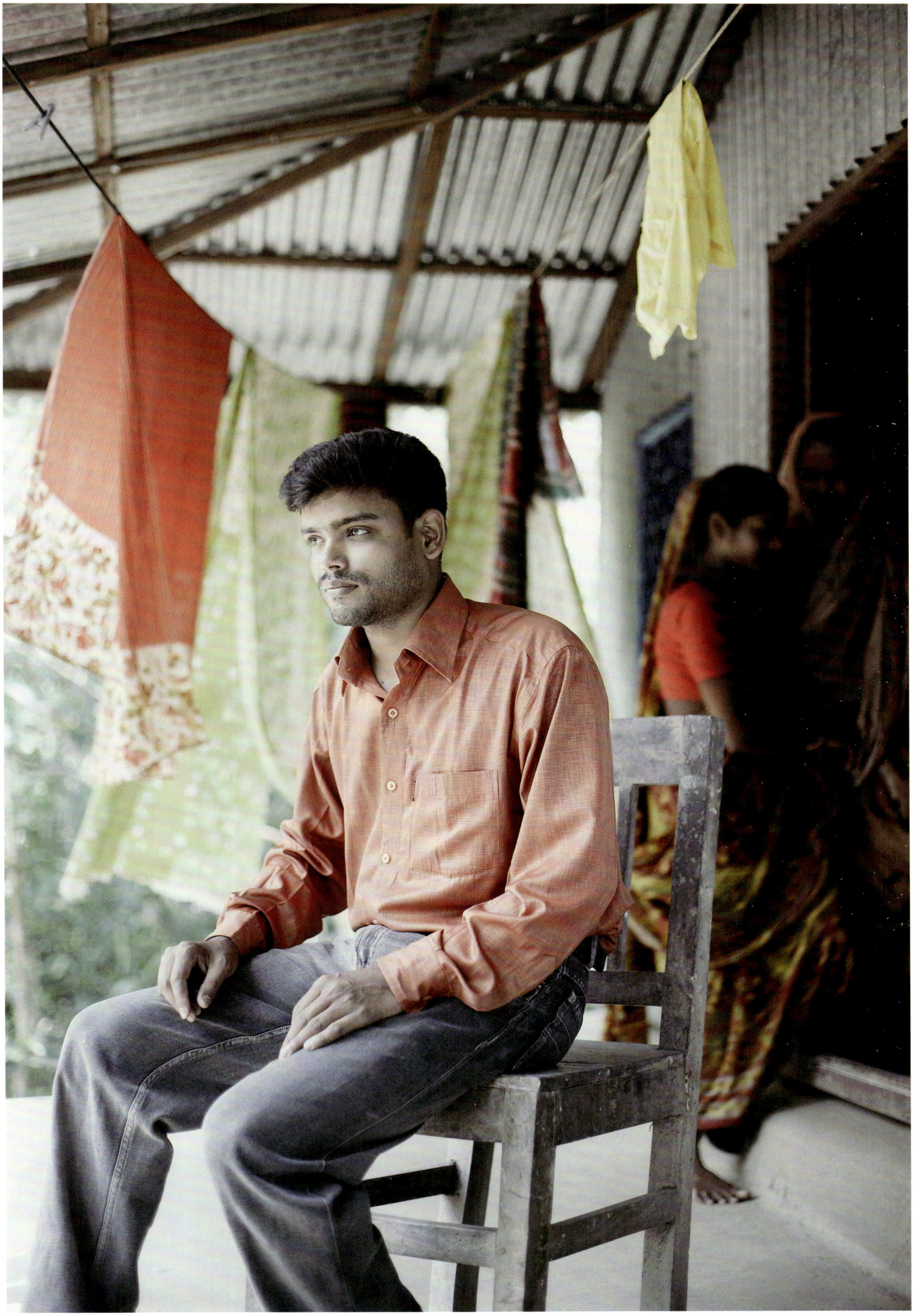

ERFOLGSFAKTOR TEAMBILDUNG

Das Grameen-Team entdeckte Teambildung als sowohl ökonomisches wie auch soziales Wundermittel in einer völlig neuen Dimension. Das Grameen-Konzept fußt nicht auf Individualkrediten, oder genauer: Wer einen Kredit erhalten will, muss vier weitere Personen finden, die sich ebenfalls mit einem Kredit mehr Selbstständigkeit und Entwicklungschancen schaffen möchten. Jedes Teammitglied erhält zwar am Ende seinen Kredit für sein eigenes kleines Geschäft, doch es ist dafür in vielfältiger Weise auf die anderen Teammitglieder angewiesen. Dies läuft so ab:

Die Initiatorin einer solchen Fünfergruppe erhält nicht als Erste, sondern als Letzte im Team den gewünschten Kredit bei Grameen. Sobald die Erste ihren Kredit erhalten hat und sich erweist, dass sie die vereinbarten Raten pünktlich zurückzahlt, kommt die Nächste an die Reihe – bis schließlich auch die Initiatorin an der Reihe ist. Alle fünf Frauen im Team bürgen füreinander, wenn auch nicht mit irgendwelchen „dinglichen Sicherheiten", wie dies in unseren Bankensystemen zu einem „Naturgesetz" erhoben ist. Die Kreditnehmer bei Grameen müssen bei ihrem ersten Kredit ganz im Gegenteil nachweisen, über keinerlei Sicherheiten zu verfügen. Damit ist nicht nur sichergestellt, dass diese Kredite tatsächlich die Ärmsten und Bedürftigsten erreichen. Die Grameen-Mitarbeiter stellten nämlich fest: Wer über keinerlei Sicherheiten verfügt, verfügt über die beste Sicherheit, und dies ist der unbedingte Wille, die niemals zuvor gekannte Chance eines solchen Kredits zu nutzen.

SUCCESS FACTOR TEAM BUILDING

The Grameen team discovered team building as both an economical and also a social miracle potion in a completely new dimension. The Grameen concept does not rest on individual loans, or more precisely: whoever wants to receive a loan must find four additional people who likewise would like to create more independence and develop more chances with a loan. Although each team member receives in the end a loan for his or her own small business, each one is, however, dependent in various ways on the other team members. This can be seen as follows:

The initiator of such a group of five does not receive the desired loan from Grameen first, but rather as the last in the team. As soon as the first one in the group has received her loan and has proven that she can pay back the agreed rate punctually, the next one comes in line until finally the initiator is also in line. All five women in the team guarantee each other, even when it is not with "material security" such as are held to be a "natural law" in our banking system. The borrowers from Grameen must prove just the opposite for their first loan, that they have no collateral whatsoever at their disposal. This method not only guarantees that this loan really reaches the poor and needy. The Grameen employees have, furthermore, discovered that those who have no collateral whatsoever at their disposal, possess the best possible collateral, this being the absolute will to use this previously undreamed-of chance of such a loan.

❧ **SCHULE AUS DEM SLUM.** Dolon besucht mit ihren 10 Jahren eine von Grameen Shikkha initiierte und geführte Slum-Schule in Dhaka. Die gesamte Schule misst ganze 20 Quadratmeter. Sie beherbergt 24 Schüler im Alter von 8 bis 10 Jahren und eine Lehrerin. Die Lehrerin ist selbst noch Schülerin an einem College und verdient sich auf diese Weise 15 Euro im Monat dazu. Es ist eine Schule im Slum – die sich bewährt als Weg aus dem Slum.

❧ **SCHOOL FROM THE SLUMS.** Dolon, 10 years old, attends a slum school in Dhaka initiated and run by Grameen Shikkha. The entire school measures all of 20 square metres. It accommodates 24 students from the ages of 8 to 10 years and one teacher. The teacher is still a student herself in a college and earns in this way 15 euros a month at the same time. It is a school in the slums that has proven itself to be a way out.

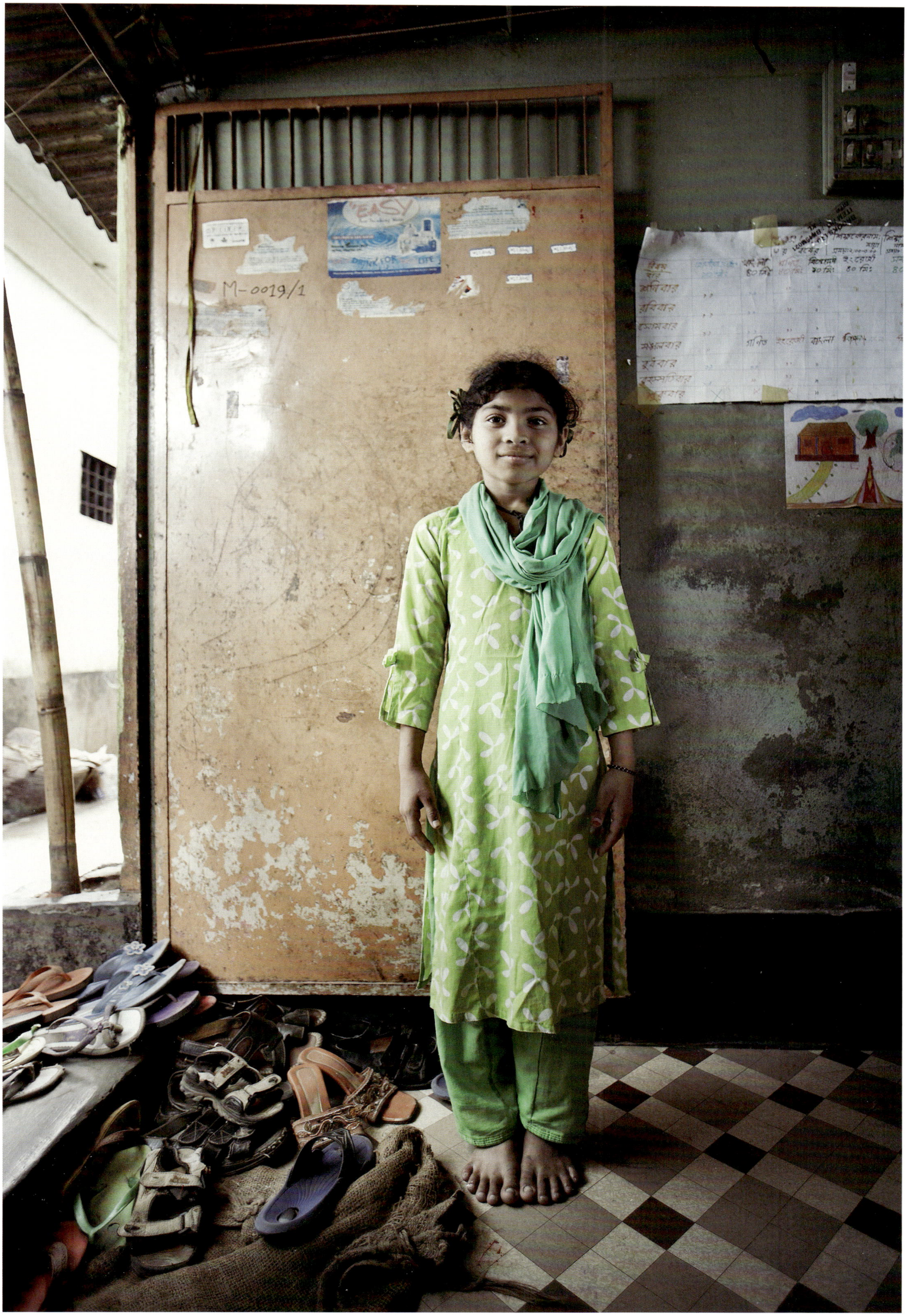
EASY
M-0019/1

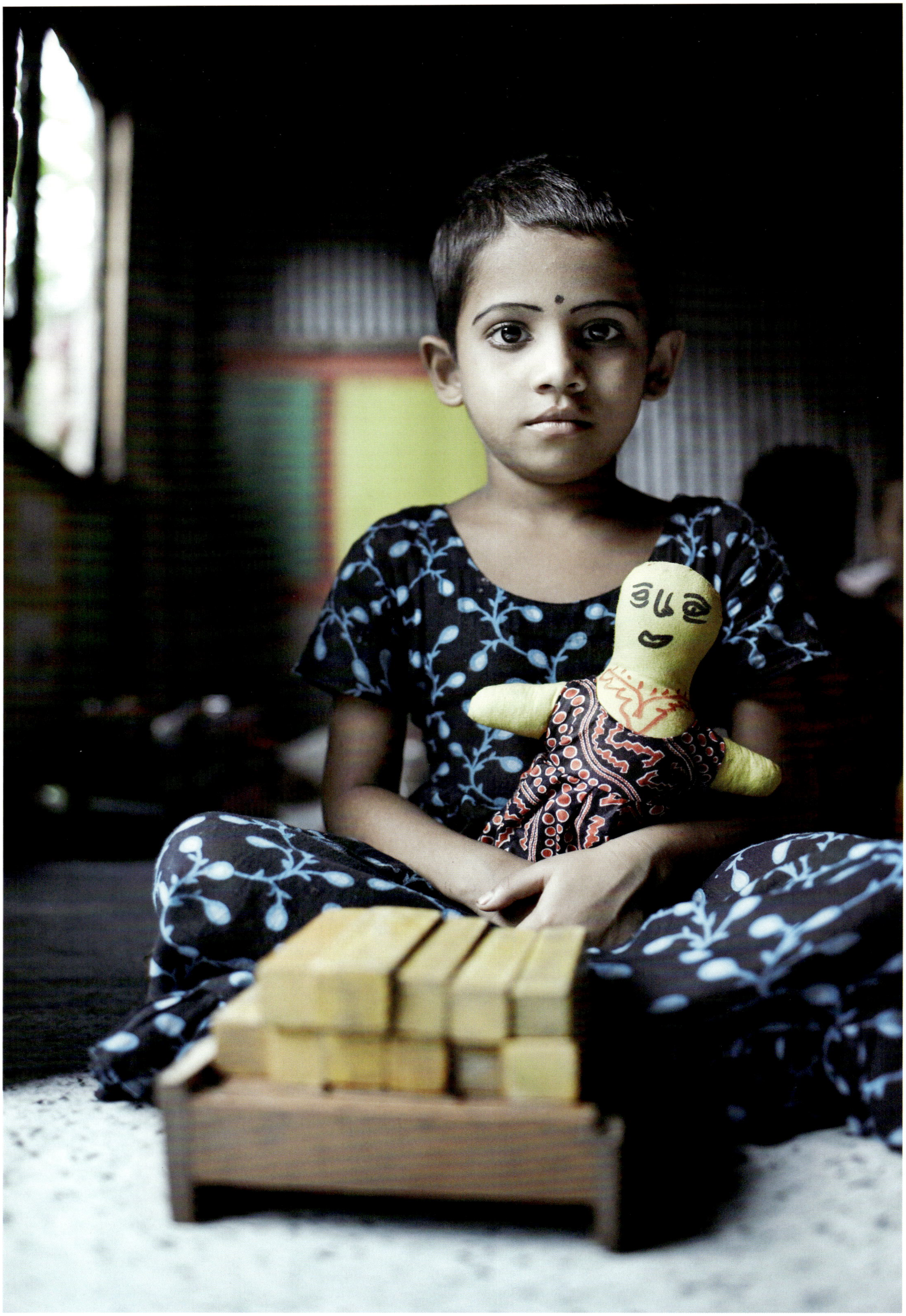

❖ **KOOPERATION VON GRAMEEN MIT PLAN INTERNATIONAL.** Nasrin, 4 Jahre alt, sitzt mit ihrer Puppe in der Hand vor einem Kasten mit Bauklötzen. Der Schulraum ist winzig und nur durch ein Fenster dringt Licht ein. Nasrins Bildungsweg beginnt schon früh, in einer Vorschule. Diese – wie zahlreiche andere Bildungseinrichtungen im Lande – werden durch die internationale Nichtregierungsorganisation Plan International gefördert und von Grameen Shikkha organisiert.

❖ **COOPERATION FROM GRAMEEN WITH PLAN INTERNATIONAL.** Nasrin, 4 years old, sits with a doll in her hand in front of a box of building blocks. The school room is tiny, and light only comes in from one window. Nasrin's educational path began very early in this pre-school. This – like numerous other educational institutions in the country – were supported through the international NGO, Plan International, and organised by Grameen Shikkha.

Durch die Fünfer-Teambildung ist der Kreditnehmer bei Grameen mit dieser Situation der großen Chance nicht allein. Denn die Situation ist schon wegen der Unvertrautheit mit den damit verbundenen Risiken nicht unproblematisch. Aufgrund der wechselseitigen Bürgschaft prüft das Team sehr kritisch und gewissenhaft das „Businessmodell" jedes Teammitglieds, aber auch dessen Haltung und Verhalten. Im Falle des Versagens eines Teammitglieds bürgen die anderen für diesen Ausfall. Sie sind dadurch auf den Erfolg jedes Teammitglieds angewiesen und dementsprechend ist ihr Verhalten untereinander durch Erfolgsorientierung geprägt. Eine Ökonomie der wechselseitigen Unterstützung wird dadurch fundiert. Das Team leistet in den Kreditgruppen bei Grameen sehr wirkungsvoll alle wesentlichen Elemente moderner Ökonomie, vom Consulting bis zum Controlling.

Die Wirkung dieser Teambildung reicht allerdings weit darüber hinaus: Die Teammitglieder denken gemeinsam darüber nach, was sich an der sozialen und sonstigen Infrastruktur ihres Dorfes verbessern kann. Wie kann man sich zusammenschließen, um gemeinsam eine bessere Bildung der Kinder sicherzustellen? Wie kann man die Kommunikation des Dorfes mit der Außenwelt verbessern, kann jemand aus dem Dorf das Telefonieren ermöglichen, indem er Handy-Telefonminuten vermietet – und vieles dergleichen mehr. Dafür schließen sich dann in einem Dorf mehrere Kreditgruppen zusammen und treffen sich regelmäßig. Das Dorf wird zu einer lebendigen, echten Gemeinschaft, die auf gemeinsamen Erfolg programmiert ist.

Yunus fasst diese Effekte der Kreditteams so zusammen: „Ein Kredit von Grameen umfasst nicht nur das reine Geld, sondern ist zugleich eine Art Passierschein zur Selbsterkenntnis und Selbsterkundung. Die Kreditnehmerin beginnt, ihre Möglichkeiten zu entdecken und ihre verborgene Kreativität zu erfahren."

By building this team of five, the borrower from Grameen is not alone with the situation of a great chance, which is in itself not unproblematic, due to the unfamiliarity of the risks allied with it. On the basis of the mutual guarantees, the team checks very critically and conscientiously the "business model" of each team member and also their attitudes and behaviour. In the case of failure of a team member, the others stand guarantee for this deficit. They are, therefore, dependent on the success of each member, and accordingly their behaviour among themselves is imprinted with orientation on success. An economy of mutual support is sustained in this way. The team very effectively accomplishes in the loan groups of Grameen all the necessary elements of a modern economy, from consulting to controlling.

The effect of this team building, however, goes much further: the team members together consider what can be improved in the social and other infrastructures of their village. How can one join together to mutually guarantee a better education for the children? How can one improve the communication of the village with the outside world? Can someone from the village make telephoning possible by renting out mobile-phone minutes? – and other similar ideas. Many loan groups in a village come together like this and meet regularly. The village becomes a lively true community that is programmed for mutual success.

Yunus summarises the effects of the loan teams in this way: "A loan from Grameen does not only comprise the money itself, but rather at the same time, a type of pass to self-knowledge and self-inquiry. The borrower begins to discover her possibilities and to experience her hidden creativity."

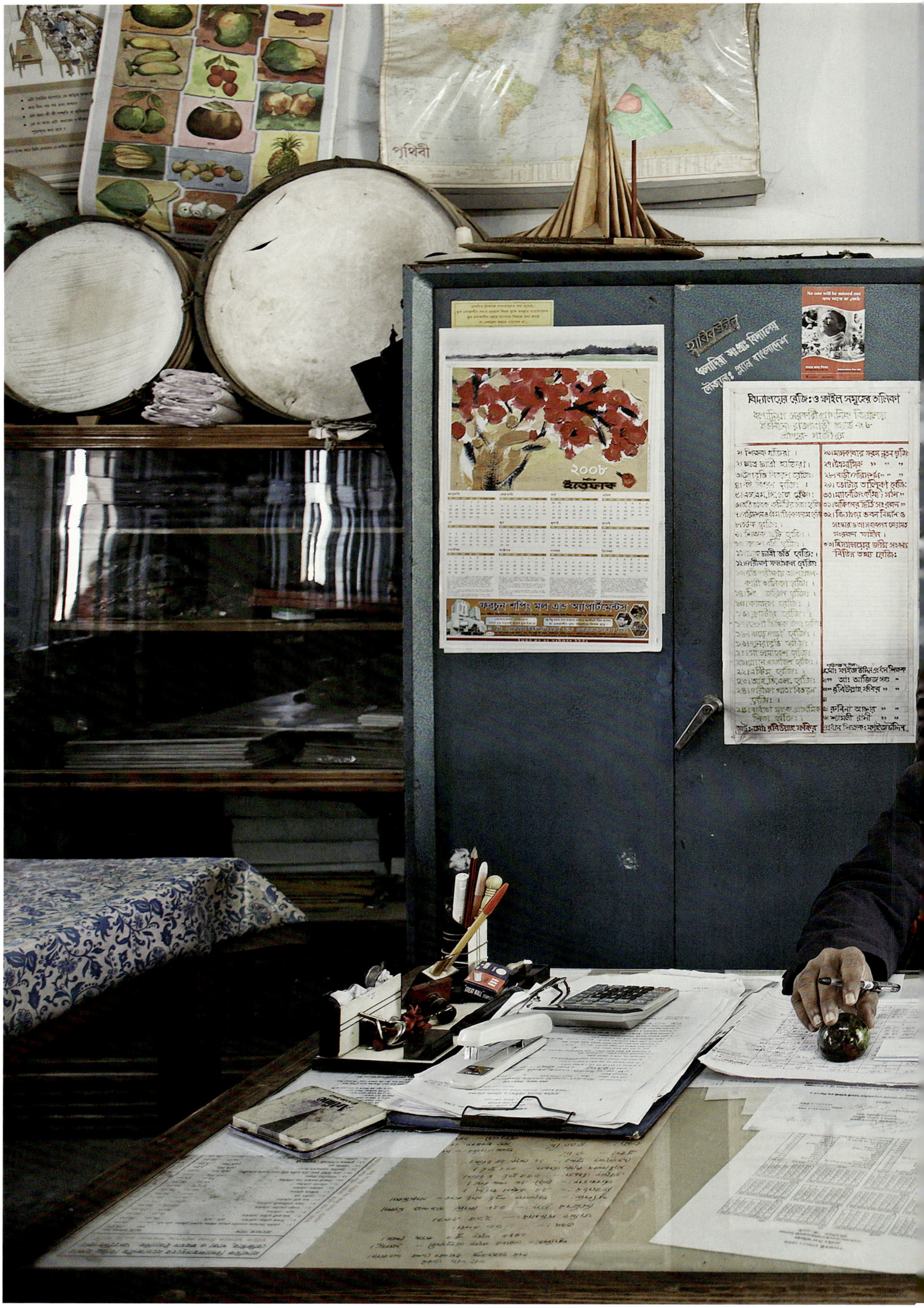
পৃথিবী
২০০৮
ইত্তেফাক

◈ **KOOPERATION MIT DEN STAATLICHEN SCHULEN.**
Muhammad Faizuddin ist Schuldirektor der Grundschule in Dhaladia. Grameen Shikkha, das staatliche Bildungssystem an dieser Stelle um ein Vorschulprogramm ergänzt, teilt sich die Gebäude mit der staatlichen Schule.

◈ **COOPERATION WITH THE STATE-RUN SCHOOL.** Muhammad Faizuddin is the school director of the elementary school in Dhaladia. Grameen Shikkha complements the state-run education system in this case with a pre-school programme and shares the building with the state-run school.

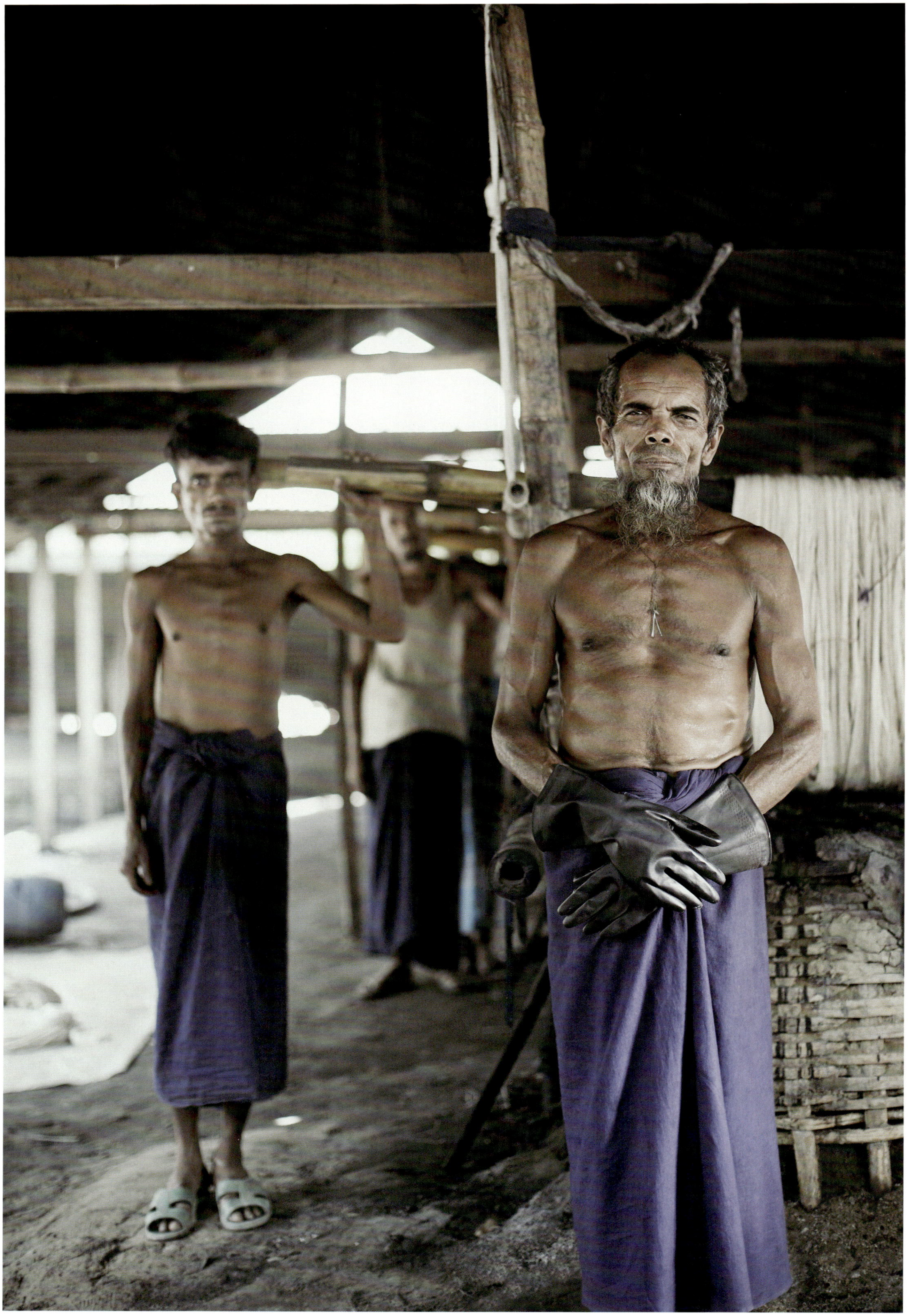

Ein weiterer zentraler Effekt dieser Teamstruktur bei der Kreditvergabe darf nicht vergessen werden: Nur dadurch sind die vergleichsweise extrem niedrigen Zinssätze möglich. Der größte Kostenpunkt bei Kreditvergaben ist normalerweise die Sicherstellung, dass die Bank ihr verliehenes Geld nicht verliert. Dafür entwickelten traditionelle Banken extrem teure Verfahren: hochkomplexe Abfragen, Verpflichtungen, Versicherungen und nicht zuletzt Sicherheitsgarantien. All dies wird bei Grameen ersetzt durch den intelligenten Einsatz von Teammechanismen.

Durch die unterschiedlichen Vorgehensweisen werden unterschiedliche Dynamiken in Gang gesetzt: Während bei „normalen" Banken die Sicherheiten zunehmend „papierener" werden, werden sie bei Grameen zunehmend menschlicher. Je mehr man sich auf Papiere verlässt, desto leichter können auch Konstrukte entstehen, bei denen niemand mehr durchblickt, so wie es bei der Subprimekrise 2007/08 in den USA der Fall war. Dort haben sich Banken dadurch „abgesichert", dass sie Kreditrisiken an Dritte weitergaben, die überhaupt keinen Kontakt mehr zu den ursprünglichen Kreditkunden hatten. Ganz pauschal vertraute man darauf, dass das Ausfallrisiko sich minimiert, wenn eine Einrichtung eine große Anzahl von Hauskrediten verwaltet, und sei dies auch völlig anonym. Diese Form der Sicherheit hebt sich irgendwann selbst auf und Billionenverluste gehen daraus hervor.

Wir haben größten Anlass, die Intelligenz unserer Systeme zu hinterfragen und zu prüfen, ob es nicht viel bessere Systeme geben kann, die sowohl menschlicher sind als auch effektiver. Traditionelle Banken haben den Ärmsten stets jegliche Kreditfähigkeit abgesprochen, weil ihre traditionellen Konzepte für Sicherheiten bei den Armen nicht greifen konnten und jegliches sonstige Konzept, sich abzusichern, viel zu aufwendig und teuer gewesen wäre. Sie schlossen daher mehr als drei Viertel der Menschheit von allen Bankgeschäften komplett aus.

Je mehr Yunus die Schlüsselbedeutung von Krediten für die Chance auf eine faire wirtschaftliche Entwicklung erkannte, desto mehr forderte er das Recht auf Kredit als ein menschliches Grundrecht ein. Vor allem mittels der Innovation der Teambildung zu Kreditgruppen wurde durch Grameen nicht weniger als die Einlösung dieses überaus zentralen Grundrechts ermöglicht.

An additional central effect of this team structure in the granting of loans should not be forgotten: by comparison, only in this way are the extremely low interest rates possible. The largest cost item in the granting of a loan is normally the security so that banks do not lose the money lent. Therefore, traditional banks develop extremely expensive processes: highly complex questioning, commitments and, last but not least, safety guarantees. All of these are replaced by Grameen through the intelligent efforts of team mechanisms.

Through the various procedures, different dynamics are set in motion: while in the "normal" banks collateral is increasingly paper values, at Grameen they are increasingly more human. The more one relies on paper, the easier it is for a financial product to develop in a way in which no one can see what is going on, the way the situation was in the sub-prime crisis 2007/08 in the United States. The banks there, by "covering themselves", gave further credit risks to third parties that had absolutely no more contact to the original credit customers. Entirely all-inclusive, one trusted that the default risk would be minimal when an institution managed a large number of house-purchase loans and they were also completely anonymous. This form of security balances itself at some point and trillions of losses follow from it.

We have the greatest reason to probe the intelligence of our system and to examine whether there are much better systems available that are more human, as well as more effective. Traditional banks have constantly denied the poorest any creditworthiness because their traditional concepts of collateral to safeguard themselves would be too complicated and expensive. They completely excluded in this way more than three-quarters of humankind from all bank activities.

The more that Yunus recognised the key significance of loans for the chance of a fair economic development, he demanded all the more the "Right to Loans" as a fundamental human right. Especially by means of the innovation of team building of loan groups was it possible through Grameen to keep this extremely central fundamental right.

❖ **ALTE WEBKUNST IN BANGLADESCH.** Abdul Jahil Mullah, 55 Jahre, der Mann mit den Gummihandschuhen im Vordergrund, arbeitet in dem Unternehmen Grameen Check in Baura, das die alte Webkunst in Bangladesch fortführt.

❖ **OLD ART OF WEAVING IN BANGLADESH.** Abdul Jahil Mullah, 55 years old, the man with the rubber gloves in the foreground, works in the enterprise Grameen Check in Baura that continues the old art of weaving in Bangladesh.

❖ **VOM WELLBLECHBÜRO MIT VENTILATOR BEI GRAMEEN CHECK ...**
Färbermeister Helal, 34 Jahre, berechnet die Menge des Farbpulvers nach den Rezeptbüchern.

❖ **FROM THE CORRUGATED IRON OFFICE WITH A VENTILATOR AT GRAMEEN CHECK ...**
Dye foreman Helal, 34 years old, calculates the amount of coloured powder from the recipe books.

Als Yunus einmal vor Führungskräften von westlichen Banken sprach, provozierte er seine Zuhörer mit der Frage, welche Probleme ihnen bisher zu Ohren gekommen seien über die Grameen Bank. Als er ihnen – nach anfänglichem Zögern – einige Problembenennungen entlockt hatte, sagte er: „Sehen Sie, dies macht den Unterschied aus. Im Westen sind Sie darauf programmiert, Probleme als etwas Problematisches zu sehen. Bei Grameen heißen wir Probleme als das willkommen, was sie wirklich sind: der Rohstoff für die Entwicklung von besseren Lösungen und wirklichen Innovationen." Die oben beschriebene Transparenz fördert genau diesen Geist. „Innovation kann nur in einer Atmosphäre der Toleranz, der Mannigfaltigkeit und der Neugier entstehen. In einer erstarrten Umgebung bleibt kein Platz für Kreativität", ist Yunus überzeugt.

Auf Seiten der Grameen Bank erzeugte dieser Geist beispielsweise eine höchst ungewöhnliche Flexibilität bei der Kreditrückzahlung. Längere Zeit legte Grameen sehr großen Wert auf absolut pünktliche Rückzahlung. Sprach doch vieles dafür, dass man nur so für eine Disziplin sorgen konnte, die für die Funktionsfähigkeit des Gesamtsystems „Grameen Bank" unentbehrlich ist. Doch die Grameen-Kunden brachten gute Gründe vor, in bestimmten Fällen mehr Flexibilität zu entwickeln. Wie konnten Flexibilität und Disziplin gleichzeitig gewährleistet werden? Auch hier war die Lösung ebenso einfach wie innovativ: Man entschied, Kredite zwar niemals abzuschreiben – um dadurch die Disziplin aufrechtzuerhalten. Doch man setzte, je nach speziellem Bedarf, Kreditrückzahlungen für einige Zeit aus, man streckte sie oder man ergänzte sie durch einen neuen Kredit. Einmal, bei der bisher größten Flutkatastrophe in Bangladesch im Jahr 1998, ging man sogar so weit: Man schloss den Bankbetrieb in den betroffenen Gebieten für mehrere Wochen komplett und bot sich den großen Hilfsorganisationen als das bestfunktionierende Verteilsystem von Hilfsgütern im Lande an. Erst nachdem die Menschen wieder im wörtlichen wie übertragenen Sinne Boden unter den Füßen gefunden hatten, setzte man die Kreditvergabe und Kreditrückzahlung fort. Und man erfand neue Kreditformen, um beispielsweise den Bau von flutsicheren Behausungen zu finanzieren.

Once when Yunus spoke before the leadership of western banks, he provoked his audience with the question about which problems they had heard until now about the Grameen Bank. As he elicited from them – after the initial hesitation – the voicing of some problems, he said: "You see, that makes the difference. In the west you are programmed to see problems as somewhat problematic. At Grameen, we welcome problems for what they really are: the raw material for the development of better solutions and important innovations." The transparency described above supports this spirit perfectly. Yunus is convinced: "Innovation can only arise in an atmosphere of tolerance, diversity and inquisitiveness. In a frozen environment, there is no room for creativity."

On the part of the Grameen Bank, the spirit generates, for instance, a highly unusual flexibility in the repayment of loans. For a long time, Grameen placed great value on absolutely punctual repayment. Much can be said for this: one can only ensure discipline in this way, which is essential for the entire system of "Grameen Bank" to function. But the Grameen clients introduced good reasons to develop more flexibility in certain cases. How could flexibility and discipline be ensured at the same time? Here again the answer was as simple as it was innovative. They decided never to write off a loan and so maintained discipline. However, they interrupted it according to special need, extending the loan repayment for some time or opening a new loan. Once, during the greatest flood disaster in Bangladesh at that time, in 1998, they even went so far as to completely close the bank operations in the affected areas for several weeks and offered themselves to the large aid organisations as the best functioning distribution system of relief supplies in the country. Only after the people found ground under their feet again – literally as well as figuratively – did they continue with the granting and repayment of loans. And they invented new forms of loans, for example to finance the construction of floodproof housing.

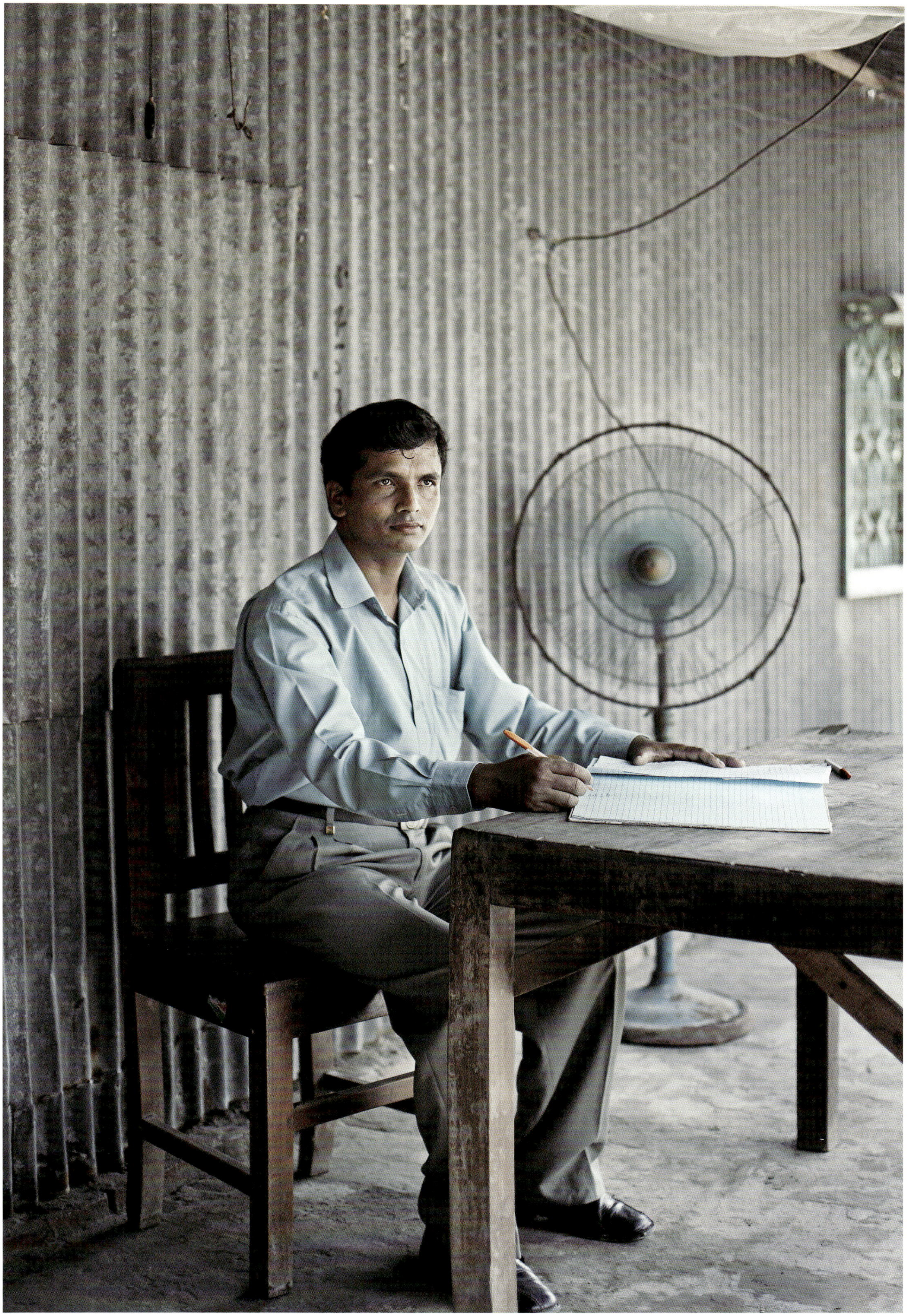

✤ **... ZUM COMPUTERARBEITSPLATZ BEI GRAMEEN KNITWEAR.**
Muhammad Shahidul Islam, 38 Jahre, ist Personalmanager für die 2.700 Mitarbeiter beim deutlich moderneren Textilunternehmen Grameen Knitwear in der Sonderwirtschaftszone von Dhaka. Er verdient 150 Euro im Monat. Selbst der Hilfsarbeiter verdient hier deutlich über dem Existenzminimum-Niveau von Bangladesch und erhält Gesundheitsvorsorge, Unfallversicherung und Hinterbliebenenrente.

✤ **... TO THE COMPUTER WORKPLACE AT GRAMEEN KNITWEAR.**
Muhammad Shahidul Islam, 38 years old, is the personnel manager for the 2,700 employees in the clearly very modern clothing business Grameen Knitwear in the special economic zone of Dhaka. He earns 150 euros a month. Even the unskilled workers here earn more than the minimum existence level of Bangladesh and are provided with health care, accident insurance and surviving dependents' pension.

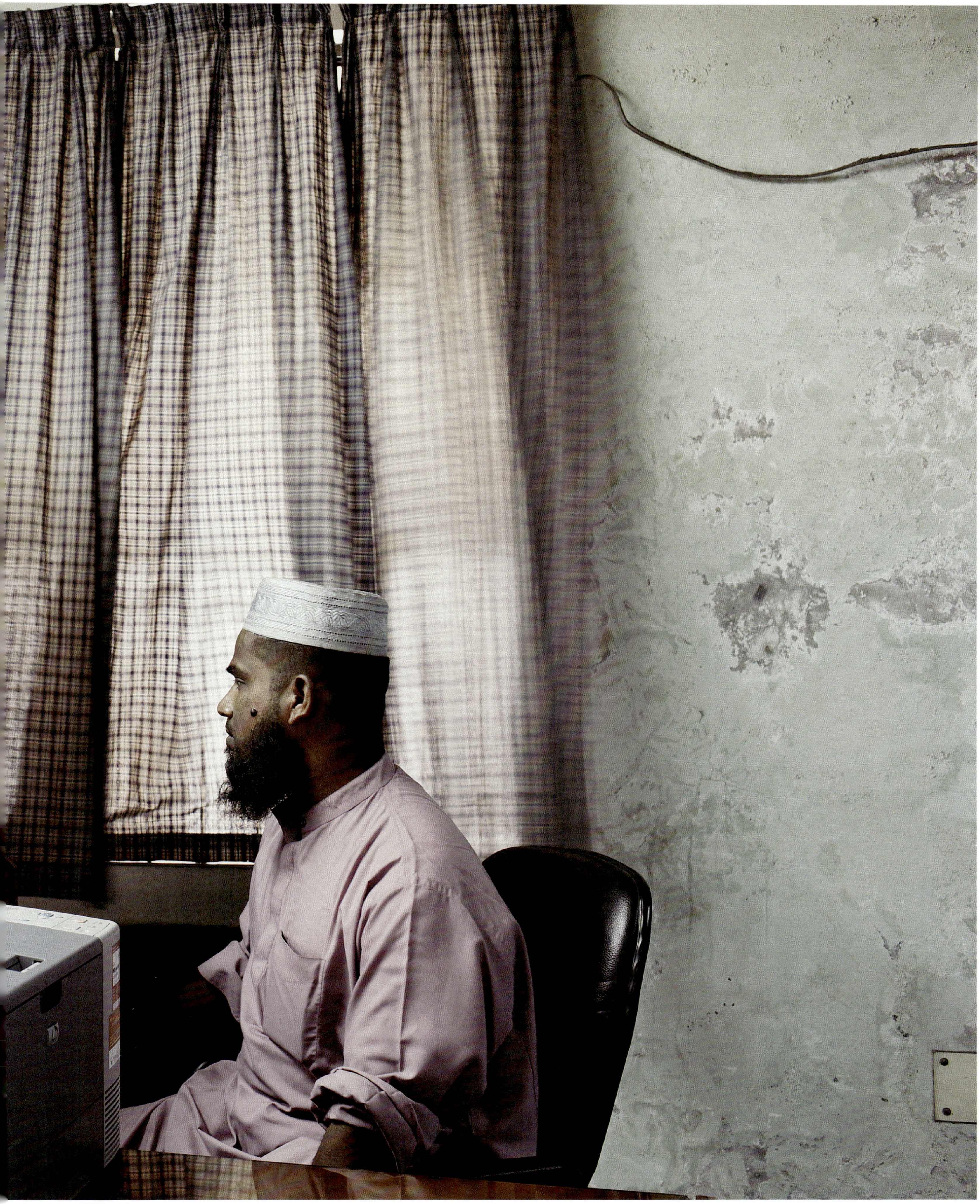

ERFOLGSFAKTOR ETHIK

Manchmal bedeutet Innovation indes auch, sich auf Erkenntnisse und Werte zurückzubesinnen, die zu einem früheren Zeitpunkt schon einmal einen Stellenwert in der Gemeinschaft hatten und dann aus irgendwelchen Gründen an Bedeutung verloren. Inzwischen besinnt man sich auch in der Wirtschaft der westlichen Industrieländer wieder darauf: Werte, Wertorientierung und Wertschöpfung gelten nicht mehr als Gegensätze, sondern werden als einander befruchtend und einander ergänzend betrachtet.

Die Kreditnehmerinnen der Grameen Bank erkannten dies schon in den 1980er-Jahren; sie drängten auf die Selbstverpflichtung aller neuen Kreditnehmerinnen auf „16 Entscheidungen" vor der Aufnahme in eine Kreditgruppe.

Manche dieser Ethikregeln klingen für westliche Ohren vielleicht allzu dirigistisch, beispielsweise die Verpflichtung, bei Hochzeiten weder Mitgift anzunehmen noch zu geben. Doch diese Festlegungen entstanden nicht durch die Lobbyarbeit religiöser Oberhäupter – wie etwa der Mullahs in dem muslimischen Land Bangladesch – und auch nicht durch gutmeinende Mitarbeiter der Grameen Bank, sondern aus den schmerzlichen Erfahrungswerten der betroffenen Menschen. Sie erkannten: Wenn sie mit den angenommenen Krediten erfolgreich ihr Leben in die eigene Hand nehmen wollen, müssen sie gleichzeitig für eine hilfreiche Werteorientierung in den Kreditgruppen Sorge tragen. An die nachfolgenden so genannten „16 Entscheidungen" von Grameen wird zwar immer wieder erinnert; doch es sind freiwillige Selbstverpflichtungen:

1. Wir werden die vier Prinzipien der Grameen Bank respektieren und anwenden: Disziplin, Einheit, Mut und harte Arbeit in allen Bereichen unseres Lebens.

2. Wir werden unseren Familien zu Wohlstand verhelfen.

3. Wir wollen nicht in einer verfallenen Unterkunft wohnen. Wir werden unsere Häuser instand halten und bestrebt sein, so schnell wie möglich neue zu bauen.

4. Wir werden das ganze Jahr über Gemüse anbauen. Wir werden viel davon essen und die Überschüsse verkaufen.

5. Während der Pflanzperiode wollen wir so viele Setzlinge wie möglich pflanzen.

6. Wir werden darauf achten, wenige Kinder zu haben. Wir wollen unsere Ausgaben einschränken und auf unsere Gesundheit achten.

SUCCESS FACTOR ETHICS

Meanwhile, innovation sometimes also means returning to insights and values that at an earlier point in time had already once had a standing in the community, and which then for some reason lost importance. In the meantime, this even applies to the economies of the western industrial countries: values, orientation on values and value generation are no longer regarded in contrast but are considered as stimulating and complementing each other.

The borrowers of the Grameen Bank realised this as early as the 1980s; they insisted on the individual commitment of all new borrowers to "16 Decisions" before being admitted into a loan group.

Perhaps some of these ethical rules sound all too rigid for western ears, for example, the commitment to neither accept nor give dowries at weddings. However, these commitments did not result through the lobbying by religious leaders – such as the Mullahs in a Moslem country like Bangladesh – and also not through the well-intentioned employees of the Grameen Bank, but from the distressing empirical values of the people affected. They realised: when they want to successfully take their lives into their own hands by accepting a loan, they must simultaneously ensure a helpful orientation on values in the loan groups. In the following "16 Decisions" from Grameen, it is constantly pointed out that they are voluntary self-commitments.

1. We shall follow and advance the four principles of the Grameen Bank: discipline, unity, courage and hard work in all walks of our lives.

2. We shall bring prosperity to our families.

3. We shall not live in dilapidated houses. We shall repair our houses and work towards constructing new houses at the earliest.

4. We shall grow vegetables all the year round. We shall eat plenty of them and sell the surplus.

5. During the planting seasons, we shall plant as many seedlings as possible.

6. We shall plan to keep our families small. We shall minimise our expenditures. We shall look after our health.

7. Wir wollen für eine schulische Ausbildung unserer Kinder sorgen und die Mittel bereitstellen, um eine solche Ausbildung zu ermöglichen.

8. Wir werden auf die Sauberkeit unserer Kinder wie auch der Umwelt achten.

9. Wir werden Abortgruben ausheben und benutzen.

10. Wir werden Wasser aus sauberen Brunnen trinken. Ansonsten werden wir das Wasser abkochen oder mit Alaun desinfizieren sowie gegen Arsen filtern.

11. Wir werden für unsere Söhne keine Mitgift verlangen, so wie wir unseren Töchtern auch keine geben werden. Die Mitgift ist in unseren Zentren verboten. Wir widersetzen uns der Verheiratung von kleinen Kindern.

12. Wir werden keine Ungerechtigkeiten begehen und uns denen widersetzen, die welche begehen wollen.

13. Wir werden gemeinsam höhere Investitionen vornehmen, um größere Einkommen zu erzielen.

14. Wir werden immer bereit sein, einander zu helfen. Wenn jemand in Schwierigkeiten gerät, wollen wir ihm alle gemeinsam helfen.

15. Wenn wir erfahren, dass die Disziplin in einem Zentrum missachtet wird, so werden wir hingehen, um sie wiederherzustellen.

16. Wir werden körperliche Ertüchtigung in unseren Zentren einführen. Wir werden gemeinsam an den gesellschaftlichen Aktivitäten teilnehmen.

Einige Jahre nach der Einführung dieser Regeln gingen mehrere wissenschaftliche Studien der Frage nach deren Einhaltung und Wirksamkeit nach. Sie stellten Folgendes fest: In allen angesprochenen Lebensbereichen hatte sich die Situation drastisch verbessert, von der Hygiene über die Ernährung bis zur Verhütung. Die Regeln hatten nicht nur Auswirkungen auf die Gemeinschaft der Grameen-Kreditnehmerinnen. In den Dörfern, in denen es Grameen-Kreditnehmer gibt, hatte sich die Kultur des Dorflebens insgesamt signifikant verändert. Die praktizierte Grameen-Ethik hatte zu einem Bewusstseinswandel beigetragen, dem sich auch die anderen Dorfbewohner nicht entziehen konnten.

7. We shall educate our children and ensure the means to pay for their education.

8. We shall always keep our children and the environment clean.

9. We shall build and use pit latrines.

10. We shall drink water from clean wells. If this is not possible, we shall boil the water or disinfect with alum and filter against arsenic.

11. We shall not take any dowry at our sons' weddings; neither shall we give any dowry at our daughters' weddings. We shall keep our centre free from the curse of dowry. We shall not practice child marriage.

12. We shall not inflict any injustice on anyone; neither shall we allow anyone to do so.

13. We shall collectively undertake larger investments for higher incomes.

14. We shall always be ready to help each other. If anyone is in difficulty, we shall all help him or her.

15. If we come to know of any breach of discipline in any centre, we shall all go there and help restore discipline.

16. We shall introduce physical training in our centres. We shall take part in all social activities collectively.

A few years after the introduction of these rules, several scientific studies investigated the question of whether they were observed and their effectiveness. In all the areas of life involved, the situation had improved drastically, from hygiene through to diet and up to contraception. The rules did not only affect the community of the Grameen borrowers. In the villages in which there were Grameen borrowers, the culture in the village life had changed significantly. The Grameen ethics put into practice had contributed to a change of awareness that the other villagers could not evade.

❂ **RITA AKTER,** 22 Jahre, schneidet die Enden von genähten Kragen ab und prüft, ob die Naht korrekt ist. Ihr Monatsgehalt liegt bei 45 Euro, das der Näherinnen bei 70 Euro.

❂ **RITA AKTER,** 22 years old, cuts off the ends of a collar and checks if the seam is correct. Her monthly salary is 45 euros, the seamstresses receive about 70 euros.

DIE SOZIALE REVOLUTION DER KLEINKREDITE

Nach einer so langen Aufzählung von positiven Wirkungen der Kleinkreditsysteme, wie sie Grameen aufgebaut hat, wird es Zeit, etwas klarzustellen: Die Grameen-Frauen sind selbstverständlich keine Engel. Sie sind unzulänglich wie wir alle, und sie sind den gleichen Versuchungen ausgesetzt wie wir alle. Sie können sehr ärgerlich werden, wenn etwas nicht nach ihren Vorstellungen läuft, und sie können selbstverständlich auch den eigenen Vorteil wichtiger nehmen als den ihres Nächsten. Auch die Armen haben ihre Statussymbole, die sie zu ihrer Selbstbestätigung brauchen, und auch Neid ist ihnen keineswegs fremd. Es geht immer um relative Verbesserungen, solange man über Menschen spricht, und niemals um Absolutheiten.

Dennoch reicht die Verbesserung des Lebens der Armen in Folge der Kreditvergabe durch die Grameen Bank an sie weit über die materielle Ebene hinaus.

Als Yunus und sein Team sich 1974 aufmachten, die Dörfer zu besuchen, hatten sie keine Möglichkeit, mit den Frauen direkt zu sprechen. Es galt für Frauen als unschicklich, mit fremden Männern zu sprechen. So funktionierte die Kommunikation nur über eine Mittelsperson. Außerdem hatten die Frauen seit jeher von allen Seiten zu hören bekommen, wie wertlos und unfähig sie seien. Nicht nur die Ehemänner und die Mullahs im Dorf, selbst die Mütter vermittelten ihren Töchtern dieses Bild. Mädchen galten den Familien als Unglück.

THE SOCIAL REVOLUTION OF MICROCREDITS

After such a long enumeration of the positive effects of the microcredit systems that Grameen has built up, the time has come to make something clear: the Grameen women are of course not angels. They are as inadequate as all of us and they are exposed to the same temptations as all of us. They can become very angry when something does not happen according to their expectations, and they of course also take their own advantages more seriously than those of their nearest. The poor also have their status symbols that they need for their self-affirmation, and jealousy is also not uncommon. It is always about relative improvements when one speaks about people and never about absolutes.

Nevertheless, the improvement in the lives of the poor resulting from loans granted by the Grameen Bank reaches further than the material level.

When Yunus and his team began in 1974 to visit the villages, they had no possibility of speaking directly with the women. It was considered improper for women to speak to strangers. So communication only functioned through an intermediary. Besides, the women had always heard from all sides how worthless and incompetent they were. Not only the husbands and Mullahs of the village, but even their mothers communicated this picture to their daughters. Girls were considered to be misfortune in the families.

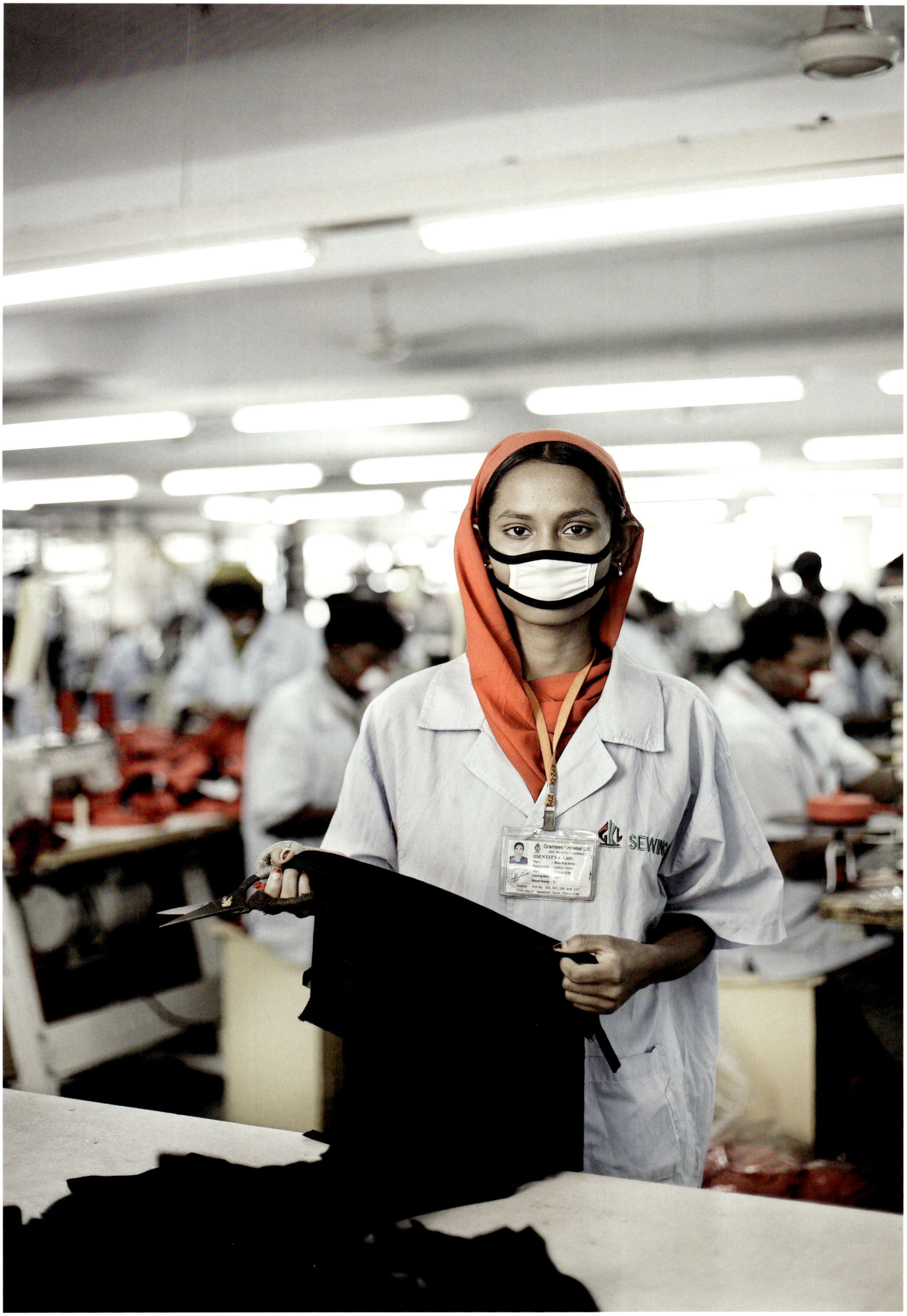
Grameen Knitwear Ltd.
IDENTITY CARD

❖ **DIE KLÄRANLAGE VON GRAMEEN KNITWEAR** entspricht internationalen Standards. Vorne ein Glas mit Wasser, wie es Grameen Knitwear verlässt, dahinter ein Glas mit Wasser des üblichen Standards in der Sonderwirtschaftszone.

❖ **THE SEWAGE WORKS OF GRAMEEN KNITWEAR** corresponds to international standards. In the foreground is a glass with water the way it leaves Grameen Knitwear, behind it is a glass with water with the usual standard in the special economic zone.

So war die Überzeugungsarbeit außerordentlich schwer, als das Grameen-Team sich entschloss, auch Frauen Kredite anzubieten. Erst nachdem das Eis bei einigen gebrochen war, begannen die ersten Kreditnehmerinnen, ihrerseits zu Botschafterinnen der neuen Idee zu werden. Eine der Ersten war Nurjahan Begum. Sie stieß bereits als Studentin zum Kernteam von Grameen, ist heute Mitglied im Vorstand der Bank und Leiterin des Bildungsprogramms Grameen Shikkha. Eine bemerkenswerte Persönlichkeit mit hellwachen Augen, glasklarem Geist und einer visionären Führungsqualität, die ihrem Partner Muhammad Yunus nicht nachsteht.

Zur Grameen Family gehören heute viele solche weiblichen Führungspersönlichkeiten – in der Leitung der Bank, in der Leitung von anderen Grameen-Unternehmen, in den zahllosen Filialen, vor allem aber als erfolgreiche Unternehmerinnen. Viele leiten heute Unternehmen mit Hunderten, Tausenden von Mitarbeitern. Aus Bettlerinnen, Analphabetinnen und Verachteten wurden erfolgreiche Geschäftsfrauen – millionenfach.

Diese Frauen verstanden es, ihre Männer klug in ihr neues Business einzubinden, so dass auch sie unmittelbare Nutznießer der neuen Situation wurden. Sie nutzten beispielsweise die traditionelle Regel, dass nur Männer auf die Märkte in den nächstgelegenen Städten gehen durften. So konnten die Männer nach außen hin den Anschein aufrechterhalten, weiterhin das Sagen zu haben. Vermutlich war es ein großes Glück, dass die Kredite, die ihre Frauen erhielten, sich so rasch auf ihre gemeinsame Lebenssituation auswirkten. Dies erleichterte die Akzeptanz des damit verbundenen Bedeutungsverlusts, der zunächst vor allem innerfamiliär stattfand.

So the work of persuasion was exceptionally difficult when the Grameen team decided to also offer loans to women. Only after the ice had been broken with some of them, did the first borrowers begin themselves to become ambassadors of the new idea. One of the first was Nurjahan Begum. She had already joined the core team of Grameen as a student, and today is a member of the board of directors and head of the education programme Grameen Shikkha. She has a remarkable personality with lively eyes, a crystal-clear mind and visionary leadership qualities, every bit as strong as her business partner, Muhammad Yunus.

Today many such female leadership personalities belong to the Grameen family – in the management of the bank, the management of other Grameen enterprises and in the countless branches, but especially as successful entrepreneurs. Many of them today manage businesses with hundreds or thousands of employees. Millionfold successful business women who were beggars, illiterates and untouchables.

These women understand how to wisely integrate their husbands into their new businesses so that they are also direct beneficiaries of the new situation. They take advantage of the traditional rule that only men are permitted to go to the markets in the neighbouring towns. In this way, the men can still maintain the outward appearance of having the final say. It was probably a great fortune that the loans their wives received had such a rapid effect on their lives together. This eased the acceptance of the loss of importance connected with it, which at first affected everything within the family.

✣ **NEUE STANDARDS FÜR BANGLADESCH.** Gruppenfoto von der Nähabteilung.

✣ **NEW STANDARDS FOR BANGLADESH.** Group photo of the sewing department.

❖ **MUHAMMAD ASHRAFUL HASSAN** ist Managing Director bei Grameen Knitwear.

❖ **MUHAMMAD ASHRAFUL HASSAN** is the Managing Director of Grameen Knitwear.

Die Frauen hatten plötzlich neue Handlungsoptionen. Sie mussten sich nicht mehr alles gefallen lassen. Irgendwann fingen die Frauen an, in den Kreditgruppen und in den Versammlungen mehrerer Kreditgruppen über häusliche Gewalt zu sprechen oder über andere Missstände. Die Stärke, die die Frauen aus diesen Versammlungen zogen, schützte sie zunehmend vor allzu gravierenden Auswüchsen und veränderte ihren Status immer schneller und schneller. Plötzlich wagten Frauen es, für politische Ämter zu kandidieren! In manchen Regionen, in denen Grameen stark vertreten war, bildeten sie gar die Mehrheit unter den Volksvertretern.

Es ist erstaunlich: Obwohl Kleinkreditprogramme keineswegs als Emanzipationsprogramme angelegt waren, erreichten sie mehr für die Frauen als jedes darauf ausgerichtete Programm, und dies ohne jegliche Zusatzkosten. Der neue Status der Frauen war dem System der Kleinkredite immanent.

Analoges lässt sich auch für einen anderen Effekt sagen. Weltweit werden immense Summen ausgegeben für Programme zur Eindämmung der Bevölkerungsexplosion. Doch all diesen Programmen steht das Faktum entgegen: Insbesondere die Ärmsten haben keine andere Form der Altersvorsorge als zahlreichen Nachwuchs. Nur so besteht eine gewisse Hoffnung, dass genügend Kinder überleben und für die Eltern sorgen, wenn diese nicht mehr für sich selbst sorgen können.

Kleinkredite an Frauen lösen dieses Dilemma, und zwar ab dem Tag, an dem die Kreditnehmerinnen mit ihrem selbstständigen Betrieb beginnen. Sie sind damit beschäftigt, ihr Geschäft erfolgreich zu führen und ihre Kreditraten zurückzuzahlen, um später einen größeren Kredit zu erhalten, mit dem sie ihr Geschäft ausweiten können. Sie spüren schnell den Erfolg ihrer unabhängigen wirtschaftlichen Tätigkeit und begreifen: Eine bessere Familienplanung mit deutlich weniger Kindern ist unter den neuen Bedingungen ein Beitrag, die wirtschaftliche Tätigkeit mit noch besserem Erfolg voranzubringen und abzusichern. Untersuchungen zeigen: Kleinkredite an Frauen sind das beste Verhütungsmittel und die beste Aufklärungskampagne – ohne dass dies zusätzliche Gelder kosten würde.

The women suddenly had new options of action. They no longer needed to put up with everything. At some time or other, the women began to talk about domestic violence or other abuses in the loan groups and in the meetings of several loan groups. The strength drawn by the women from these gatherings increasingly protected them from all too serious excesses and changed their status faster and faster. Suddenly women risked running for political office: in some areas in which Grameen was strongly represented, they even formed a majority of the representatives of the people.

It is remarkable: although the microcredit programme was not by any means structured as an emancipation programme, it has accomplished more for the women than any other programme so oriented, and this at no extra cost. The new status of the women was inherent in the system of microcredits.

Analogies can also speak for another effect. Enormous amounts are spent worldwide on programmes to curb the population explosion. However, there is a factor standing in the way of all of these programmes: the poor in particular have no other provision for their retirement other than numerous offspring. Only in this manner can a certain hope exist that enough children will survive to care for their parents when they can no longer care for themselves.

Microcredit for women solves this dilemma, namely on the day on which the borrowers start their own company. They are busy successfully managing their business and paying back their loan instalments in order to receive a larger loan later with which they can expand their business. They quickly feel the success of their independent economic activity and understand that better family planning with clearly fewer children is, under the new conditions, a contribution to advance and secure their economic activity with even greater success. Studies show that microcredits for women are the best contraceptive and the best sexual education campaign without costing any additional money.

Ein großes Problem in den Armutsregionen der Welt ist der chronisch niedrige Wert einfacher menschlicher Arbeit. Die Globalisierung hat diese Situation für viele Regionen nur noch weiter verschärft, weil Global Player sich für solche Arbeit jenen Platz auf diesem Planeten aussuchen können, an dem die Arbeiter mit den geringsten Löhnen und den schlechtesten Arbeitsbedingungen zufrieden sind. Die Drohung, weiterzuziehen, sobald die Arbeiter bessere Bedingungen verlangen, wirkt höchst disziplinierend. Somit stellt sich die Frage: Wie wirkt sich die Ausbreitung von Kleinkreditsystemen auf den Wert der Arbeit aus?

Im Zuge der Grameen-Revolution wurden in Bangladesch Millionen neue Arbeitsplätze geschaffen in den Familienbetrieben, die mit den Kleinkrediten gegründet wurden. Selbstverständlich arbeiten die Ehegatten und Kinder von Kreditnehmern viel lieber im eigenen kleinen Familienbetrieb als in den Sweatshops der Global Player oder der einheimischen Industrie, die längst gleichfalls unter dem Lohndruck der unkontrolliert wuchernden Globalisierung steht. Weil sie im Familienbetrieb mehr vom Wertschöpfungsprozess haben, bleibt ihnen eindeutig mehr zum Leben.

Zahlt dann der Rest des Arbeitsmarkts die Zeche für den Erfolg der Grameen-finanzierten Unternehmen? Keineswegs. Durch den Wechsel von zunehmend mehr Arbeitern in diesen neuen Sektor der Wirtschaft wird Arbeit zu einem knapperen Gut und damit teurer. In wenigen Jahren stellte man selbst bei der Gruppe der Tagelöhner eine Steigerung der Löhne um den Faktor fünf fest. Wer also die Löhne in den Entwicklungsländern auf ein humaneres Niveau anheben will, sollte auf das Instrument der Kleinkredite setzen!

A major problem in the regions of poverty in the world is the chronic low value of simple human labour. Globalisation has only aggravated the situation for many regions because a global player can choose any place on this planet for such work in which the labourer is willing to accept the lowest wages and the worst working conditions. The threat to move on, as soon as the workers demand better conditions, has a highly disciplinary effect. Consequently, the question is: how does the spread of the microcredit system affect the value of labour?

In the course of the Grameen revolution, millions of new workplaces have been created in the family companies in Bangladesh that were founded with microcredits. Naturally, the married partner and the children of the borrowers prefer to work in their own small family business rather than in the sweatshops of the global players or the local industry, that likewise is under the wage pressure of the uncontrolled rampant globalisation. Because they have more from the process of added value in the family business, clearly more remains for them to live on.

Does the rest of the labour market pay the bill for the success of the Grameen financed enterprises? Not at all. Through the change of increasingly more workers in this new sector of the economy, jobs become scarce and are therefore expensive. In a few years, one noticed that amongst the group of day labourers there was an increase in wages by a factor of five. Whoever wants to raise wages in the developing countries to a more human level should trust the instrument of microcredits.

❂ Junge Männer prüfen die Stoffqualität.
❂ Young men check the quality of the material.

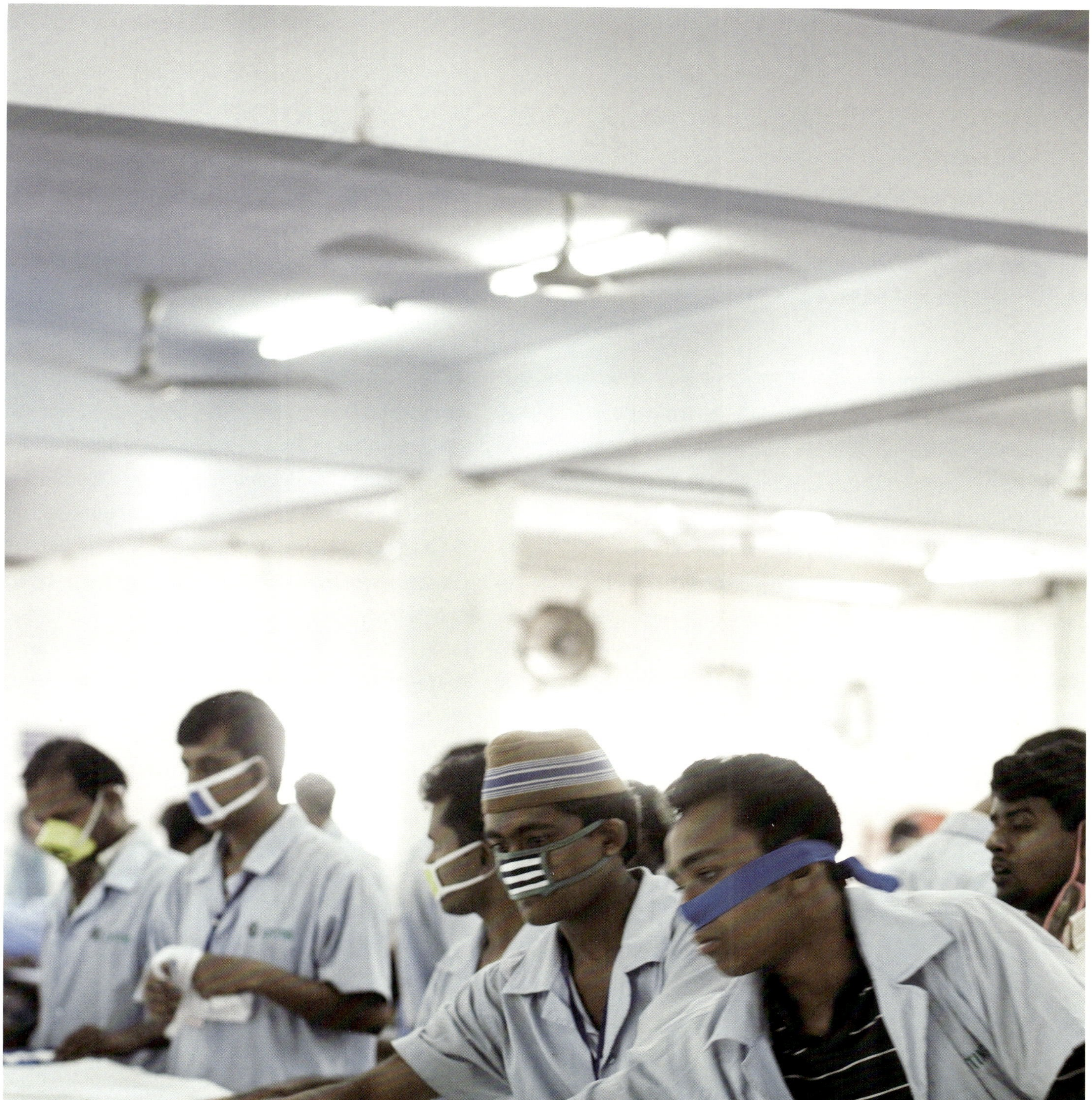

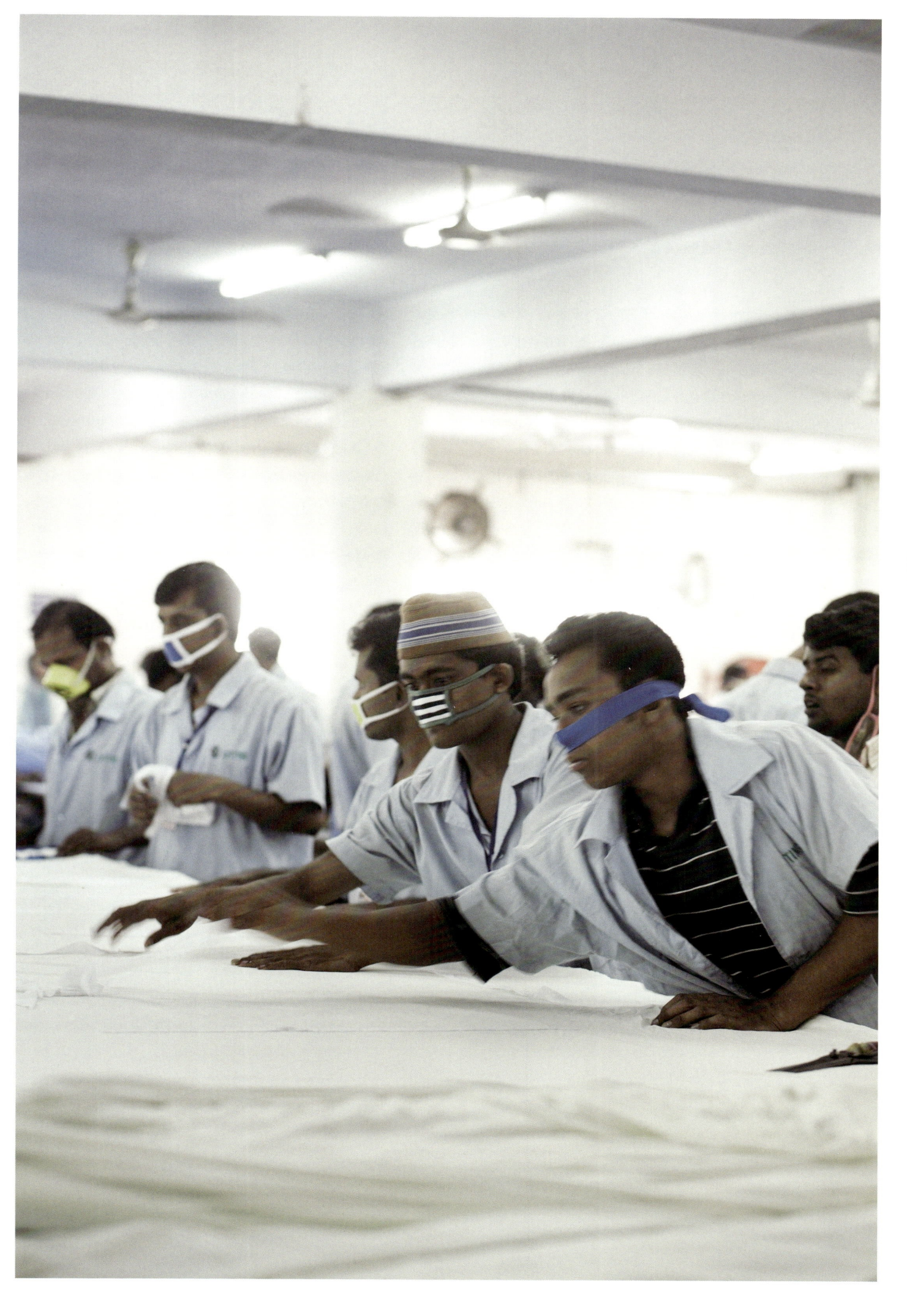

❋ **GLEICHE ARBEITSBEDINGUNGEN** vom Chef bis zur Servicekraft. Rohol Amin, 22 Jahre, sorgt für den Papierfluss zwischen den Abteilungen.

❋ **THE SAME WORKING CONDITIONS** for the boss and the service employees. Rohol Amin, 22 years old, takes care of the flow of paper between the departments.

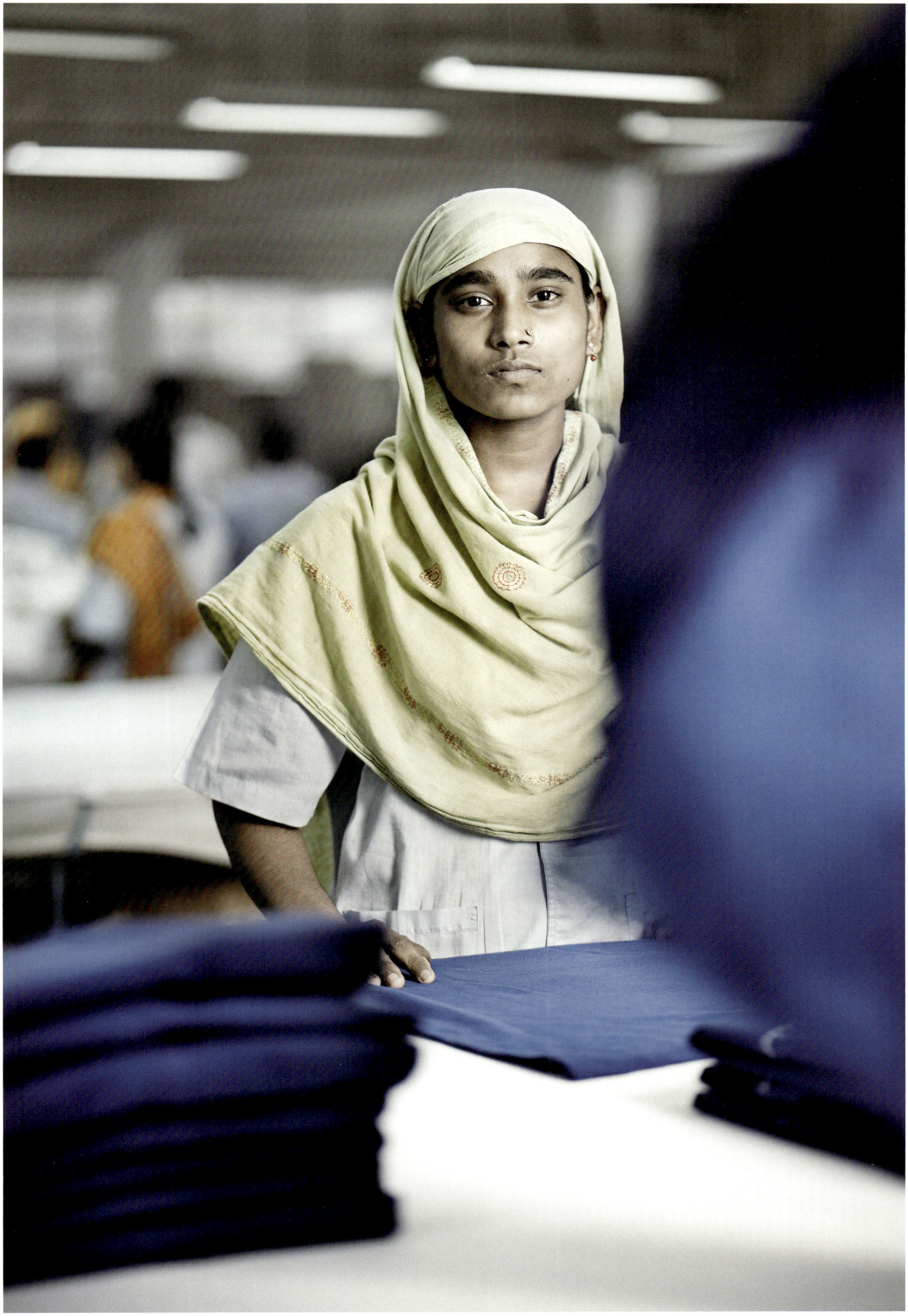

❖ **FIRMENGRÜNDER PROF. MUHAMMAD YUNUS** an seinem Arbeitsplatz.
❖ **THE COMPANY FOUNDER PROFESSOR MUHAMMAD YUNUS** at his workplace.

ES FUNKTIONIERT ÜBERALL

Immer wieder wurde Yunus gefragt, ob sein System der Kleinkredite überall auf der Welt und bei allen Bevölkerungsgruppen funktioniere. Hier seine Antworten:

Er fragte seine größten Kritiker, welcher Ort der Welt ihrer Ansicht nach am ungeeignetsten sei für den Aufbau eines erfolgreichen Kleinkreditprogramms. Ihre einmütige Antwort: der Bundesstaat Uttar Pradesh in Nordindien. Also wählte er diese Gegend für sein nächstes Projekt. Und auch dort war er erfolgreich.

Als schwierigste Bevölkerungsgruppe, auch da herrschte Einigkeit, würden sich wohl die Bettler erweisen. Also startete Grameen ein spezielles Kreditprogramm für Bettler. Das Ergebnis: Ein kleinerer Teil der Bettler gab schon nach kurzer Zeit das Betteln auf und konzentrierte sich ganz auf das neue Geschäft. Die Mehrzahl arbeitet allerdings noch zweigleisig: als Halbtags-Bettler und als Halbtags-Unternehmer. Sie verkaufen an den Haustüren Produkte, die sie sich von ihrem Kredit leisten können. Und wenn sie an einer Türe nichts verkaufen können, wechseln sie in ihr vertrautes „Business" des Bettelns über. Nichts geht von heute auf morgen, doch der Wechsel vom Betteln zur Kleinselbstständigkeit fällt zunehmend leichter.

Die Innovation der Kleinkreditidee funktioniert. Durch sie werden soziale Problemfelder – die wir längst abgeschrieben hatten – zu Feldern der Hoffnung und Zukunftsgestaltung.

IT FUNCTIONS EVERYWHERE

Time and again, Yunus was asked whether his system of microcredits functions everywhere and in all sections of the population. Here are his answers.

He asked his greatest critics which city in the world, in their opinion, was the most unsuitable for the creation of a successful microcredit programme. Their unanimous answer: the federal state of Uttar Pradesh in Northern India. So he selected this area for his next project. He was also successful there.

The most difficult section of the population, here agreement prevailed too, would prove to be the beggars. Grameen also started a special loan programme for beggars. The result: after only a short time, a smaller part of the beggars had already given up begging and concentrated completely on their new business. Most of them, however, still worked in two directions, part-time as beggars and part-time as employees. They sold products that they could afford from their loan door-to-door. And when they couldn't sell anything, they changed over to their familiar "business" of begging. Nothing happens overnight, but the change from begging to small-time self-employment became continually easier.

The innovation of the microcredit idea works. Social problem areas that we wrote off long ago will become areas of hope and future planning.

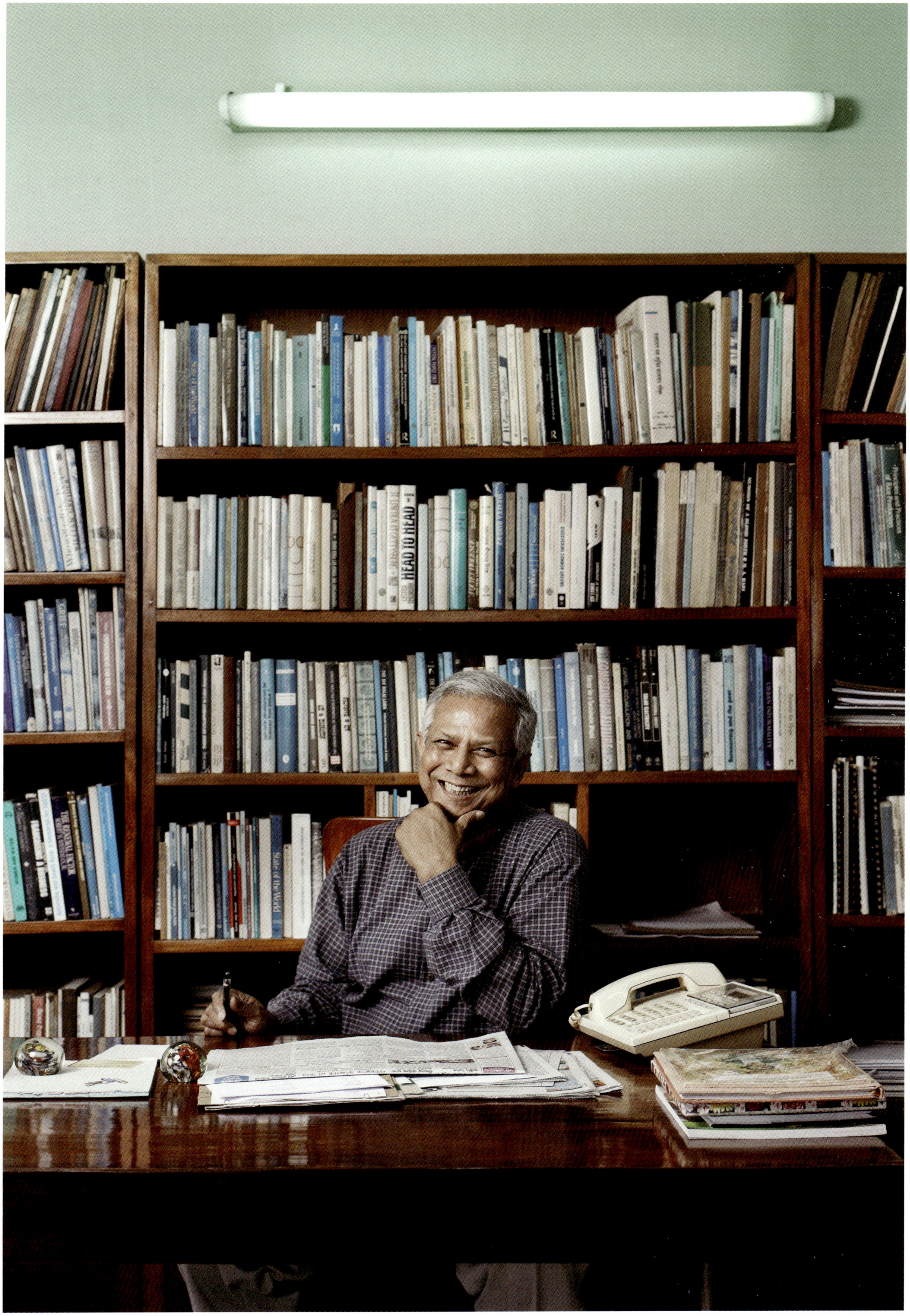
HEAD TO HEAD

SOCIAL BUSINESS – „JUST TRY IT!"

Donnerstag, 9. November 2006, Bogra, Bangladesch. Eingeladen: die Fußballlegende Zinedine Zidane. Zidane reist nach Bangladesch, tief in die nördlichen Provinzen bis zur Kleinstadt Bogra. Dort ist für diesen Tag eine Weltpremiere angesagt. Er soll ein Unternehmen einer völlig neuen Art eröffnen, ein Unternehmen, das bisherige zentrale Prinzipien der Ökonomie außer Kraft setzen und neue an ihrer Stelle etablieren wird.

Zur Eröffnung sind auch jene zwei Männer angereist, die dieses Unternehmen miteinander ausgeheckt haben: Franck Riboud, Chef des internationalen Lebensmittelkonzerns Danone, und Muhammad Yunus. Sie feiern gemeinsam die Eröffnung von Grameen Danone, einem Social Joint Venture, wie es nach dem Willen Yunus' künftig Tausende geben soll. Hier steht nicht nur ein Fabrikgebäude, das selbst strengste Umweltauflagen in Europa erfüllen würde. Hier steht ein neues Unternehmensmodell, das nach dem Wunsch von Yunus die Weltwirtschaft aufmischen soll.

DIE VERSÖHNUNG VON WIRTSCHAFT UND SOZIALEM

„In einer verrückten Welt muss man verrückt sein, um normal sein zu können." Mit diesem Satz beschreibt der Begründer der Zukunftsforschung Robert Jungk eine merkwürdige Eigenart des menschlichen Gehirns: In einer Welt und Zeit, in der Sklaverei „normal" ist, denkt die überwältigende Mehrheit: Eine Welt ohne Sklaverei ist undenkbar! Und wenn Sklaverei dann endlich überwunden ist, verkehrt sich unser Denken ins genaue Gegenteil, und eine überwältigende Mehrheit meint – Gott sei Dank: Eine Welt mit Sklaverei ist undenkbar! Will man dazu beitragen, dass die Menschheit an mehr Stellen und in schnellerer Abfolge solche Phasen des „Denkwandels" vollzieht, lautet die Devise daher: „In einer verrückten Welt muss man verrückt sein, um normal sein zu können."

SOCIAL BUSINESS – "JUST TRY IT!"

Thursday, 9 November 2006, Bogra, Bangladesh. The soccer legend Zinedine Zidane has been invited. Zidane travelled to the small town, Bogra, deep in the northern province of Bangladesh. A world premiere has been announced for this day. A totally new type of business will be opened, a business that replaces the known central economic principles and establishes new ones in their place.

Two other men have also travelled there who have hatched out this business with each other: Frank Riboud, director of the international food processing company Danone, and Muhammad Yunus. Together they are celebrating the opening of Grameen Danone, a social joint venture It is Yunus' intention that thousands like it should exist in the future. Not only a company building stands here that would fulfil even the most intensive environmental regulations in Europe. Here is a new company model that is Yunus' desire for the world industry to become involved with.

THE RECONCILIATION OF BUSINESS AND SOCIAL ASPECTS

"In a crazy world one must be crazy to seem normal." With this sentence, the founder of futurology, Robert Jungk, describes a curious characteristic of the human brain: in a world and time in which slavery is "normal", the overwhelming majority of the people think that a world without slavery is inconceivable! And when slavery is finally overcome, our thinking becomes the opposite, and the overwhelming majority thinks – thank goodness: a world with slavery is unthinkable! One wants to say that humanity takes place in several locations and in rapid sequences of such phases of "thinking changes", which is why the slogan rings true: "In a crazy world one must be crazy to seem normal."

❖ **DAS BÜROGEBÄUDE** der Firmenzentrale von Grameen in Dhaka.

❖ **THE OFFICE BUILDING** at the company centre of Grameen in Dhaka.

✣ **GLEICHE ARBEITSBEDINGUNGEN** vom Chef bis zur Servicekraft. Rohol Amin, 22 Jahre, sorgt für den Papierfluss zwischen den Abteilungen.

✣ **THE SAME WORKING CONDITIONS** for the boss and the service employees. Rohol Amin, 22 years old, takes care of the flow of paper between the departments.

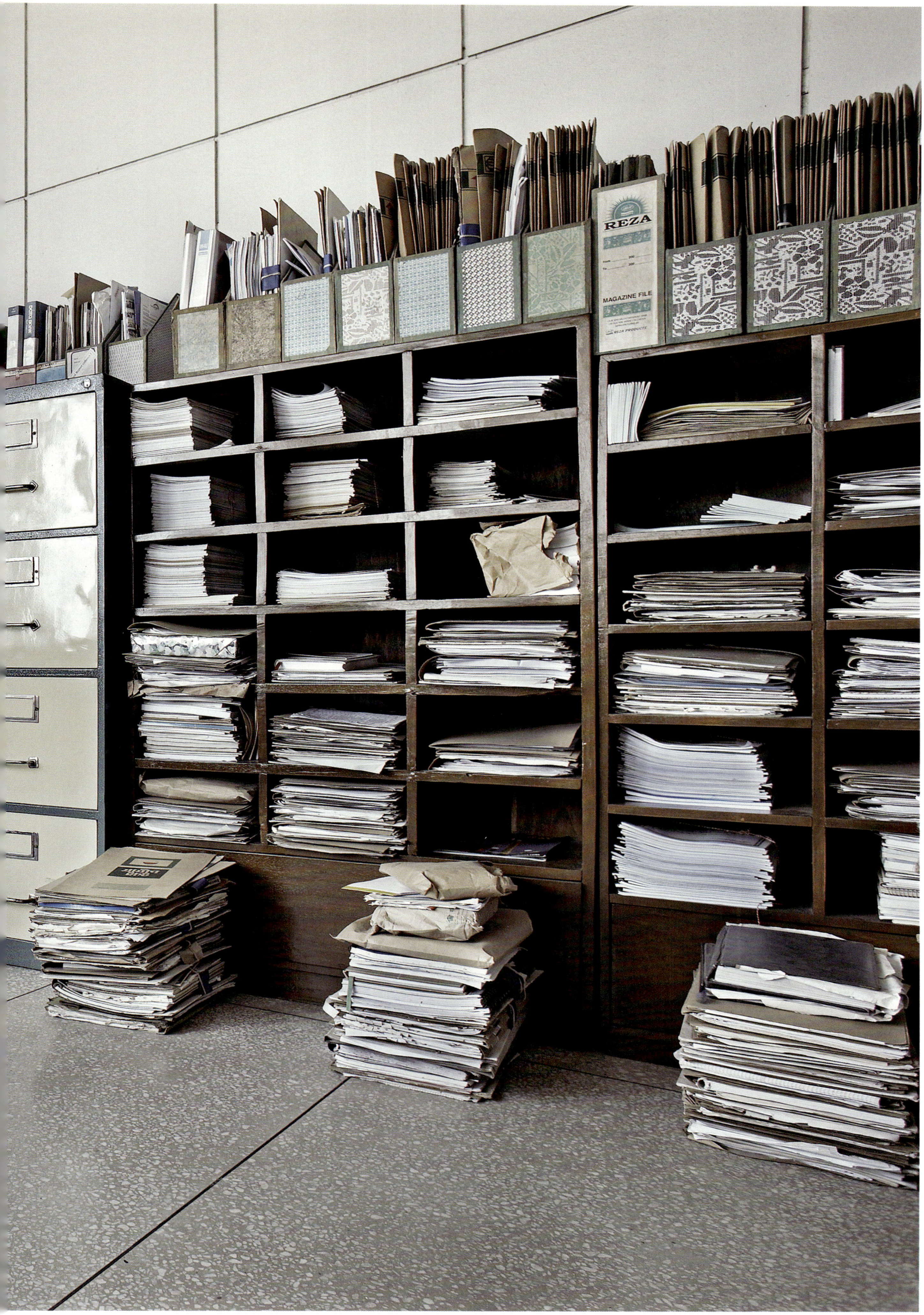
REZA
MAGAZINE FILE

Ganz ähnlich sieht Joseph Schumpeter, einer der Väter der Marktwirtschaft, den Prozess jeglichen Fortschritts. Sein ebenfalls provozierender Begriff dafür lautet: „kreative Zerstörung". Innovation ist für ihn die kreative Zerstörung bisheriger Denkmuster.

Mit seiner Grameen Bank hat Yunus ein ausgesprochen hartnäckiges Denkmuster auf dem Weg zu einer Welt ohne Armut bereits ausgeräumt: Nachdem inzwischen weltweit mehr als 100 Millionen bettelarme Menschen Kleinkredite erhalten und damit ihr Leben selbst erfolgreich in die Hand genommen haben, kann man nicht mehr ernsthaft behaupten, ein Banking ohne Sicherheiten sei undenkbar.

Mit dem Beispiel von Grameen Danone tritt Yunus nun einen zweiten Feldzug in seinem Kampf gegen die Armut an. Dazu nimmt er die Vorstellung ins Visier, Wirtschaft und Kapitalismus könnten nur mit Unternehmen funktionieren, die auf Profitmaximierung angelegt sind. Seine Gegenthese lautet: „Social Business", „Sozialunternehmen" funktionieren sowohl wirtschaftlich als auch gesamtgesellschaftlich besser.

Yunus glaubt an den alten Ludwig-Erhard-Traum „Wohlstand für alle". Allerdings: In einer offenen Weltgesellschaft kann dies nur noch global funktionieren. „Wohlstand für alle", jedoch nur innerhalb eines Landes – dafür hat die Globalisierung die Voraussetzungen zerstört. Mit offenen Weltmärkten steuern wir entweder auf tief in Arme und Reiche gespaltene Gesellschaften in jedem Land zu – oder auf eine besser ausbalancierte Gesellschaft in allen Ländern.

Joseph Schumpeter, one of the fathers of the market economy, sees the process of any progress similarly. His term for this is equally provoking: "creative destruction". Innovation is for him the creative destruction of previous patterns of thought.

With the Grameen Bank, Yunus had already removed one distinctly persistent pattern of thinking on the way to a world without poverty: in the meantime, since more than 100 million destitute people worldwide have received microcredits and therefore have successfully taken their lives in their own hands, one can no longer seriously claim that banking without collateral is unthinkable.

With the example of Grameen Danone, Yunus is now entering a second campaign in his battle against poverty. In addition, he is targeting the idea that commerce and capitalism can only function with businesses that are structured to maximise profits. His countertheory reads: "Social Business", "Social Enterprises" can only function properly if the economy relates to society as a whole.

Yunus believes in the old Ludwig Erhard dream, "prosperity for all". Although in an open world society, this can still only function worldwide. "Prosperity for all" within only one country is not possible, as globalisation has destroyed the prerequisites for that situation. Under the precondition of open world markets, we are steering either into the depths of poor and rich divided societies in each land, or into a better balanced society in all countries.

❊ **ABTEILUNG FÜR INTERNATIONALE KONTAKTE.** Abdur Razzaque telefoniert, Muhammad Moslehuddin bearbeitet den Posteingang.

❊ **THE DEPARTMENT FOR INTERNATIONAL CONTACTS.** Abdur Razzaque telephones and Muhammad Moslehuddin answers the mail.

✤ **EINE VON VIELEN STARKEN FRAUEN.** Nurjahan Begum, 53 Jahre, ist eine der Gründerinnen von Grameen. Sie ist General Manager der Internationalen Programme von Grameen sowie Managing Director von Grameen Shikkha.

✤ **ONE OF MANY STRONG WOMEN.** Nurjahan Begum, 53 years old, is one of the founders of Grameen. She is General Manager of the international programme of Grameen, as well as Managing Director of Grameen Shikkha.

167

✿ **EIN TYPISCHER ARBEITSPLATZ** in der Grameen-Zentrale. Hier arbeitet Muhammad Ansaruzzaman.

✿ **A TYPICAL WORKPLACE** in the Grameen Centre. Muhammad Ansaruzzaman works here.

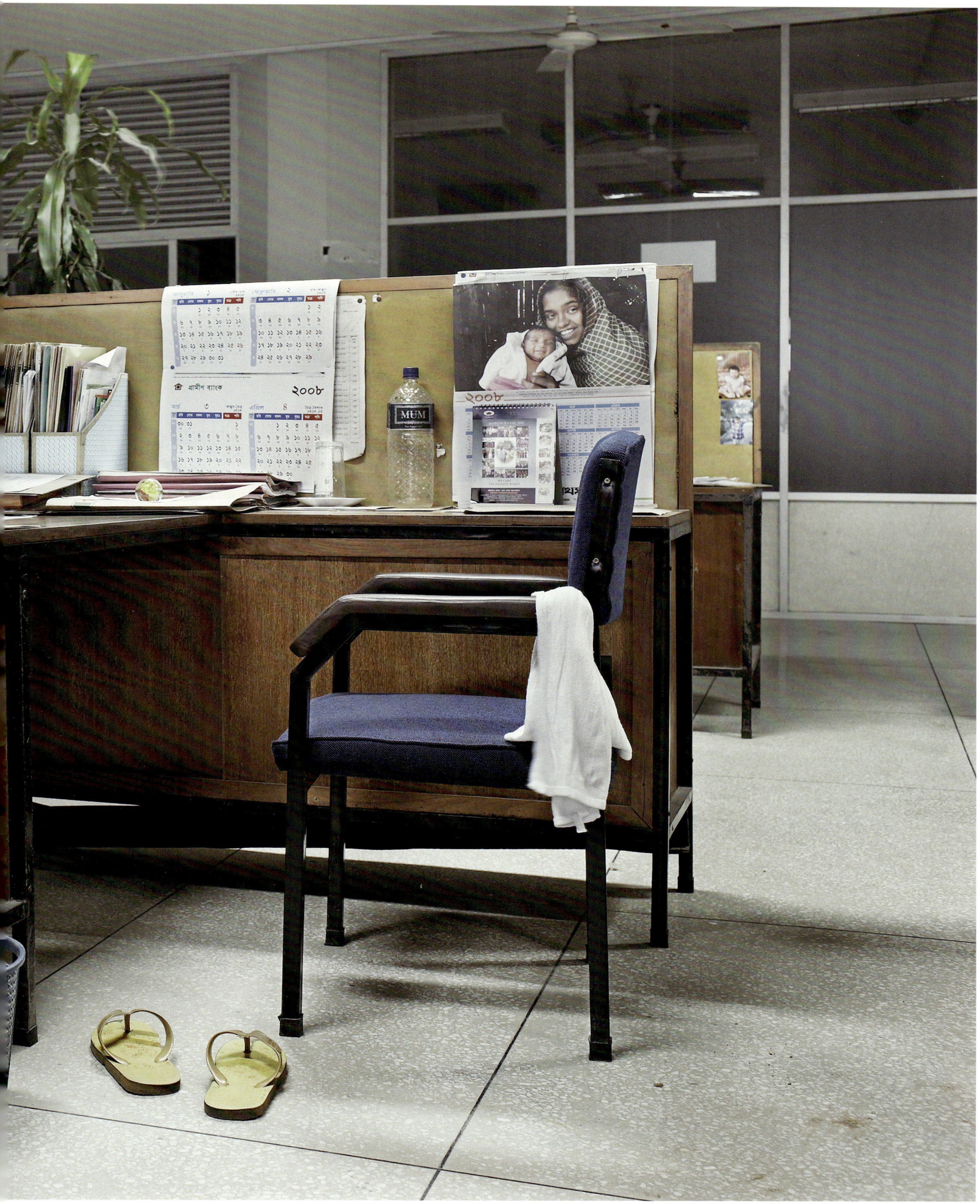
২০০৮
MUM
২০০৮

Yunus ist eine Art „globalisierter Ludwig Erhard", denn die Überwindung weltweiter Armut ist in Zeiten der Globalisierung die Voraussetzung, um aus dem neoliberalen Teufelskreis der sozialen Spaltung wieder herauszufinden und zu einem „Wohlstand für alle – diesmal global" zu kommen: In einem offenen Weltarbeitsmarkt können bei uns die Löhne nur dann dauerhaft hoch bleiben, wenn sie im Rest der Welt rasch steigen. In einer offenen Handelswelt sind Exportnationen nur dann zukunftsfähig, wenn der Rest der Welt aus der Armut herauswächst. „Zukunft für uns" und „Welt in Balance" werden in Zeiten der Globalisierung systemnotwendig zu Synonymen. Daher sollten wir schon aus purem Eigennutz an nichts stärker interessiert sein als an Wissen über die Zusammenhänge funktionierender Systeme. Brennend interessieren sollten uns folgende Fragen: Wie kann die Armut weltweit überwunden werden? Wie können die Einkommen in den bisher wenig entwickelten Regionen der Welt steigen – und wie kann daraus auch die Nachfrage nach unseren Produkten dauerhaft gesichert werden?

Die zweite soziale Revolution von Yunus namens „Sozialunternehmen" liefert dazu ein höchst effektives Instrument. Sozialunternehmen unterscheidet Yunus von „normalen" Unternehmen durch zwei Merkmale. Erstens: Ihre Mission ist ganz auf die „Lösung eines gesellschaftlichen Problems" ausgerichtet, sei es der Zugang zu Kleinkrediten, zu sauberem Wasser, zu erneuerbarer Energie usw. Zweitens: Die Investoren in Sozialunternehmen erwarten nicht mehr als „Return on Invest", also die Rückzahlung ihrer Investition. Darüber hinausgehende Gewinne verbleiben im Unternehmen für Investitionen in die Ausweitung der Mission. Ansonsten sollen Sozialunternehmen wie jedes andere Unternehmen arbeiten, also effizient und effektiv gewinnorientiert.

Yunus is a kind of "globalised Ludwig Erhard", because the overcoming of international poverty is, in times of globalisation, the pure prerequisite in order to again find a way out of the neo-liberal vicious circle of social division and to come to a position of "prosperity for all – this time globally": in an open world labour market, the wages for us could then only permanently remain high when they rapidly rise in the rest of the world. In an open world of commerce, exporting nations are only compliant with the future when the rest of the world grows out of poverty. "Future for us" and "World in balance" would be necessary system synonyms in times of globalisation. Therefore, out of pure self-interest we should not be interested in anything more than know-how. Urgently interested, we should ask ourselves: how can worldwide poverty be overcome? How can incomes increase in the less developed countries in the world – and from that how can the demand for our products also be permanently secured?

The second social revolution, which Yunus named "Social Business", delivers a highly effective instrument. Yunus distinguishes "social enterprises" from "normal enterprises" through two characteristics. First: their mission is entirely directed to "a social solution of a social problem"; it could be access to microcredits, to clean water, to renewable energy. Second: the investors in social enterprises do not expect more than "return on investment", that is, the repayment of their investment. Profits exceeding that amount remain in the enterprise for investments in the widening of the mission. Otherwise, the social enterprises should work like other enterprises, just as efficiently and effectively profit-oriented.

Yunus unterliegt nicht der Illusion, alle Unternehmen der Welt könnten nun zu solchen Sozialunternehmen mutieren. Doch er sieht ein sehr großes Potenzial für die Entwicklung von Sozialunternehmen:

- Bestehende Unternehmen unterschiedlicher Form und Größe werden eigene Sozialunternehmen gründen. Einige von ihnen werden sich entschließen, im Rahmen ihrer sozialen Verantwortung (Corporate Social Responsibility) einen Teil ihres Jahresgewinns in Sozialunternehmen zu investieren.

- Andere Unternehmen werden Sozialunternehmen ins Leben rufen, um neue Märkte zu erschließen und gleichzeitig den Benachteiligten zu helfen.

- Stiftungen werden für die Investition in Sozialunternehmen Fonds einrichten, die parallel zu ihrer bisherigen philanthropischen Arbeit tätig sind. Die Vorteile eines solchen Fonds bestehen darin, dass seine Mittel nicht erschöpft werden, obwohl er dazu dient, sozialen Gewinn zu erzielen. Die Kapazität der Stiftung, gute Werke zu unterstützen, wird dadurch laufend erneuert und erweitert.

- Einzelne Unternehmer, die mit gewinnorientierten Unternehmen Erfolg gehabt haben, werden sich entschließen, ihre Kreativität, ihr Talent und ihre Managementkenntnisse an einem Sozialunternehmen zu erproben. Möglicherweise wollen sie der Gemeinschaft, die sie reich gemacht hat, etwas zurückgeben, oder sie verspüren einfach den Drang, etwas Neues zu versuchen. Wenn sie Erfolg haben, wiederholen sie die Erfahrung möglicherweise und bauen ein Sozialunternehmen nach dem anderen auf.

- Wohlhabende Ruheständler werden in den Sozialunternehmen eine attraktive Investitionsmöglichkeit erkennen. Reiche Erben oder Personen, die große Investitionsgewinne erzielen, können eine verlockende Möglichkeit darin sehen, ein Sozialunternehmen zu gründen oder in einen solchen Betrieb zu investieren.

- Idealistische Hochschulabsolventen, die eine Chance sehen, die Welt zu verändern, werden sich entschließen, statt eines herkömmlichen Unternehmens ein Sozialunternehmen zu gründen.

Yunus is not subject to the illusion that all enterprises in the world could now mutate into social enterprises. However, he sees a very large potential for the development of such social enterprises:

- Existing enterprises of various forms and size could establish their own social enterprises. Some of them could decide, within the framework of their corporate social responsibility, to invest a part of their annual profits in social enterprises.

- Other enterprises would create social enterprises to develop new markets and help disadvantaged ones at the same time.

- Foundations would be established for the investment in social enterprise funds actively parallel to their philanthropic work. The advantage of such a fund exists in the respect that its resources cannot be exhausted, even when it serves to achieve social profits with them. The capacity of the foundation to support good deeds would be continually renewed and expanded.

- Individual entrepreneurs, who are successful with profit-oriented businesses, would decide to test their creativity, their talent and their management experience in a social enterprise. Perhaps they would like to give something back to the society that made them rich or they feel the desire to try something new. When they succeed, perhaps they would repeat the experience and create one social enterprise after another.

- Wealthy retired persons would recognise an attractive investment possibility in the social enterprises. Rich heirs or people who scored a large investment profit could see in it a tempting possibility to establish a social enterprise or to invest in such a business.

- Idealistic university graduates who see a chance to change the world would decide to establish a social enterprise instead of a conventional business.

GEBETSZEIT IM BÜRO. Mitarbeiter Moslehuddin kommt seinen Pflichten als gläubiger Muslim nach. Die ausrangierte Schreibmaschine am Fußboden tut ihren Dienst noch als Halterung für die Schnur des Rollos.

PRAYER TIME IN THE OFFICE. Employee Moslehuddin follows his responsibility as a religious Moslem. The discarded typewriter on the floor still finds service as a holder for the cord of the blinds.

Schon kurze Zeit nach dem „Social Business"-Impuls von Yunus ist all dies bereits in vollem Gange; eine rapide wachsende und völlig heterogene Szene hat sich aufgemacht, diese Vision umzusetzen.

Yunus baut vor allem auf zwei Entwicklungen: Einerseits suchen immer mehr Menschen nach „Gewinn" jenseits des Materiellen, also nach Sinngewinn und gesellschaftlichem Gewinn. Hier bieten Sozialunternehmen eine ideale Ergänzung oder gar Alternative, denn die Mitarbeiter sollen dort keineswegs weniger verdienen als in normalen Unternehmen. Yunus ist sich sicher, dass Motivation und Leistungsbereitschaft in Sozialunternehmen sogar deutlich höher sein werden und damit auch die Wirtschaftlichkeit; er bietet seine eigenen Unternehmen als entsprechende Studienbeispiele an.

Eine andere Entwicklung, die dem Phänomen „Sozialunternehmen" in die Hände spielt: Der indische Wirtschaftswissenschaftler C. K. Prahalad, einer der erfolgreichsten strategischen Berater global agierender Unternehmen, führte anhand mehrerer Beispiele den Nachweis: Die Zukunft der Global Player und der starken mittelständischen Unternehmen, die sich auf den neuen globalen Märkten positionieren möchten, hängt in zunehmendem Maße davon ab, wie schnell und wie gut sie es verstehen, sich auf die Märkte am untersten Ende der sozialen Pyramide der Weltgesellschaft einzustellen. Hier handelt es sich um die stärksten potenziellen Wachstumsmärkte der Zukunft – und um nicht weniger als zwei Drittel der Menschheit. So viel ist klar: Auf diese Märkte kann man sich nicht einstellen, indem man Konzepte, die man für die Märkte in den reicheren Sektoren der Weltgesellschaft entwickelt hat, schlicht und einfach anpasst. Prahalad sieht hier vielmehr eine radikale Infragestellung bisheriger Produkt- und Vermarktungskonzepte zwingend geboten.

Only a short time after the "Social Business" impetus came from Yunus, all of this is already completely in operation; a rapidly growing and totally heterogeneous scene has set out to put this vision into practice.

Yunus builds especially on two developments: on the one hand, more and more people are searching for "profit" beyond the material, such as a gain in meaning and social profit. Here, social businesses offer an ideal supplement or an alternative because the employees should not by any means earn less than in normal businesses. Yunus is certain that motivation and commitment in social enterprises would even be clearly higher and with it, the economy, too; he offers his own enterprises as appropriate study examples.

A different development that plays into the hands of the phenomenon "social enterprises": the Indian economist, C. K. Prahalad, one of the most successful strategic advisers of globally operating enterprises, delivered the proof on the basis of several examples that the future of global players and the strong medium-sized businesses wanting to position themselves on the new global markets, depends to an increasing degree on how fast and how well they understand how to position themselves in the market at the lowest end of the social pyramid of the world society. Here it is a matter of the strongest potential growth markets of the future – no less than two-thirds of humankind. So much is clear: for these markets one cannot prepare oneself simply by adapting concepts developed for the markets in the wealthier sections of the global society. Rather, Prahalad sees here as urgently needed a radical questioning of current product and marketing concepts.

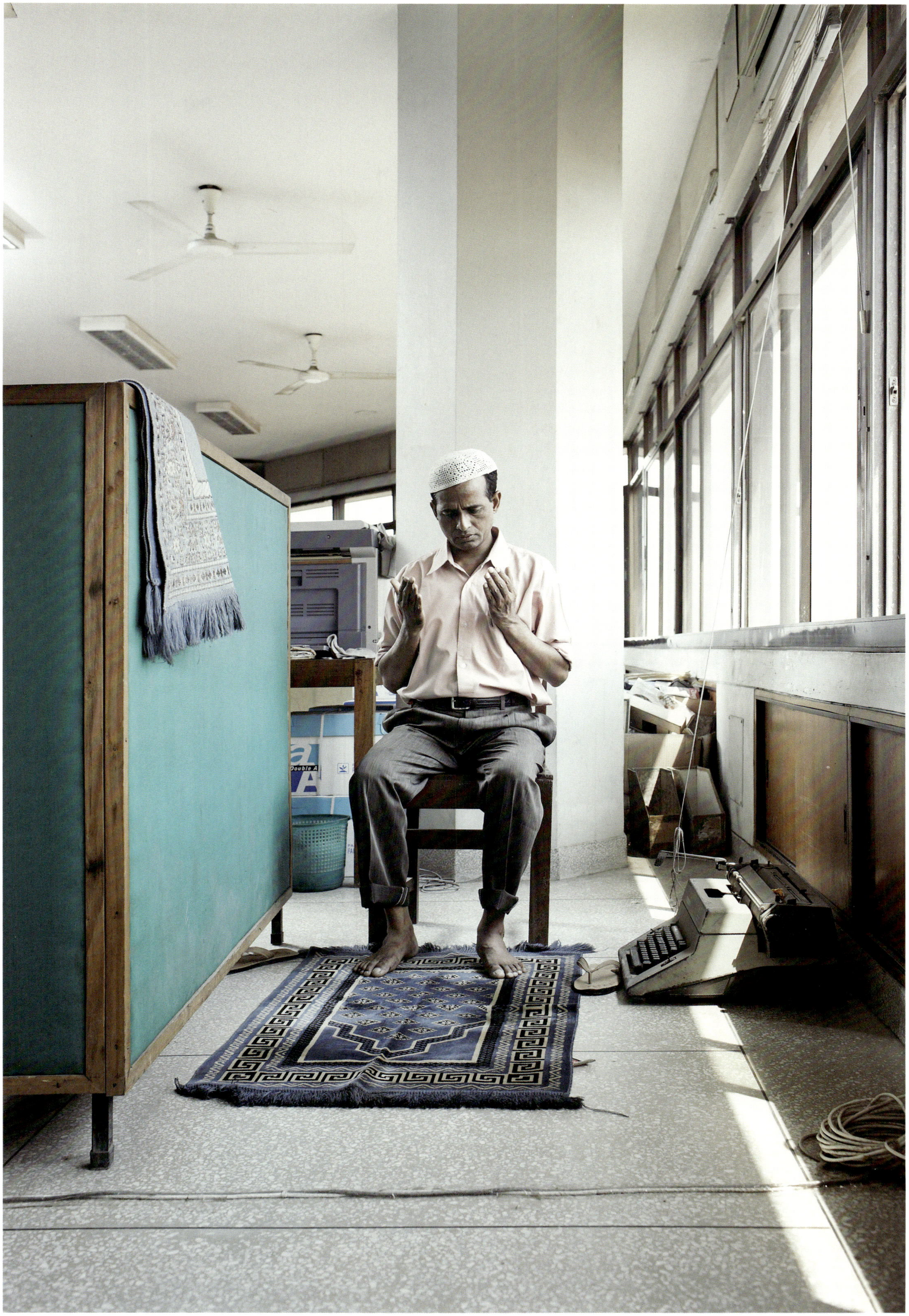
Double A

❀ **PROFESSOR H. I. LATIFEE** ist Managing Director des Grameen
Trust und einer der engsten Weggefährten von Professor Yunus.

❀ **PROFESSOR H. I. LATIFEE** is Managing Director of Grameen Trust
and one of the closest companions of Professor Yunus.

Wer also die noch so ungewohnten und noch völlig unerschlossenen „Märkte der heute noch Armen" erschließen will, ist auf das Know-how der Grameen-Unternehmen und ähnlicher Sozialunternehmen angewiesen. Nachdem Danone es vormachte und sich damit weit mehr als nur einen Imagevorsprung in diesen Märkten schuf, klopft jetzt ein Unternehmen nach dem anderen bei Grameen an. Immer mehr erkennen: Niemand bietet wertvolleres Know-how zu der Frage, wie mehr als zwei Drittel der Menschheit in die Weltökonomie integriert werden können.

Neue Einrichtungen wie GENISIS Institute for Social Business and Impact Strategies und das Grameen Creative Lab, beide in Berlin angesiedelt, helfen dabei, die Potenziale solcher Unternehmen und den Erfahrungsschatz der Grameen Family kreativ zusammenzuführen.

Als sich Yunus und Riboud im Oktober 2005 in Paris trafen, entwickelte Yunus spontan die Idee zu einem Gemeinschaftsunternehmen, das einen besonderen Jogurt produzieren sollte. Dieser Jogurt sollte all jene Bestandteile enthalten, die in der normalen Nahrung der Ärmsten fehlen, aber für eine gesunde Ernährung wichtig sind. Er sollte so preiswert sein, dass die Armen ihn sich leisten können. Und selbst an einem neuartigen Becher sollte Danone arbeiten: Dieser sollte essbar sein, um die Umwelt nicht zu belasten.

Wirklich kritisch aber würde eine andere seiner Forderungen sein, so fürchtete Yunus. Er konzipierte dieses Gemeinschaftsunternehmen als ein richtiges Sozialunternehmen: Danone solle sein Know-how einbringen und einen Großteil der Finanzierung übernehmen. Doch Danone solle seine Anteile ganz an Grameen übergeben, sobald es seine Investitionen wieder herausgeholt habe. Zur Überraschung von Yunus willigte Riboud auch in diesen Vorschlag sofort ein. Bereits weniger als ein Jahr später fand die Eröffnung des ersten Grameen-Danone-Werks statt. Das Modellprojekt in Bogra soll nun flächendeckend für das ganze Land umgesetzt werden – mit mehr als 70 Regionalfabriken.

Therefore, whoever wants to develop the unusual and still completely underdeveloped "markets for the poor today" is dependent on the know-how of the Grameen enterprises and similar social organisations. Since Danone showed how to do it, creating far more than just an image improvement in these markets, one enterprise after another is knocking on the Grameen door. Many more realize that no one offers more valuable know-how as to how to integrate more than two-thirds of humankind into the world economy.

New organisations like the GENISIS Institute for Social Business and Impact Strategies and the Grameen Creative Lab, both established in Berlin, help increasingly to bring together the potential of such businesses and the treasure of experiences of the Grameen family.

When Yunus and Riboud met in Paris in October 2005, Yunus on the spur of the moment developed the idea of a joint venture to produce a special yogurt. This yogurt should contain all of those components missing in the food of the poorest but which are important for a healthy diet. It should be so reasonably priced that even the poor could afford it. And Danone should even work on a new type of container: it should be edible, so as not to pollute the environment.

But Yunus feared they would be really critical of another of his stipulations. He conceived this joint venture as a true social enterprise: Danone should contribute its know-how and assume a large part of the financing. But then Danone should surrender its shares entirely to Grameen, as soon as it had regained its investment. To Yunus' surprise, Riboud agreed to this suggestion immediately. Less than a year later, the opening of the first Grameen Danone factory had already taken place. The model project in Bogra could now be put into practice covering the entire country with more than 70 regional factories.

Als Nächstes folgte ein Social Joint Venture mit dem französischen Wasserkonzern Veolia. Bangladesch leidet an arsenverseuchtem Grundwasser. Grameen Veolia soll sauberes, aber bezahlbares Wasser für die Ärmsten liefern. Grameen ist an sehr vielen weiteren Social Joint Ventures interessiert – insbesondere auch daran, dass analoge Gemeinschaftsunternehmen überall in der Welt zwischen anderen Partnern entstehen. Nur eines ist Yunus wichtig dabei: Auf der untersten Ebene der sozialen Pyramide, also bei der einen Milliarde absolut Armer, sollten sich nur echte Sozialunternehmen etablieren, die mit einem reinen „Return on Invest" zufrieden sind. Für entscheidend hält er dies, damit dieser Teil der Weltbevölkerung so schnell wie möglich die Armutsgrenze hinter sich lassen kann. Danach, so Yunus, können die „normalen" Unternehmen noch genügend Geld verdienen mit denselben Menschen, die dann nicht mehr auf derartige Einstiegsprodukte angewiesen sind.

Dies betrifft vor allem die Social Joint Ventures, bei denen sich traditionelle Großunternehmen mit Sozialunternehmen wie Grameen zusammenfinden, um ein Gemeinschaftsprojekt oder Gemeinschaftsunternehmen als Sozialunternehmen zu gründen. Daneben will Yunus mit seinem neuen Impuls eine Gründerwelle von Sozialunternehmen auslösen, bei denen die Gründer Einzelpersonen, Investorengruppen, Stiftungen oder auch Nichtregierungsorganisationen sind.

Next came a social venture with the French water group, Veolia. Bangladesh suffers from arsenic contamination in the groundwater. Grameen Veolia should deliver clean but affordable water for the poorest. Grameen is interested in very many additional social joint ventures, especially those in analogous community businesses everywhere in the world which form between other partners. One thing is important for Yunus while doing this: on the lowest level of the social pyramid, in other words the billions of absolute poor, only real social enterprises should be established that are satisfied with a pure "return on investment". He considers this to be decisive so this part of the world's population can leave the poverty level behind them as rapidly as possible. Afterwards, according to Yunus, the "normal" businesses can earn enough money with the same people who are no longer dependent on such gateway products.

Above all, this concerns the social joint ventures in which traditional big business comes together with social enterprises like Grameen to establish a joint project or joint venture as a social enterprise. In addition, Yunus wants to activate with his new impetus a wave of founders of social businesses in which the founders are individuals, investor groups, foundations or also NGOs.

❧ **JANNAT E. QUANINE** ist stellvertretende General Managerin der Grameen Bank und Leiterin der Abteilung Internationale Programme.

❧ **JANNAT E. QUANINE** is Deputy General Manager of the Grameen Bank and Chief of the department of international programmes.

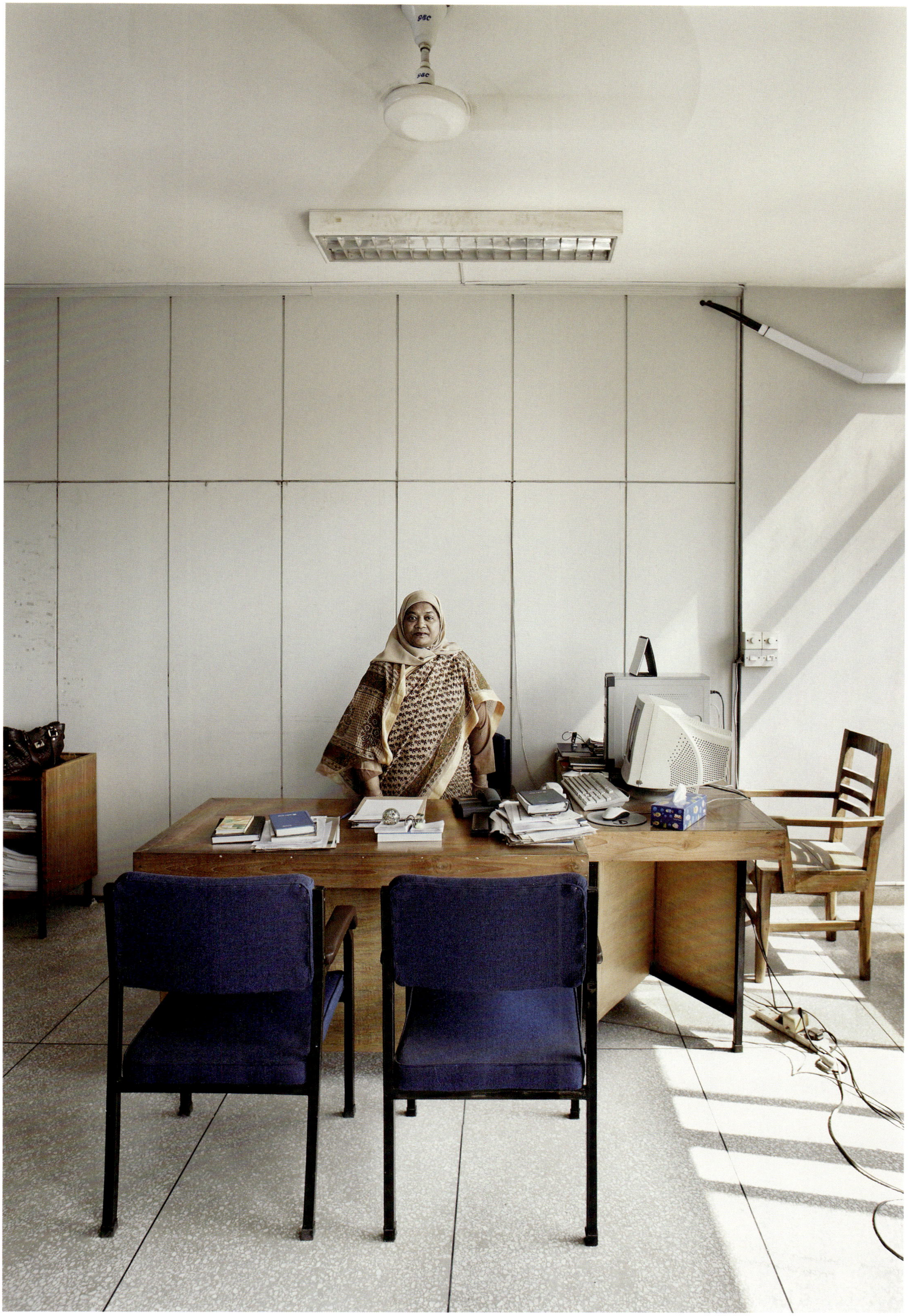

SOZIALUNTERNEHMEN

Was sind Sozialunternehmen konkret? Die Grameen Family selbst bietet eine Reihe von Anschauungsbeispielen.

GRAMEEN SHAKTI

„Shakti" bedeutet „Energie". Grameen Shakti ist das Energieunternehmen innerhalb der Grameen Family und konzentriert sich auf mehrere Systeme alternativer Energiegewinnung.

Das erfolgreichste Modell sind die „Solar Home Systems". Solarmodule, die auf einer stabilen Bambusstange montiert sind, liefern so viel Strom, dass dies für den Bedarf eines Haushalts ausreicht. Sie bringen Licht in das Leben dieser Familien – im wörtlichen wie im übertragenen Sinne.

Bis heute haben 70 Prozent der Bevölkerung von Bangladesch keinen Zugang zu den Stromnetzwerken. Oft reicht das Geld nicht, sich auch nur für die elementarsten Dinge andere Energieformen zu leisten als ein offenes Feuer aus gesammeltem Holz. Und wenn es für andere Energie reicht, stehen meist nur die teuersten und umweltschädlichsten Quellen zur Verfügung, wie Kerosin, Diesel oder Batterien. Nur wenige Menschen in der Welt sind sich der Tatsache bewusst, dass ausgerechnet die Ärmsten der Welt die höchsten Energiepreise bezahlen müssen, zum Beispiel für Licht aus Kerzen das Drei- bis Hundertfache – je nach Berechnungsgrundlage – im Vergleich zu Glühbirnen, die durch Überlandleitungen mit Strom versorgt werden.

Regenerative Energieformen sind in der Regel dezentral und daher besonders geeignet, in ländlichen Regionen von Entwicklungsländern eingeführt zu werden, solange es dort keine Stromnetze gibt. Solar Home Systems sind Fotovoltaikanlagen, also Solarzellen, die von anderen Ressourcen unabhängig machen und im besten Sinne nachhaltig sind.

Daher engagieren sich viele Umweltorganisationen für die Einführung von Solar Home Systems in diesen Regionen. Sie sammeln Spendengelder oder organisieren Unterstützungsgelder von staatlichen Einrichtungen in der Überzeugung, dass den Ärmsten am besten geholfen ist, wenn ihnen solche Anlagen kostenfrei zur Verfügung gestellt werden. Die Wahrheit ist jedoch: So verbreiten sich Solar Home Systems nur relativ langsam in der Welt – denn die Gebermittel sind begrenzt. Ferner lässt die Identifikation der solchermaßen Beschenkten mit diesen umsonst erhaltenen Systemen – und damit auch deren notwendige Pflege und Wartung – sehr zu wünschen übrig.

SOCIAL BUSINESSES

What are social businesses exactly? The Grameen family offers a number of illustrative examples.

GRAMEEN SHAKTI

"Shakti" means "energy". Grameen Shakti is an energy enterprise within the Grameen family which concentrates on several alternative systems for the generation of energy.

The most successful models are the solar home systems. Solar modules are installed on a stable bamboo pole and deliver enough electricity to cover the needs of a household. They bring light into this family – literally, as well as figuratively.

Up until now, 70 per cent of the population of Bangladesh are not connected to the electrical supply system. Frequently there is not enough money for energy other than for an open fire from collected wood. And when there is enough for another kind of energy, only the most expensive and environmentally damaging sources are available, such as kerosene, diesel or batteries. Only a few people in the world are aware that the poorest of the world, of all people, must pay the highest price for energy, for example for light from candles at three to one hundred times the amount – according to calculations – in comparison to light bulbs which are supplied with electricity through overhead power cables.

Renewable forms of energy are as a rule decentralised forms of energy, and as such especially suitable for rural areas in developing countries, while there are no power supply systems there. Solar home systems are photovoltaic conversion installations, solar cells that make them independent from other resources and, in the best sense of the word, sustainable.

That is why many environmental organisations commit themselves to introducing solar home systems in these areas. They collect money from donations or organise support payment from government organisations in the conviction that the poorest can best be helped when such equipment is made available for free. The reality is, however, that solar home systems are only spreading out in the world relatively slowly, since the charity is limited. Furthermore, there remains a lot to be wished for in the identification of such donors in this gift-giving system – and with it also the necessary care and repair.

Der naheliegende sozialunternehmerische Ansatz in einer solchen Situation ist: Man berechnet, was arme Familien bisher für Energie ausgeben, und setzt das in Relation zu den Kosten eines Solar Home Systems. Dipal C. Barua, der Chef von Grameen Shakti, machte dies und kam zu einem verblüffenden Ergebnis: Ein Solar Home System rechnet sich für die Armen auf dem Lande von Bangladesch schon nach drei Jahren. Das Darlehenskonzept für Solar Home Systems war also schnell entwickelt: Die Familien zahlen drei Jahre lang exakt jene monatliche Rate zurück, die ihren bisherigen Energiekosten entspricht. Ohne jegliche Mehrbelastung werden sie Besitzer von Solar Home Systems, die allerdings mindestens fünf Jahre halten und bei guter Wartung noch deutlich länger.

1996 wurde Grameen Shakti gegründet. Bis 2008 konnten mit diesem einfachen Kreditsystem bereits 200.000 Solar Home Systems installiert und problemlos finanziert werden – ohne staatliche Hilfe und ohne Spendengelder. Solche Gelder können nunmehr viel sinnvoller in den Aufbau von Schulungszentren gesteckt werden, um Frauen mit dem nötigen Ingenieurswissen auszustatten, so dass sie die Lebenszeit der Anlagen noch mehr ausweiten können. Bereits bis 2012 will Grameen Shakti mehr als eine Million Solar Home Systems installiert haben.

Mit dieser einfachen Sozialunternehmenslogik kann nunmehr eine weltumspannende Welle der Einführung regenerativer Energiesysteme in Hunderten Millionen von Haushalten armer Familien organisiert werden – zu einem Bruchteil der Kosten des bisherigen Verschenksystems, bei wesentlich besserer Akzeptanz und Nachhaltigkeit. Ferner wird es durch die Darlehensinnovation von Grameen Shakti für Hersteller von Solarzellen viel interessanter, in diese neuen Märkte einzusteigen und ihrerseits mit Innovationen zu deren Ausweitung beizutragen. Ein Beispiel: Durch die einfache Frage, welche Kosteneinsparungen bei der Herstellung von Solarzellen erzielt werden können, wenn diese nicht alle Kundenwünsche in Industrieländern – wie zum Beispiel glänzende Oberflächen – erfüllen müssen, sondern nur die Anforderungen für den Einsatz in Entwicklungsländern, brachte Yunus einen Solarzellenhersteller auf eine viel versprechende neue Businessidee.

The obvious social entrepreneurial assessment in such a situation is that one calculates what poor families paid for energy up to now and place it in relation to the costs of a solar home system. Dipal C. Barua, director of Grameen Shaki, did this and arrived at an amazing result: a solar home system paid off for the poor in the countryside of Bangladesh after only three years. The loan concept for solar home systems was therefore quickly developed: the families paid back over three years exactly that monthly rate corresponding to their energy costs until then. Without any additional burden, they became owners of solar home systems that last at least five years and even, with good maintenance, considerably longer.

Grameen Shakti was founded in 1996. By 2008, 200,000 solar home systems had already been installed with the help of this simple loan system and financed without problems, and without government help or donated money. Such money could now be more appropriately invested in the construction of education centres to provide women with the necessary engineering knowledge to be able to extend the lifetime of the installations. Grameen Shakti wants to install more than a million solar home systems by 2012.

With this simple logic of social enterprise, a global wave of introducing renewable energy systems into hundreds of millions of households of poor families can now be organised, and at a fraction of the cost of previous donation systems and with considerably better acceptance and renewability. Furthermore, through the loan innovation of Grameen Shakti, it is more interesting for the manufacturers of solar cells to enter this new market and to contribute with innovations for their distribution. For example, Yunus brought a solar cell manufacturer to a very promising new business idea through the simple question about which cost savings in the manufacturing of the solar cells could be reached when they did not need to fulfil the wishes of clients in the industrialised countries – such as shiny surfaces – but rather only the requirements for use in the developing countries.

GRAMEEN SHIKKHA

Unsere Phantasie läuft zu schmalspurig, wenn es darum geht, beim Design von Sozialunternehmen innovativ zu sein. Ein Extrembeispiel: Der Bildungssektor gilt nahezu allen Menschen als untauglich für unternehmerische Ansätze, zumindest wenn es um die Förderung von Bildung in den Entwicklungsländern geht. Tausende von Nichtregierungsorganisationen sehen hier eines ihrer wichtigsten Betätigungsfelder und Millionen von Spendern unterstützen Bildungsmaßnahmen in den Armutsregionen der Welt, etwa durch die Übernahme von Patenschaften.

Grameen Shikkha ist das „Bildungsministerium" innerhalb der Grameen-Welt und fördert Bildung auf sehr vielfältige Weise. Grameen Shikkha ist zum Teil jedoch auch ein Bildungsunternehmen – mit Dienstleistungen für Familien, die sehr weit davon entfernt sind, eine gute Schulausbildung mit Hochschulabschluss für ihre Kinder finanzieren zu können. Für Familien, die in der Lage sind, für ein späteres Bildungsdarlehen für ihre Kinder zunächst etwas Geld anzusparen, hat Grameen dazu passende Darlehensformen entwickelt. Auf diese Weise haben bereits mehr als 20.000 Kinder aus Grameen-Darlehensnehmerfamilien studieren können – und weitere etwa 8.000 kommen inzwischen jährlich hinzu. Aber was ist mit Familien, die dazu nicht in der Lage sind?

Für diese hat Grameen Shikkha das klassische Patenschaftsmodell entwickelt. Menschen aus den reicheren Ländern können nun Darlehens-Patenschaften eingehen. Sie können bei Grameen einen Betrag ab rund 1.000 Euro anlegen und dieses Darlehen nach einer vereinbarten Zeit wieder zurückerhalten. Das Patenschaftsdarlehen funktioniert so: Die Ausbildung eines Kindes wird aus der Verzinsung des Darlehens finanziert. Da die Anleger von Patenschaftsdarlehen ihr Geld nicht verlieren, birgt dieses innovative Modell sehr viel mehr Potenziale als etwa die Spendenpatenschaften. Ferner kann Grameen seinen Klienten Mischmodelle anbieten: Ein Teil von Bildungsdarlehen wird über externe Patenschaftsdarlehen finanziert, ein anderer Teil über langfristige Kredite an jene, die durch ein solches Konstrukt ein Studium absolvieren können. Diese jungen Akademiker verdienen nach ihrer Ausbildung so viel, dass es für sie keine ernsthafte Belastung darstellt, von ihrem künftigen Einkommen einen Teil in die Darlehensrückzahlung zu geben. Der individuelle wie der volkswirtschaftliche Nutzen solcher Modelle ist immens.

GRAMEEN SHIKKHA

Our imagination is too constricted to be innovative when it comes to designing social enterprises. An extreme example: the educational sector was considered by almost everyone to be unsuitable for entrepreneurial attempts, at least when it was about the promotion of education in the developing countries. Thousands of NGOs see this as one of their most important fields of activity, and millions of donations support educational measures in the poorest areas of the world, for instance through providing sponsorships.

Grameen Shikkha is an "education ministry" within the Grameen world, and supports education in many various ways. Grameen Shikka is partially, however, an education business, too, with services for families who are a long way from being able to finance a good education with a university degree for their children. For families who are in the position to first save some money for a later education loan, Grameen has developed the appropriate loans. In this way, more than 20,000 children from Grameen borrower families have already been able to study, and a further 8,000 are added annually. But what about the families who are not in this position?

For them, Grameen Shikkha has shaped the classical sponsorship model. People from wealthier countries can now enter loan sponsorships. They can invest with Grameen an amount of about 1,000 euros and receive this back after an agreed period. The sponsorship loans function in this way: the education of a child is financed through the interest on the loan. Since the investors of sponsorship loans do not lose their money, this innovative model guarantees much more potential than the donation sponsorships, for example. Grameen can further offer its clients mixed models: one part of the education loan is financed through outside sponsorship loans, another part through long-term loans to those who can complete their studies through such a model. These young university graduates earn so much after their training that it does not represent any serious burden to allot a portion of their future income to repay the loan. The individual as well as the economic benefits of such a model are enormous.

❖ **GOLAM MORSHED MUHAMMAD** ist Mitarbeiter in der Abteilung Internationale Programme und führt insbesondere Gästegruppen aus dem Ausland durch die Grameen-Welt.

❖ **GOLAM MORSHED MUHAMMAD** is an employee in the department of international programmes and leads special groups of guests from foreign countries through the Grameen World.

❂ **MUHAMMAD IMAMUS SULTAN** ist Managing Director von Grameen Health Care Services Ltd.
❂ **MUHAMMAD IMAMUS SULTAN** is Managing Director of Grameen Health Care Services Ltd.

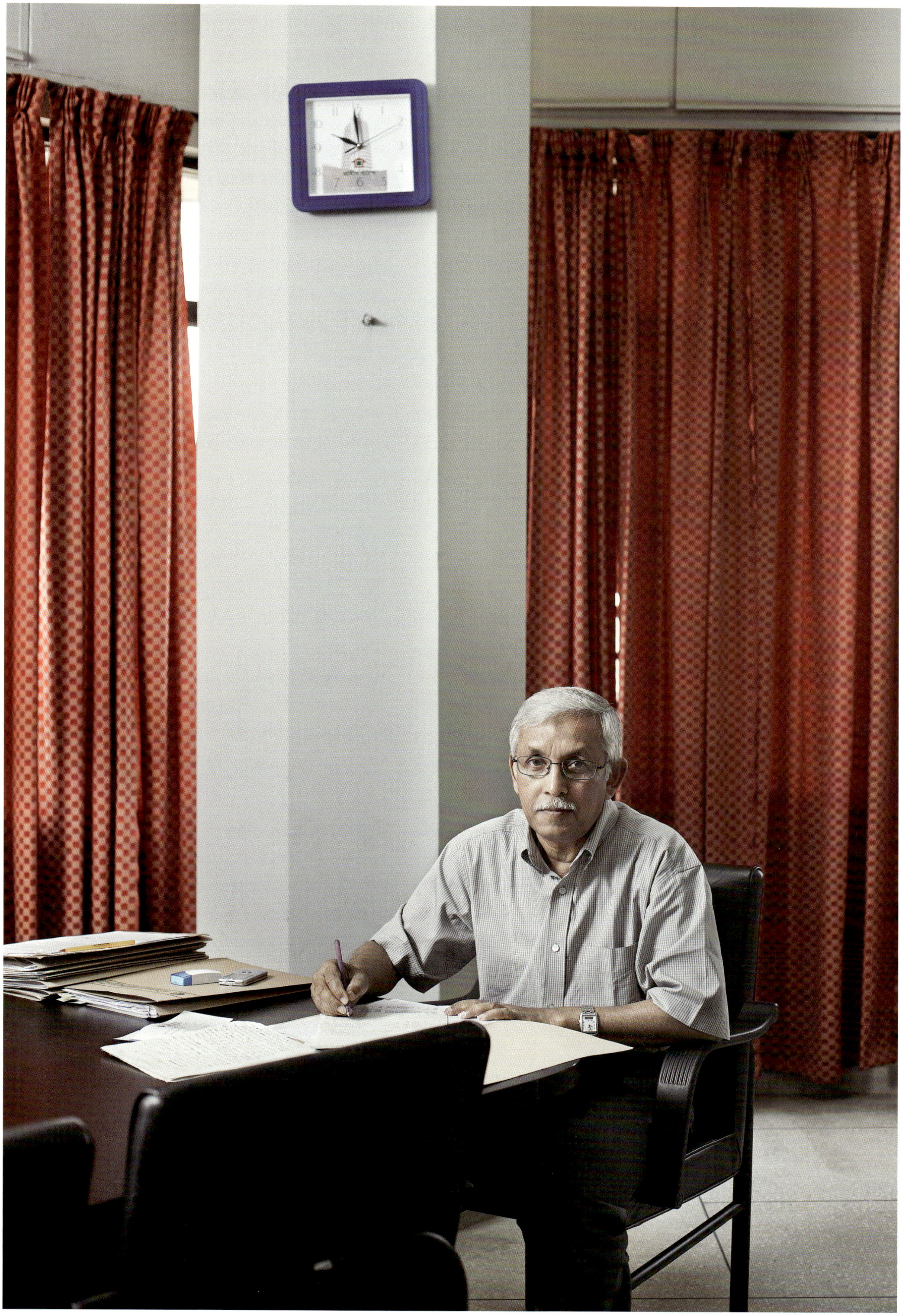

❖ **MEHR ALS 250 VIDEOAUFNAHMEN** von Sendungen gibt es über Grameen. Muhammad Ekramul Haque ist Leiter des Büros für audiovisuelles Material in der Abteilung Internationale Programme.

❖ **MORE THAN 250 VIDEO RECORDINGS** from programmes about Grameen. Muhammad Ekramul Haque is head of the office for audiovisual material in the department of international programmes.

189

Auch bei der Konferenz selbst, an der die Öffentlichkeit nicht teilhaben kann, geschieht viel Überraschendes. Muhammad Yunus, Friedensnobelpreisträger, einstiger Wirtschaftsprofessor und späterer Gründer der Grameen Bank, wird von den sonst so nüchternen, coolen Wirtschaftsstudenten und Nachwuchsforschern gefeiert wie ein Superstar. Auch wenn er das Wissen, das sie sich an den Elitehochschulen der Welt erworben haben, fundamental in Frage stellt.

Yunus trifft diese Nachwuchselite am Nerv ihres Selbstwertgefühls, wenn er über die Grameen-Unternehmensfamilie sagt: „Wir bereichern uns nicht auf Kosten der Armen." Ihnen selbst stehen Traumgehälter bevor, die sie als Nachweis ihrer Leistung zu sehen gelernt haben. Dann tritt ihnen ein Ökonom gegenüber, der sie auffordert, eine Ökonomie zu betreiben, die vor allem zum Ziel hat, jenen Menschen, die bisher „out of economy" stehen, den Weg zu einem würdevollen und ökonomisch selbstständigen Leben zu bereiten: „Wir sollten uns fragen, wie kann ich ein Geschäft aufziehen, das den armen Menschen dabei hilft, ihrer Armut zu entfliehen. Sie nur als Möglichkeit zum Geldverdienen zu sehen, geht aber genau in die entgegengesetzte Richtung."

So demontiert er mit wenigen Sätzen einen Glaubenssatz der Wirtschaftswissenschaften und der Wirtschaftstreibenden nach dem anderen. Er wirft den Bänkern der Welt vor, ihr Geschäft offensichtlich nicht zu verstehen, wenn sie nicht auch dem Ärmsten Kredite gewähren können und stattdessen die Steuerzahler in der Welt nötigen, für ihre Milliarden- und Billionen-Defizite geradezustehen wie in der Subprimekrise nach 2007. Er kritisiert das Gros aller anderen Ökonomen, wenn sie bis heute nur höchst selten an Businessmodellen tüfteln, die auch den Armen Nutzen bringen.

Doch trotz derartiger Provokationen genießt Yunus auf diesem Treffen der Elite und Nachwuchselite höchsten Respekt. Er hat eindrucksvoll nachgewiesen, dass seine so völlig anderen Grundannahmen über Banking und Ökonomie tatsächlich funktionieren. Dem kann man sich nicht mehr entziehen, wenn man seine intellektuelle Redlichkeit erkannt hat. Ein weiteres Moment kommt hinzu: Ein Blick in die Augen von Yunus, und man kann nur schwerlich übersehen: Dieser Mann ist mit seinem Job zweifellos glücklicher als all die Wirtschaftstheoretiker und -praktiker, die die Ökonomen normalerweise kennenlernen. Daher gehen viele der Jungökonomen auch weiter: Sie äußern sich so bewegt von den Gedanken dieses Mannes, dass sie nun ernsthaft erwägen, eine gänzlich andere Karriereplanung zu betreiben. Es dreht sich etwas an der Spitze der Weltökonomie.

Also at the conference itself in which the public cannot participate, many surprises occurred. Muhammad Yunus, Nobel Peace Prize winner, once professor of economics and later founder of the Grameen Bank, was celebrated like a superstar by the usually so sober and cool economics students and young professional researchers – even when he fundamentally placed in question the knowledge they had gained at the elite universities of the world.

Yunus struck a nerve amongst the young up-and-coming elite and their sense of self-esteem when he spoke about the Grameen family enterprises: "We don't become rich ourselves at the expense of the poor. You yourselves have dream salaries awaiting you that you have learned to expect as proof of your performance. Then an economist appears across from you who requests that you proceed with an economy that has as its primary goal to prepare those people, who until now have stood 'out of economy', for the way to a dignified and economically independent life. We should ask ourselves, how can I open a business that can help poor people to escape their poverty? To describe them only as a possibility to earn money, however, goes in exactly the opposite direction."

In this way, he dismantled with just a few sentences the economic dogma and the economic hustle and bustle, one after another. He reproached the bankers of the world for obviously not understanding their business when they refuse loans to the poorest, and instead force the taxpayers of the world to answer for their billon and trillion deficits, as in the sub-prime crisis after 2007. He criticised the majority of all other economists because, until today, they only extremely seldom fiddle around on business models that also bring advantages for the poor.

But in spite of such provocations, Yunus enjoyed the highest respect at this meeting of the elite and up-and-coming elite. He had impressively proven that his so completely different assumptions about banking and the economy actually function. One cannot evade them when one does not want to betray one's intellectual honesty. In addition, another moment came: a look in Yunus' eyes that one can only overlook with difficulty; this man is undeniably happier with his job than all the other economics theoreticians and practitioners that economists usually get to know. That is why many of the young economists then said they were so moved by the thoughts of this man that they would seriously consider proceeding on a completely different career path. Something is changing at the summit of the world economy.

Dieser Eindruck setzt sich fort bei der Beobachtung der Gespräche unter den fünfzehn Nobelpreisträgern in Lindau. Etwa, wenn Joseph Stiglitz, der bekannte Globalisierungskritiker, Wirtschaftsnobelpreisträger des Jahres 2001, frühere Chefökonom der Clinton-Administration und später der Weltbank, Yunus beipflichtet: „Die Bänker haben total versagt. Sie haben die aktuelle Finanzkrise selbst heraufbeschworen, weil sie ihr eigenes Geschäft nicht verstanden haben. Weil sie sehr, sehr schlechte Risikoanalysen zu dessen Grundlage gemacht haben."

Sein Doktorvater, Robert Solow, ebenfalls Nobelpreisträger der Ökonomie, pflichtet dem bei: „Mir scheint, dass eine der grundlegenden Ursachen der aktuellen Finanzkrise die Banken selbst sind. Das Finanzsystem hat es verstanden, sehr komplizierte und riskante Geschäfte zu entwickeln. Es hat begonnen, Risiken zu verursachen, anstelle die Finanzierungsrisiken der Wirtschaft mit ihren Produkten im Griff zu behalten, was eigentlich ihre Aufgabe wäre." Von einem, der lange Zeit als Stütze des heutigen Systems galt, lässt ein solches Statement aufhorchen. Auch ein anderer der anwesenden Nobelpreisträger, der Bankierssohn Daniel McFadden, kommt ins Grübeln. Bei Tisch erzählt er, sein Vater habe „das finanzielle Wohl seiner Kunden so im Auge gehabt, wie ein Arzt die Gesundheit seiner Patienten. Ich glaube, das ist heute anders."

So verwundert es nicht mehr ganz so sehr, wenn die Rat suchenden Blicke innerhalb der Runde in Lindau weniger den anderen Ökonomie-Nobelpreiskollegen gelten, sondern sich vor allem auf Yunus, den Friedensnobelpreisträger, richten. Weiß er nicht Rat – zumindest für einige der Baustellen der Weltökonomie? Man erhofft sich von ihm Orientierung, wo andere Ökonomen mit den ihnen vertrauten oder auch den von ihnen entwickelten Theorien nicht recht weiter wissen angesichts der offensichtlichen Defizite und Verwerfungen bei der gegenwärtigen Form der Globalisierung.

Yunus erinnert an das Ökonomie-Nobelpreisträgertreffen zwei Jahre zuvor – an die damaligen Worte des deutschen Bundespräsidenten Horst Köhler: Dieser hatte die versammelte Wirtschaftsintelligenz gemahnt, die Ökonomie müsse sich daran messen lassen, welchen Beitrag sie zur Lösung von Armut, Klimawandel, sozialer Ungleichheit oder Migration leiste. Ökonomie, die nicht dem Menschen diene, habe ihr Ziel verfehlt.

Zeigt das Nobelpreisträger-Treffen von Lindau bereits jene historische Wendemarke an, an der es sich die Ökonomie zu ihrer vornehmsten Aufgabe macht, alle Menschen zu Teilhabern und Nutznießern wirtschaftlicher Entwicklung werden zu lassen?

This impression continued in the observation of the talks among the fifteen Nobel Prize winners in Lindau. When Joseph Stiglitz, the well-known globalisation critic, Nobel Prize winner in economics in 2001, former head economist in the Clinton administration and later of the World Bank, agreed with Yunus: "The bankers have totally failed. They have caused the current financial crisis themselves because they did not understand their own business and made as a fundamental mistake very, very poor analyses of the risks."

His doctoral supervisor, Robert Solow, likewise Nobel Prize winner in economics, agreed with him: "It appears to me the fundamental causes of the current financial crisis are the banks themselves. The finance system understood how to develop very complicated and risky businesses. It had begun to cause risks instead of keeping a grip on the financial risks of their products, which was actually their responsibility." From someone who was considered to be a pillar of the present system for a long time, such a statement causes one's ears to prick up. Another of the Nobel Prize winners present, the banker's son, Daniel McFadden, also began to brood. At the table he related how his father had kept his eyes on "the financial welfare of his clients like a doctor does for the health of his patients. I believe this is different today."

So it was not very surprising when the advice-seeking glances within the company in Lindau were meant less for the other economics Nobel Prize winners but rather were directed at Yunus, the Nobel Peace Prize Laureate. Does he at least have advice for some of the building blocks of the world economy? One hoped to gain an orientation from him where other economists did not really know what to do with their known or also developing theories in the face of obvious deficits and faults in the present system of globalisation.

Yunus might have remembered the economists' summit of the Nobel Prize winners from two years earlier – on the words at that time from the President of the Federal Republic of Germany, Horst Köhler: he had admonished the assembled economic intelligentsia, saying the economy had to be measured by how much it generated as an answer to poverty, environmental changes, social inequalities or migration. An economy that does not serve the people has missed its goal.

Did the Nobel Prize winner summit in Lindau already indicate the historical turning point in which the economists determined, as their primary task, that everyone should become participants and beneficiaries of the economic development?

❊ **GRAMEEN PHONE** – das größte Unternehmen des Landes. Muhammad Mosharaf Hossain, 20 Jahre, kommt aus dem Dorf Natiyapara. Er ist einer von Tausenden von Mitarbeitern von Grameen Phone, dem größten Arbeitgeber und Steuerzahler des Landes.

❊ **GRAMEEN PHONE** – the largest enterprise in the country. Muhammad Mosharaf Hossain, 20 years old, comes from the village of Natiyapara. He is one of thousands of employees of Grameen Phone, the largest employer and taxpayer in the country.

VON DER SCHWIERIGKEIT, EINE INNOVATION WIRKLICH ZU VERSTEHEN

ABOUT THE DIFFICULTY OF REALLY UNDERSTANDING AN INNOVATION

Donnerstag, 10. April 2008, ZDF-Hauptstadtstudio in Berlin. Prof. Muhammad Yunus kommt zur Promotion seines neuen Buches „Die Armut besiegen" für zwei Tage nach Deutschland. Mit diesem Buch will er seine Popularität nach der Verleihung des Friedensnobelpreises nutzen, um eine weitere weltweite Initiative zu lancieren. Nach jener für Kleinkredite für die Ärmsten in der Welt geht es nun um „Social Business". Ein neuer, ergänzender Zweig in der Weltwirtschaft soll entstehen, der sich das Ziel vornimmt, mit ökonomischem Denken und Handeln die sozialen Probleme der Welt zu lösen. „Sozialunternehmen" sollen intelligentere Antworten geben, als es traditionelle Hilfsprojekte vermögen. Zum Auftakt dieser neuen Mission ist er in Deutschland als Special Guest in der Talkshow „Maybrit Illner". Thema des Abends: „Das Geschäft der Gierigen. Kann man Banken noch vertrauen?"

Die weltweite Bankenkrise steht zur Diskussion, im Fachjargon „Subprimekrise" genannt. Maybrit Illner überrascht ihr Millionen-TV-Publikum mit einer ungewöhnlichen Konstellation. Während sonst stets vier bis sechs Gäste links und rechts neben ihr zur Diskussionsrunde Platz nehmen, sitzt ihr diesmal zunächst nur ein Gast gegenüber: der „Bänker der Armen" Muhammad Yunus.

Thursday, 10 April 2008, ZDF-TV main studio in Berlin. Muhammad Yunus came to Germany for two days to promote his new book, "Die Armut besiegen" (The Defeat of Poverty). With this book, he wants to use his popularity since receiving the Nobel Peace Prize to launch an additional worldwide initiative which is now about "Social Business". A new supplementary branch in the economy should arise that takes as its goal solving the social problems of the world with economic thinking and acting. "Social Business" (social enterprises) should give more intelligent answers than traditional aid projects are capable of giving. For the start of this new mission, he was in Germany as a special guest on the talk show "Maybrit Illner". Theme for the evening: "The business of the greedy. Can one still trust the banks?"

The worldwide bank crisis was up for discussion, in the specialised lingo called "sub-prime crisis". Maybrit Illner surprised her TV public of millions with an unusual constellation. Usually during the discussion round, four to six guests take their places to her left and right, but this time only one guest sat opposite her at first, the "banker of the poor", Muhammad Yunus.

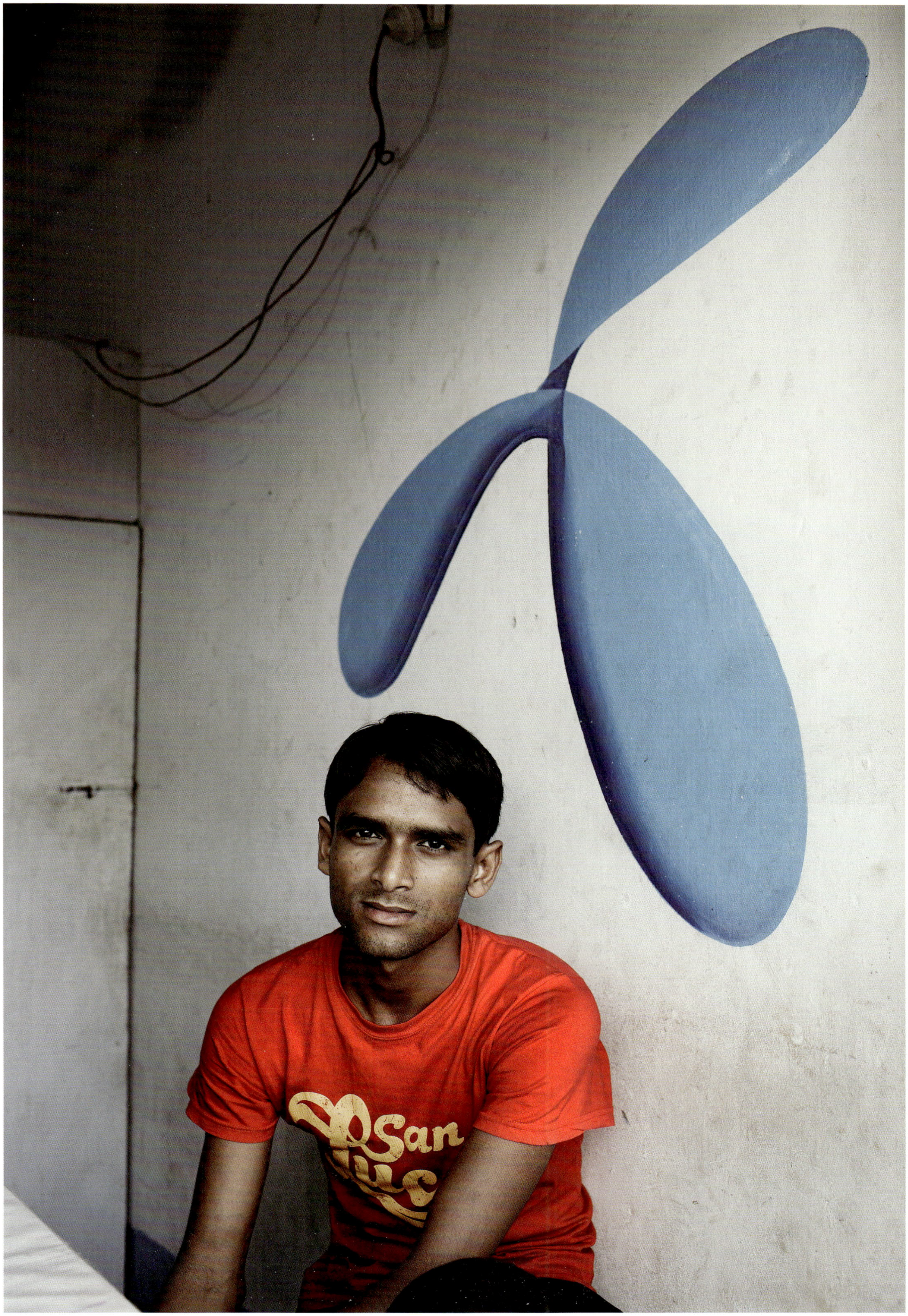
San

শিলা
বৃষ্টি

Maybrit Illner, bekannt für ihre forschen Fragen, bereitet Yunus gekonnt die Gelegenheit, seine so völlig andere Bank und ihre Funktionsweise darzustellen. Yunus ist in Bestform. Mit einfachen Worten und mit überzeugenden Fakten zeigt er prägnant auf, wie und warum sein „Banking des Vertrauens" selbst bei den Allerärmsten funktioniert.

In den ihm zur Verfügung stehenden 17 Minuten werden zentrale Eckpunkte für den Erfolg seiner Innovation für jeden Zuschauer sehr anschaulich nachvollziehbar. Das Publikum im Studio applaudiert – staunend, ergriffen, hochachtungsvoll. Der Moment macht den sonst eher polarisierenden Charakter dieser Sendung für kurze Zeit vergessen. Auch die später hinzukommenden Mitdiskutanten applaudieren mit offenbar aufrichtiger Bewunderung. Doch haben sie wirklich verstanden, was Yunus ihnen da erklärte?

Nach einer kurzen Videoeinspielung nehmen neben Maybrit Illner und Yunus in der jetzt erweiterten Talkrunde Platz: der frühere Chef des Bundesverbands der Deutschen Industrie, Michael Rogowski, der Präsident des Deutschen Sparkassen- und Giroverbands, Heinrich Haasis, der Chef der SPD im nördlichsten deutschen Bundesland Schleswig-Holstein und Finanzexperte, Ralf Stegner, und die Wirtschaftsjournalistin Christiane Oppermann. Die Atmosphäre ändert sich jäh: Schnell ist man wieder beim altbekannten TV-Talkshow-Schlagabtausch.

Maybrit Illner, well-known for her searching questions, prepared Yunus masterly for the opportunity to portray his so completely different bank and its functions. Yunus was on his best form. With simple words and with convincing facts, he succinctly showed how and why his "bank of trust" functions even for the poorest.

In the 17 minutes placed at his disposal, central cornerstones of the success of his innovations became very illustratively comprehensible. The audience in the studio applauded – astonished, moved and with great respect. This moment made the usually rather polarised character of this programme forgotten for a short time. Even the later arriving discussion participants applauded with obviously sincere admiration. But have they really understood what Yunus explained to them?

After viewing a short video, the others took their places next to Maybrit Illner and Yunus in the now expanded discussion round: the previous head of the Federation of German Industry (BDI), Michael Rogowski; the President of the Deutschen Sparkasse and Giroverbands, Heinrich Haasis; the head of the SPD (political party) in the most northern federal state, Schleswig-Holstein, and financial expert Ralf Stegner and the economy journalist, Christiane Oppermann. The atmosphere changed abruptly: one was rapidly back into the well-known TV talk show exchange of words.

❧ **DER TRAUM VON DER STADT DER ZUKUNFT.** Gemälde auf der Seitenfront und Tür eines LKW.
❧ **THE DREAM OF CITY OF THE FUTURE.** Painting on the front side and door of a truck.

Die Frage lautet jetzt offensichtlich nicht mehr: Wie können wir eine Innovation besser verstehen, die es so offensichtlich verstanden hat, mit dem so genannten „Subprime", also mit dem deutlich weniger vermögenden Teil der Weltgesellschaft, klug und erfolgreich umzugehen? Die Frage lautet jetzt: Wie kann man Schuld abwälzen? Und die Antworten sind bekannt:

Schuld an dem globalen Verlust der Subprimekrise von mehr als einer Billion US-Dollar – das sind immerhin eine Million mal eine Million – tragen selbstredend die anderen. Die Krise war so nicht vorhersehbar ... man selbst habe sich verantwortungsvoll verhalten auf der Grundlage der vorliegenden Zahlen ... und auf der Grundlage der vorhandenen Regelwerke und Kontrollmechanismen ... usw. Und welche Lehre ist zu ziehen aus diesen Erfahrungen? Wie kann man verhindern, künftig noch einmal Millionen relativ armer kleiner Hausbesitzer um ihr jahrelang Erspartes zu bringen? Einer der Diskutanten, Heinrich Haasis, fasst die Lehre, die man aus der Subprimekrise ziehe, so zusammen: Man müsse halt noch besser darauf aufpassen, dass „die Nicht-Kreditwürdigen" auf gar keinen Fall mehr Kredite erhalten!

The question now was obviously no longer: how can we better understand an innovation that had so obviously understood the sub-prime, that is, to treat the clearly less wealthy section of the global society intelligently and successfully? The question now was: how can one unload the blame? And the answers are well-known:

Blame the global loss of the sub-prime crisis of more than a trillion US dollars – that is at least a million times a million – on the others, of course. The crisis as such was not foreseeable ... each one conducted himself responsibly on the basis of the available numbers ... and on the basis of the existing set of rules and regulations and controlling mechanism. And what lessons can be gained from this experience? How can one in the future prevent a million relatively poor small homeowners of being robbed again of their savings of many years? One of the members of the panel, Heinrich Haasis, grasped the lesson that one can take from the sub-prime crisis: one must pay better attention that "the non-creditworthy" should not in any case receive more loans.

❖ **DIE GEGENWART IM SLUM VON DHAKA.** Muhammad Imman Uddin, 70 Jahre, bezog einmal einen Kredit von ASA, einem Konkurrenzunternehmen von Grameen. Sein Einkommen als Schneider auf der Straße liegt in guten Zeiten bei 20 Euro in der Woche. Wegen seiner Herzprobleme kann er derzeit jedoch nicht voll arbeiten.

❖ **PRESENT TIME IN THE SLUMS OF DHAKA.** Muhammad Imman Uddin, 70 years old, once received a loan from ASA, an enterprise competing with Grameen. His income as a dressmaker on the streets was 20 euros a week during good times. Due to a heart problem, he cannot work full-time at the moment.

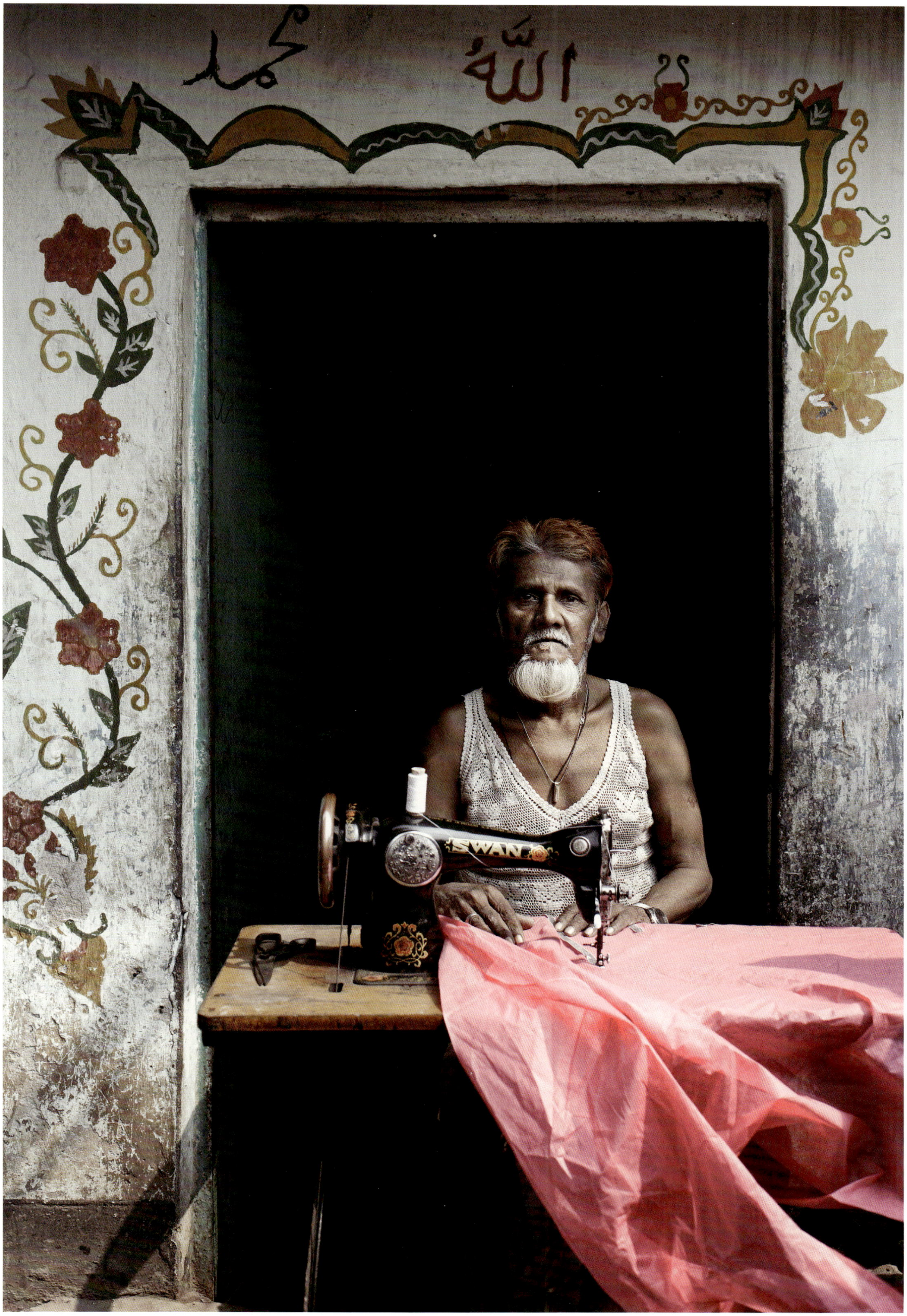
محمد
الله
SWAN

Jetzt wird es spannend. Sprach da nicht jemand, nur wenige Minuten zuvor, von der inzwischen hundertmillionenfach bewiesenen Kreditwürdigkeit jener, die man gerade wieder einmal als „die Nicht-Kreditwürdigen" einstuft? Haben wir nicht soeben – vor Millionen Zeugen an den Bildschirmen – erklärt bekommen, ohne dass jemand der Diskutanten in der Runde auch nur leisesten Widerspruch angemeldet hätte: Diese Menschen sind kreditwürdig – wenn wir die Systeme des Bankings nur einigermaßen intelligent auf sie einstellen? Doch der öffentliche Rat unserer Experten zum Umgang mit der Subprimekrise lautet wie gehabt: Wir müssen die alten Systeme nur noch konsequenter durchführen. Die „Nicht-Kreditwürdigen" müssen wieder konsequent zu dem werden, was sie so lange Zeit zuvor schon waren: die Parias des Weltfinanzsystems!

In den Ohren von Yunus muss dieser Rat wie blanker Zynismus geklungen haben. Da wird er auf der einen Seite verehrt für seine Innovationen im Umgang mit „den Nicht-Kreditwürdigen". Und dann wissen dieselben Fachleute keinen besseren Rat für das Problem, für das er längst bestens bewährte Lösungen entwickelt und umgesetzt hat, als den noch konsequenteren Ausschluss der Armen von den Entwicklungspotenzialen, die mit vernünftig eingesetzten Krediten verbunden sind.

Von den anderen Fachleuten auf der Bühne kommt kein substanzieller Widerspruch zum Haasis-Statement. Die Unterschiede beschränken sich allenfalls darauf, an welcher Stellschraube des bisherigen Systems man drehen müsse. Einzig Yunus widerspricht grundlegend:

„Subprime ist das Problem?", fragt er, noch immer in seiner warmen, herzlichen Art, aber diesmal in ernstem Ton und in der Sache sehr provozierend. „Ich arbeite im Bereich von Subsubsubprime und habe dort keine Probleme mit der Vertrauenswürdigkeit und Kreditrückzahlung von Menschen, die ökonomisch weit unter der unteren Mittelschicht in den USA stehen. Warum haben die Banken nun weltweit eine Krise mit der weitaus leichteren Ebene der Subprime?"

Now it became exciting. Didn't someone speak just minutes before about the hundred-million times proven creditworthiness of those who just now were again classified as "the non-creditworthy"? Were we not just told on the screen, before millions of witnesses, without any of the participants in the group asserting even the slightest objection, that these people are creditworthy when we only reasonably and intelligently adjust our systems of banking to them? However, the public advice of our experts in the dealings with the sub-prime crisis reads as it was: we only need to follow the old systems more consistently. The "non-creditworthy" must again become what they already were for such a long time before: the pariahs of the world financial systems!

In Yunus' ears, this advice must have sounded like pure cynicism. On the one hand, he was admired for his innovations in his associations with the "non-creditworthy". And then the same experts did not know any better advice for the problem, for which he has long developed and practiced the best proven solutions, as an even more consistent exclusion of the poor from the developmental potentials that are connected with sensibly established loans.

From the other experts on the stage, there was no substantial contradiction to Haasis' statement. The differences were limited, at best, to which screws in the current system one must turn. Yunus alone contradicted fundamentally:

"Sub-prime is the problem?" he asked, still in his warm and friendly manner, but this time with a serious very provoking tone in the affair. "I work in the area of the sub-sub-sub-prime and have no problems with the trustworthiness and loan repayments from people who are economically far below the lower middle class in the USA. Why do the banks worldwide now have a crisis with the far easier level of the sub-prime?"

Es ist offensichtlich: Irgendwie haben die mit ihm zusammensitzenden Wirtschafts- und Bankexperten bei seinen vorherigen Ausführungen nicht wirklich zugehört, denn sie haben ihn nicht verstanden. Sie haben kein einziges Argument von ihm aufgegriffen, bei keinem nachgefragt, keines weitergedacht, keine Erkenntnis aus der Welt der Kleinkredite des Muhammad Yunus in das eigene Denken integriert. Alle seine Erläuterungen über „die Nicht-Kreditwürdigen" fanden keinen wirksamen Eingang in ihre Reflexionen.

Auch die Erfolge in den alten Industrieländern können daran offensichtlich nichts ändern: Bei Maybrit Illners Einstiegsinterview führte Yunus die Tatsache an, dass es in mehreren Metropolen des Westens inzwischen erfolgreiche Grameen-Modelle gibt, seit Anfang 2008 gar eine funktionierende Grameen-Filiale in der Weltfinanzmetropole New York. Spätestens nach der Verleihung des Friedensnobelpreises an Yunus im Jahr 2006 hat jeder einigermaßen gebildete Mensch etwas von den Grundzügen seiner sensationellen Innovation gehört. Warum dann dieses Desaster des Nichtverstehens?

Ganz offensichtlich ist es nicht so einfach, sich vom traditionellen Denken zu lösen. Irgendwie versperrt sich unser Denken den Innovationen von Yunus und Grameen.

Natürlich gibt es Menschen, die die Innovationen eines Yunus verstanden haben, und natürlich wächst deren Zahl ständig, und erfreulicherweise auch mit zunehmender Geschwindigkeit. Aber dies sind jene, die bereit sind, sich mit dem innovativen Charakter der Grameen-Welt mit der unbedingt erforderlichen Demut zu befassen. Der Direktor des Wissenschaftszentrums Berlin, Wolf Lepenies, diagnostizierte einmal eine tragische Deformation unseres westlichen Denkens aufgrund unserer lang anhaltenden Überlegenheit in vielen Bereichen. Wir haben eine Tendenz entwickelt, uns fraglos als Weltmeister aller relevanten Disziplinen zu sehen – ganz besonders in den Bereichen Wissenschaft, Ökonomie und Politik. Diese Überheblichkeit, die uns selbst häufig nicht bewusst ist und die wir nicht selten in der Attitüde des gut meinenden Helfers vor uns hertragen, macht es uns schwer, ausgerechnet den Gedanken eines Bangladeschi auf gleicher Augenhöhe zu begegnen. Noch schwerer fällt es, ihnen zu folgen, wenn es darum geht, sie in Gestalt äußerst einschneidender Innovationen für uns selbst zu akzeptieren.

Wenn wir die Innovationen von Grameen endlich in vollem Umfang nutzen wollen, dann bedarf das vor allem in zwei Bereichen einer Denkwende: erstens in unserem Verständnis von Hilfe, zweitens in unserem Verständnis von Ökonomie.

It was obvious: somehow or other the economists and the bank experts sitting together with him had not really listened to his prior explanations because they had not understood him. They had not taken up a single one of his arguments, had not inquired about anything, thought about anything further, had not integrated into their own thoughts any knowledge from Muhammad Yunus' world of microcredits. All of his explanations about the "non-creditworthy" found no effective entrance into their reflections.

Even the successes in the old industrialised countries obviously cannot change anything: in Maybrit Illner's opening interview, Yunus presented the fact that in many capitals in the west there exist, in the meantime, successful Grameen models. Since the beginning of 2008, there is even a functioning Grameen branch in the world financial capital of New York. After Yunus was awarded the Nobel Peace Prize in 2006, every well-educated person had heard something about the essential features of his innovation. Why then this disaster of not understanding?

Quite evidently, it is not so easy to free oneself from traditional thinking. Somehow our thinking blocks the innovations from Yunus and Grameen.

Naturally there are people who have understood Yunus' innovations, and naturally their number grows constantly and, happily, also with increasing speed. But these are those who are prepared to occupy themselves with the innovative character of the Grameen world with the absolutely necessary humility. The director of the Science Centre Berlin, Wolf Lepenies, once diagnosed a tragic deformation in our western thinking owing to our long continuous superiority in many areas. We have developed a tendency to see ourselves unquestionably as world champions in all the relevant disciplines – most particularly in the areas of science, economy and politics. This arrogance that we ourselves frequently are not aware of and too often carry before us in the attitude of the good meaning helper makes it difficult for us to respond to the thoughts of a Bangladeshi, of all people, on the same level. It is even more difficult to follow him when it is about accepting them for ourselves in the form of extremely important innovations.

When we finally want to use to the full extent the innovations from Grameen, then it is necessary to have a change of ideas, especially in two areas: first, in our understanding of help, and secondly, in our understanding of economy.

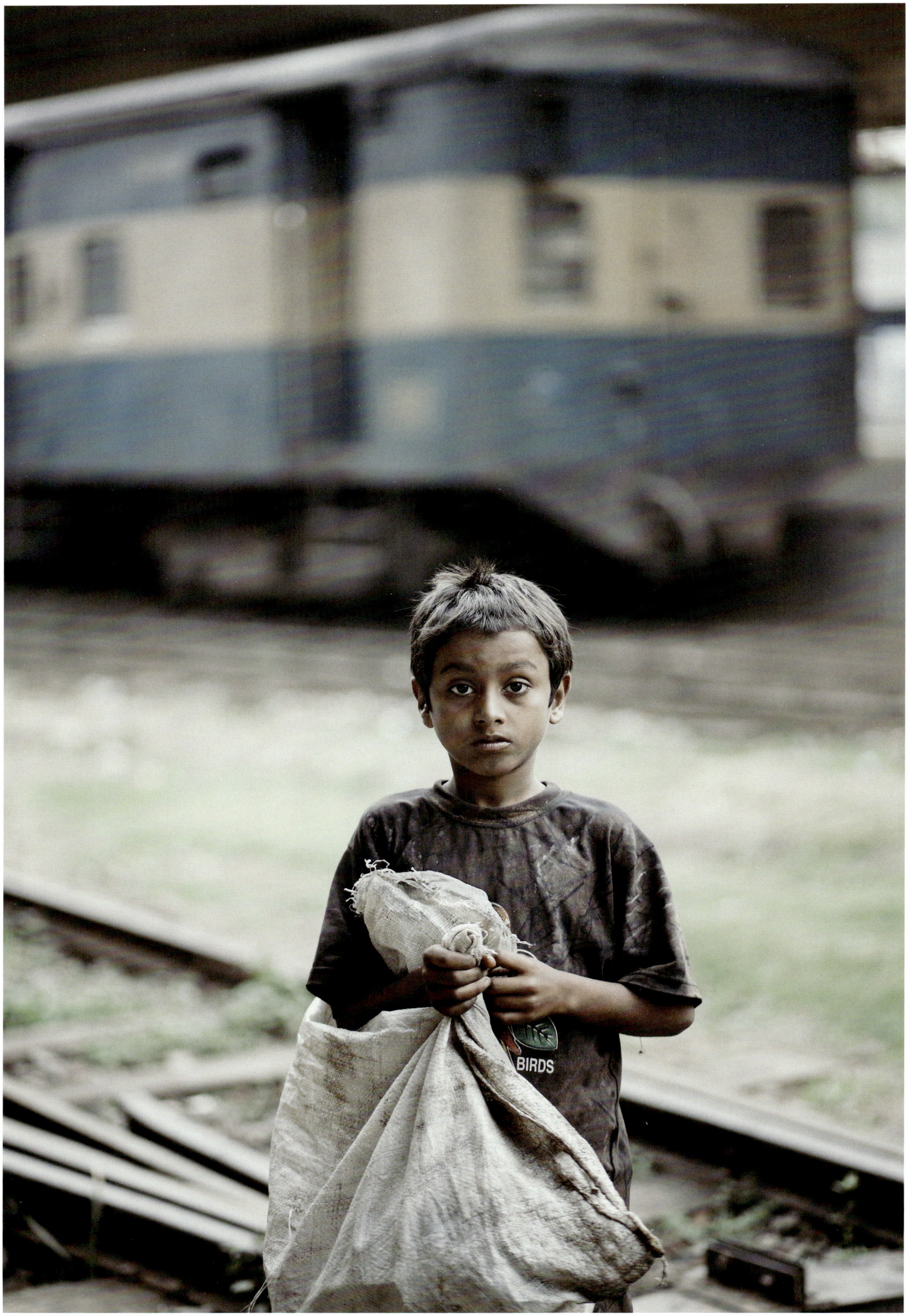
BIRDS

❀ **LEBEN ZWISCHEN DEN GLEISEN.** Bappi, 10 Jahre, sammelt zwischen den Gleisen im Bahnhof Kamlapur von Dhaka Papier. Er kommt ursprünglich aus Bogra und lebt seit einem Jahr in Dhaka. Seine Mutter ist verstorben, von seinem Vater ist er fortgelaufen, nachdem dieser neu geheiratet hatte. Bappi verdient 40 bis 60 Taka am Tag, davon kann er 5 Taka zur Seite legen. Sein Schlafplatz wird von einer Nichtregierungsorganisation gestellt. Dort bekommt er auch Essen sowie zwei Stunden Schulunterricht. Alltag für Tausende von Kindern in der Großstadt.

❀ **LIFE BETWEEN THE TRACKS.** Bappi, 10 years old, collects paper between the tracks in the Kamlapur train station in Dhaka. He originally came from Bogra and has now lived in Dhaka for a year. His mother died and he ran away from his father after he remarried. He has a place to sleep from an NGO. He can also eat there and gets two hours of school lessons. This is everyday life for thousands of children in the big city.

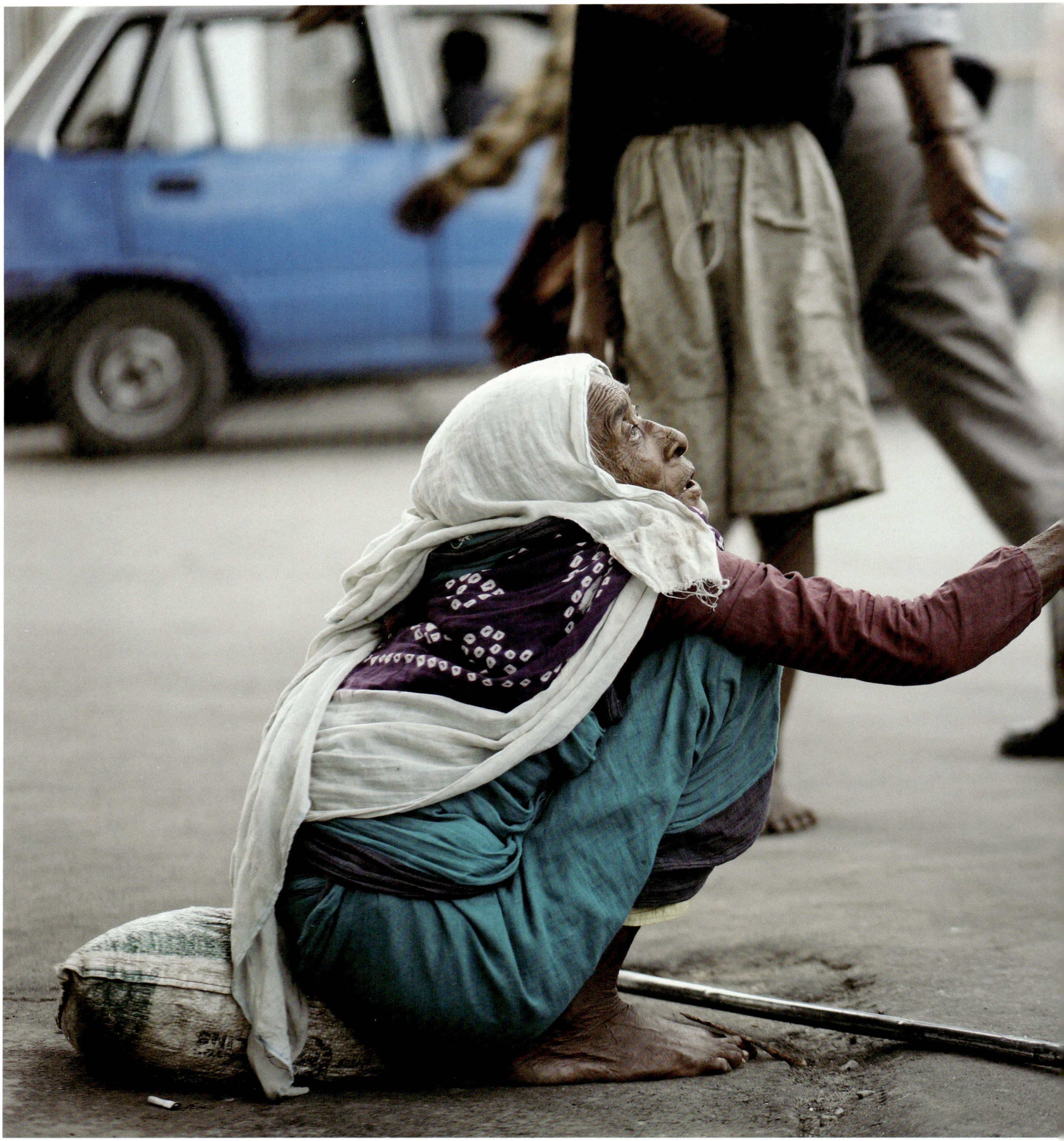

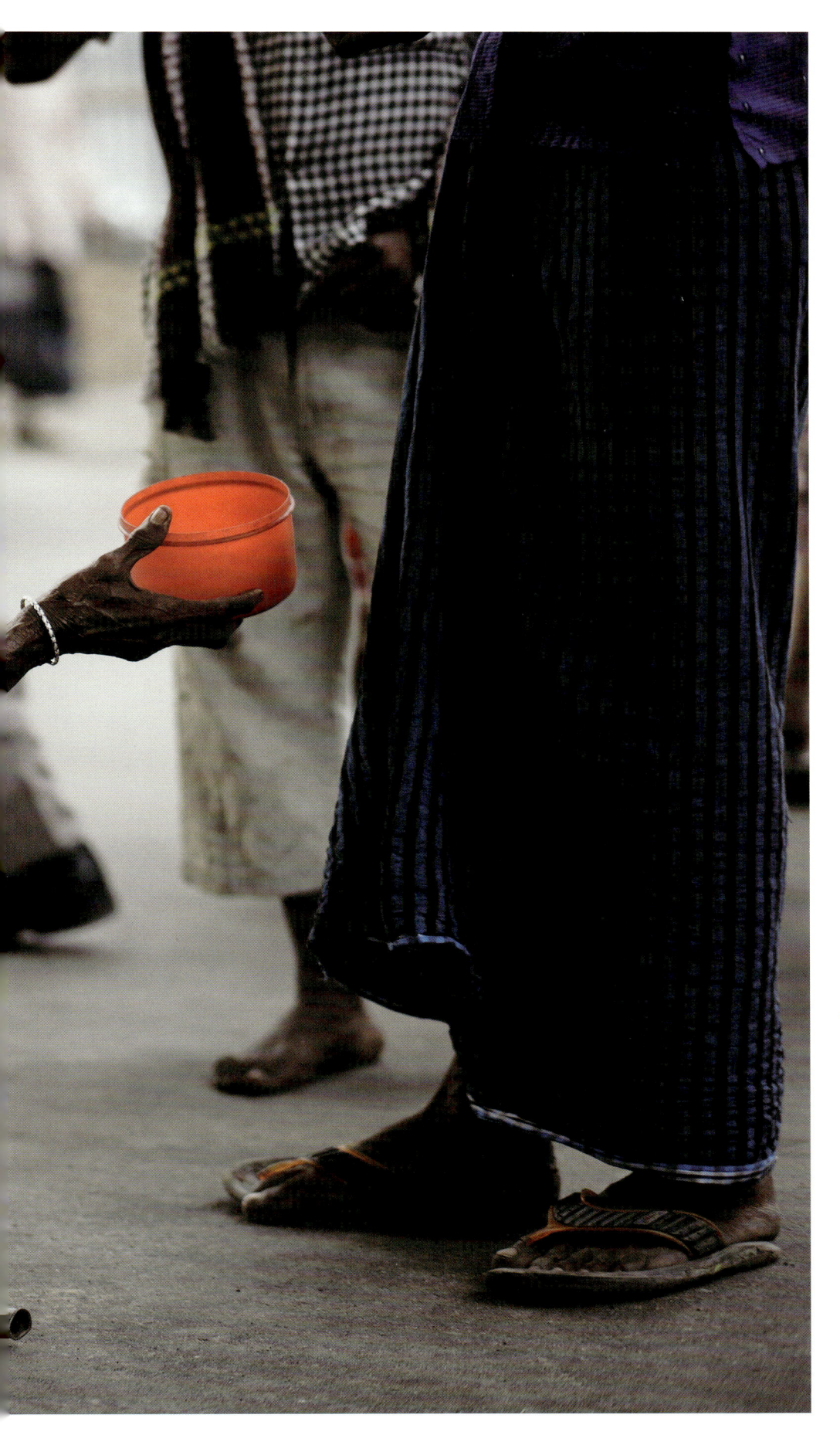

✣ **ALLGEGENWART DES BETTELNS** in den Straßen von Dhaka. Wenn Bodrun Nesa nach ihrem Alter gefragt wird, gibt sie „130 Jahre" an. Sie hat keine Verwandten mehr. Sie fristet ihr Dasein als Bettlerin vor dem Bahnhof Kamlapur in Dhaka.

✣ **BEGGING IS OMNIPRESENT** on the streets of Dhaka. When Bodrun Nesa is asked about her age, she says, "130 years old". She does not have any relatives now. She ekes out an existence as a beggar in front of the Kamlapur train station in Dhaka.

HILFE — VON ABHÄNGIGKEIT ZUR SELBSTSTÄNDIGKEIT

Abertausende von Hilfsorganisationen haben wir bislang geschaffen, um dem Hunger und der Armut in der Welt zu Leibe zu rücken. Viele Milliarden fließen auf diesem Wege jedes Jahr in die Armutsregionen der Welt. Wir in den reichen Ländern haben Ministerien geschaffen, die sich der Überwindung der eklatanten sozialen Kluft verschrieben haben; der Geldstrom beläuft sich derzeit auf rund 70 Milliarden US-Dollar jährlich. Wir haben Weltbank, Internationalen Währungsfonds, regionale Entwicklungsbanken und viele weitere Einrichtungen etabliert mit der Mission, den Armen unter die Arme zu greifen. Doch all diese Waffen im Kampf gegen die Armut erwiesen sich – über all die Jahrzehnte ihres Wirkens hinweg – als merkwürdig stumpf. Helfen Kleinkredite aus diesem Patt? Sind sie das lange ersehnte Wundermittel? Wie stehen die Hilfsorganisationen zur Idee der Kleinkredite?

Weil die Erfolge der Pioniere der Kleinkreditidee spätestens seit den 1990er-Jahren in der weltweiten Entwicklungsszene nicht mehr zu übersehen waren, etablierten zunehmend mehr Hilfsorganisationen eigene Kleinkreditprojekte; es entstanden zahlreiche neue Kleinkreditorganisationen. Deren Zahl wird inzwischen auf mehr als 10.000 weltweit geschätzt. Doch nicht jedes Kleinkreditprogramm funktioniert, und nicht jedes funktionierende Kleinkreditprogramm erzielt vergleichbar große Wirkungen. Die Unterschiede sind beträchtlich – was die Hoffnungen auf das vermeintliche „Wundermittel" schnell wieder dämpfen kann. Man muss genauer hinsehen, dann werden zwei Ursachen deutlich, warum nicht alle Kleinkreditprogramme gleich wirksam sind.

Bei den Hilfswerken spielt das traditionelle Charity-Denken noch immer eine zu große Rolle, auch dann, wenn sie mit dem Instrument der Kleinkredite operieren. Sie bringen dadurch zu viel Elemente der Fortführung von Abhängigkeiten in ihre Kleinkreditprogramme ein – sowohl auf organisatorischer und struktureller Ebene als auch auf zwischenmenschlicher Ebene. Dies reduziert, je nach Abhängigkeitsgrad, die Effekte und Erfolge des Kleinkreditprogramms. Solange Charity-Denken noch eine Rolle spielt beim Einsatz von Kleinkrediten, so lange wirkt dies wie Sand im Getriebe.

HELP — FROM DEPENDENCY TO INDEPENDENCE

Thousands upon thousands of aid organisations have been able until now to tackle the hunger and poverty in the world. Many billions flow in this manner each year into the poverty regions of the world. In the wealthy countries, we have created ministries devoting themselves to overcoming the glaring social gulf; the monetary flow currently amounts to about 70 billion US dollars annually. We have the World Bank, the International Monetary Fund, regional development banks and many more institutions established with the mission to help the poor. However, all these weapons in the battle against poverty have shown, over all the decades of their work, to be curiously dull. Can microcredits help us out of this stalemate? Are they the longed-for miracle cure? What is the position of the aid organisations on the idea of microcredits?

The success of the pioneers of the microcredit ideas could not be overseen anymore since the 1990s worldwide development of the scene, so increasingly more aid organisations have established their own microcredit projects: there arose numerous microcredit organisations. Their number is estimated in the meantime to be more than 10,000 worldwide. However, not every microcredit programme functions and not every functioning microcredit programme achieves comparably large effects. The differences are considerable, which can swiftly subdue the hopes for a supposed "miracle cure". When one looks more precisely, two reasons become evident as to why all microcredit programmes are not equally effective.

In the relief organisations, traditional charity mentality still plays too large a role, even when they operate with the instrument of microcredits. Thus they bring too many elements for the continuation of dependency into their microcredit programmes – on the organisational as well as the structural level, and even on the interpersonal level. As long as the charity mentality plays a role in the assignment of microcredits, so long will this malfunction like sand in the gearbox.

Der hier notwendige Wandel im Denken stellt für alle Menschen, die Soziales und Charity noch allzu sehr gleichsetzen, die größte Herausforderung dar, wenn es darum geht, die eigentliche Innovation von Yunus zu erfassen. Für Yunus ist jedes Verhalten, das zwar sozial gemeint ist, aber im Effekt dann doch Abhängigkeiten fortsetzt, kein soziales Verhalten mehr. Wir leben, sagt er, in einer Welt mündiger Menschen und in einer Welt, in der eine Entwicklung aller Menschen in Richtung großer Selbstständigkeit sehr wohl möglich ist. Für ihn ist der entscheidende soziale Sprung eines Menschen der Sprung in eine umfassende Selbstständigkeit. Er weiß, wovon er spricht: Genau dies funktioniert überall, wo er diese klare Erkenntnis umsetzt.

Vielleicht liegt hier auch ein Grund für unsere Widerstände gegenüber diesem Denken – für unsere Schwierigkeiten mit der Idee der Kraft umfassender Selbstständigkeit. Viele Menschen bei uns trauen sich für ihr eigenes Leben einen solchen Sprung nicht zu, wie viel weniger dann für Menschen, die doch viel hilfsbedürftiger scheinen als sie selbst. Andererseits: Mehr als einhundert Millionen Menschen haben es geschafft, sich aus den denkbar schwierigsten Lebensbedingungen heraus ökonomisch und sozial selbstständig zu machen. Dies zu sehen, kann uns zu einem überaus wertvollen Lernschritt verhelfen: Warum sollte nicht auch für mich persönlich wie für unsere Gesellschaft insgesamt der Schritt zu selbständigerer Lebensgestaltung – als Schritt zu einem weitaus kreativeren, aufregenderen und selbstbestimmteren Leben – möglich sein?

Selbstverständlich braucht eine funktionierende Gesellschaft auch ein System des Auffangens, wenn jemand in Not gerät. Entscheidend für den Erfolg einer Gesellschaft ist freilich ein funktionierendes System der Entwicklungsförderung jedes einzelnen ihrer Mitglieder.

Einigen Hilfsorganisationen gelingt der Umgang mit den hier angesprochenen Innovationen sehr gut, sie können anderen als Beispiel dienen. So vergab die Andheri-Hilfe ähnlich früh Kleinkredite an Arme wie die Grameen Bank. Und kurz nach der Yunus-Initiative für Sozialunternehmen entschied sich die Andheri-Hilfe, ihre Palette an Projekten nunmehr um Sozialunternehmen zu ergänzen, beginnend im Sektor „Einsatz regenerativer Energieformen".

The necessary change in thinking here confronts everyone, the social and the charitable still resembling each other too much; the greatest challenge is when it comes to grasping the actual innovations from Yunus. For Yunus, every behaviour is no longer social behaviour when it is meant to be social but in effect still continues dependency. He says we live in a world of responsible people and in a world in which development for all people in the direction of increased independence is very well possible. For him, the decisive social leap of a person is a leap into complete independence. He knows what he is talking about: exactly this functions everywhere he has implemented this clear insight.

Perhaps here, too, lies the reason for our resistance towards this way of thinking, for our difficulties with the idea of the force of embracing independence. Many people amongst us do not trust themselves to take such a leap for their own lives, even fewer then for people who appear more in need of help than they themselves. On the other hand, more than a hundred million people have accomplished this, out of inconceivably difficult living conditions to be economically and socially independent. To see this can guide us to an extremely valuable step in learning: why should it not be possible for me personally, as well as for our society altogether, to take the step to a more independent life plan, as a step to a far more creative, stimulating and self-determined life?

Naturally, a functioning society also needs a social net when someone ends up in need. Decisive for the success of a society, of course, is a functioning system of developmental stimulations for every one of its members.

Individual relief organisations manage very well in their dealings with the here mentioned innovations, they can serve others as an example. Andheri Help gave microcredits to the poor as early as the Grameen Bank. And shortly after the Yunus initiative for social business, Andheri Help decided to extend their palette of projects to include social businesses, starting in the sector of a commitment to renewable forms of energy.

❖ **BETTLER WERDEN UNTERNEHMER.** Bettlerin Baronbebe, 65 Jahre, nimmt an einem neuen Programm von Grameen teil, das speziell Bettlern Kleinkredite gibt. Zunehmend mehr schaffen den Sprung vom Bettler zum Unternehmer oder werden zumindest Teilzeitbettler plus Teilzeitunternehmer. Baronbebe besitzt jetzt 10 Hühner und verkauft Eier in einem Vorort von Dhaka.

❖ **BEGGARS BECOME BUSINESS PEOPLE.** The beggar Baronbebe, 65 years old, participates in a new programme from Grameen that gives beggars, especially, a small loan. Increasingly more accomplish the jump from beggar to business person or become at least part-time beggar plus part-time worker. Baronbebe now owns 10 chickens and sells eggs in a suburb in Dhaka.

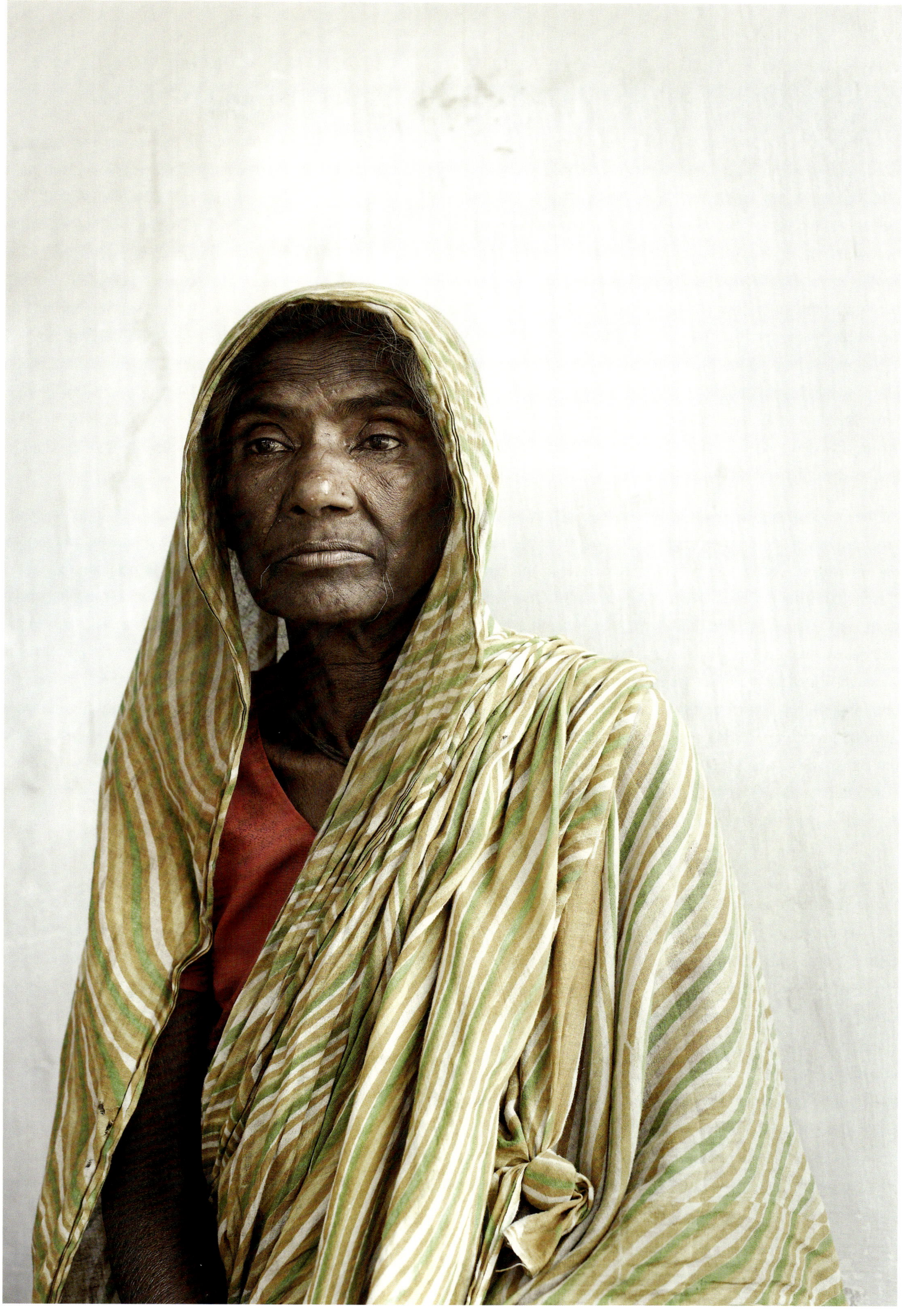

210

✾ **DIE DORFBANK GRAMEEN KOMMT IN DIE STADT.** Lange Zeit galt die Banklizenz ausschließlich für die ländlichen Regionen des Landes. Erst jetzt darf Grameen auch in den Städten arbeiten. Topon Sheel, 22 Jahre, einer der wenigen männlichen Kreditnehmer von Grameen, finanzierte mit dem Kredit seinen Friseursalon in Shingair am Stadtrand von Dhaka.

✾ **THE VILLAGE BANK ENTERS THE CITY.** For a long time the bank licence was exclusively for the rural areas of the country. Only now is Grameen also permitted to work in the cities. Topon Sheel, 22 years old, one of the few male borrowers from Grameen, financed a hairdresser shop with his loan in Shingair on the outskirts of Dhaka.

❊ **MINIJOB-GESCHÄFTSMODELL WAAGE.** Siddik Mia ist 70 Jahre alt und lebt davon, dass Menschen sich oder ihre Waren bei ihm wiegen – für 2 Taka, das sind 2 Euro-Cent. Die Kunden sind häufig Jogger und Händler. Immer dabei: ein Öllämpchen, links unten, und ein Regenschirm.

❊ **MINI-JOB BUSINESS MODEL SCALE.** Siddik Mia is 70 years old, and lives by weighing people or their goods for 2 Taka, that is 2 euro cents. The clients are frequently joggers and dealers. Always close by: an oil lamp, below left, and an umbrella.

213

SLUMS am Stadtrand von Dhaka.

SLUMS in the outskirts of Dhaka.

215

✤ **ÜBERGANG** von der Stadt zum Land bei Dhaka.

✤ **THE TRANSITION** from the city to the countryside near Dhaka.

217

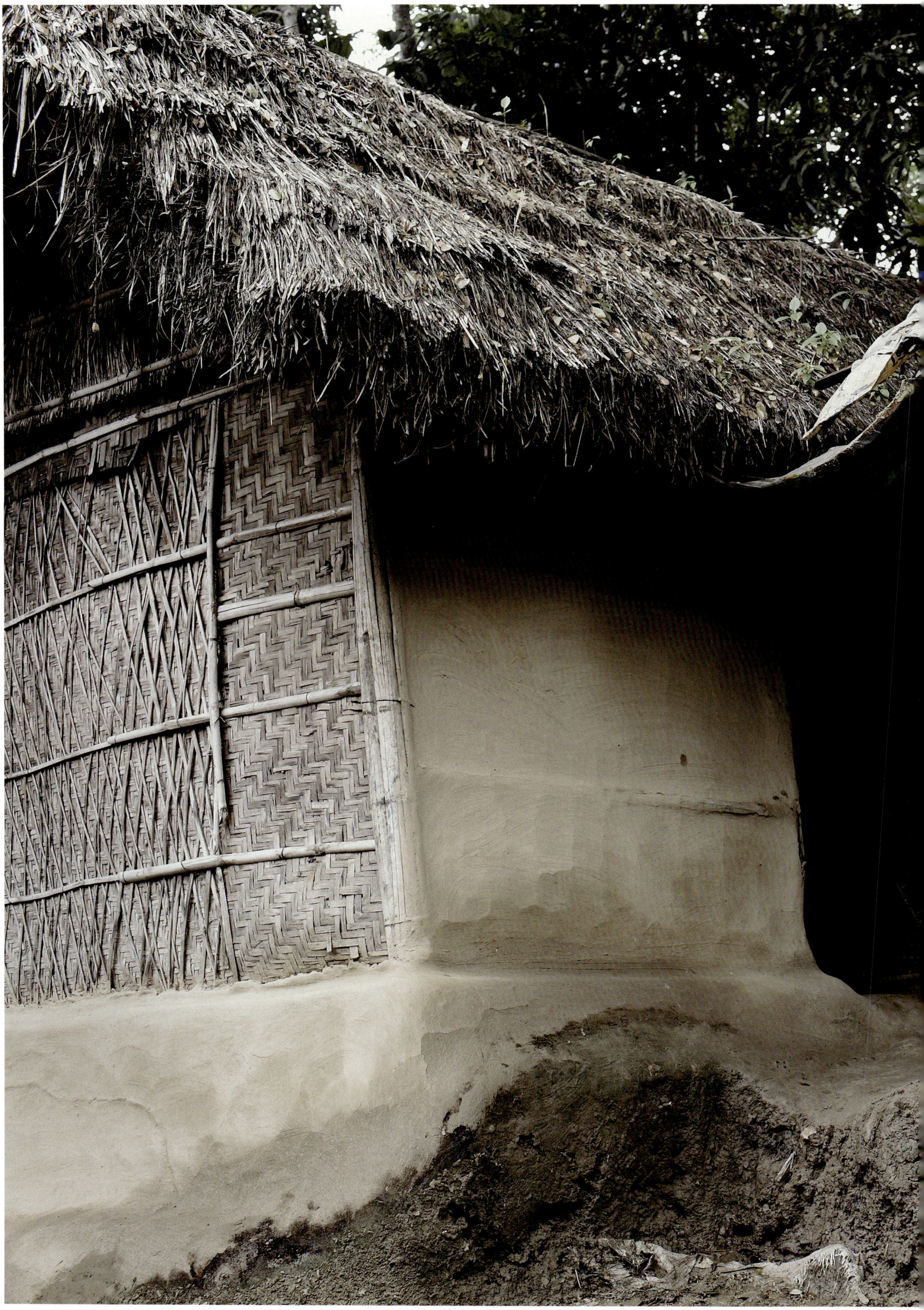

✥ **BLICK IN EINE HOFFNUNGSVOLLE ZUKUNFT.**
Sharola Rema, 31 Jahre, sitzt vor ihrem Haus im Dorf Gul Para. Mit den 50 Euro Familieneinkommen und durch die Zusammenarbeit mit der Grameen Family kommt sie Stück für Stück weiter auf ihrem Weg in eine bessere Zukunft.

✥ **VIEW OF A PROMISING FUTURE.** Sharola Rema, 31 years old, sits in front of her house in the village of Gul Para. With the 50 euros family income and through working with the Grameen family, she is treading, step by step, further on the path to a better future.

❖ **DAS KLEINE MÄDCHEN SMRITE.** Sie lebt auf der Insel Baghai Kande. Wie wird ihr Land im Jahr 2030 aussehen?
❖ **THE LITTLE GIRL SMRITE.** She lives on the island of Baghai Kande. What will her country look like in the year 2030?

221

DIE KRAFT DER WÜRDE — THE POWER OF DIGNITY

1. Auflage 2008
Die Deutsche Bibliothek – CIP-Einheitsaufnahme
Ein Titelsatz für diese Publikation
ist bei der Deutschen Bibliothek erhältlich.

ISBN 978-3-89901-169-2

J. Kamphausen

Die Kraft der Würde – The Power of Dignity · Herausgeber: **Hans Reitz** · Essay: **Peter Spiegel** · Fotografie: **Roger Richter**
© J. Kamphausen Verlag & Distribution GmbH, Bielefeld, Dezember 2008 · info@j-kamphausen.de · www.weltinnenraum.de
Übersetzung ins Englische: Susan Polzer · Lektorat (deutsch): Adele Gerdes · Lektorat (englisch): AdverTEXT
Design: 99° www.99grad.de · Druck & Verarbeitung: fgb – freiburger graphische betriebe GmbH & Co. KG

Alle Rechte der Verbreitung, auch durch Funk, Fernsehen und sonstige Kommunikationsmittel, fotomechanische
oder vertonte Wiedergabe sowie des auszugsweisen Nachdrucks vorbehalten.